The Modern Data Warehouse in Azure

Building with Speed and Agility on Microsoft's Cloud Platform

Matt How

Apress®

The Modern Data Warehouse in Azure: Building with Speed and Agility on Microsoft's Cloud Platform

Matt How
Alton, UK

ISBN-13 (pbk): 978-1-4842-5822-4   ISBN-13 (electronic): 978-1-4842-5823-1
https://doi.org/10.1007/978-1-4842-5823-1

Managing Director, Apress Media LLC: Welmoed Spahr
Acquisitions Editor: Jonathan Gennick
Development Editor: Laura Berendson
Coordinating Editor: Jill Balzano

Cover image designed by Freepik (www.freepik.com)

Distributed to the book trade worldwide by Springer Science+Business Media New York, 233 Spring Street, 6th Floor, New York, NY 10013. Phone 1-800-SPRINGER, fax (201) 348-4505, e-mail orders-ny@springer-sbm.com, or visit www.springeronline.com. Apress Media, LLC is a California LLC and the sole member (owner) is Springer Science + Business Media Finance Inc (SSBM Finance Inc). SSBM Finance Inc is a **Delaware** corporation.

For information on translations, please e-mail rights@apress.com, or visit http://www.apress.com/rights-permissions.

Apress titles may be purchased in bulk for academic, corporate, or promotional use. eBook versions and licenses are also available for most titles. For more information, reference our Print and eBook Bulk Sales web page at http://www.apress.com/bulk-sales.

Any source code or other supplementary material referenced by the author in this book is available to readers on GitHub via the book's product page, located at www.apress.com/9781484258224. For more detailed information, please visit http://www.apress.com/source-code.

Printed on acid-free paper

To my wife Amy and our children,
for the continual love and support.

Table of Contents

About the Author xi

About the Technical Reviewer xiii

Acknowledgments xv

Introduction xvii

Chapter 1: The Rise of the Modern Data Warehouse 1

Getting Started 2

    Multi-region Support 3

    Resource Groups and Tagging 3

    Azure Security 4

    Tools of the Trade 4

    Glossary of Terms 5

    Naming Conventions 7

Chapter 2: The SQL Engine 9

The Four Vs 9

Azure Synapse Analytics 11

    Understanding Distributions 12

    Resource Management 20

    Workload Management 25

    PolyBase 26

Azure SQL Database 29

    The Cloud-Based OLTP Engine 30

    The Benefits of Azure SQL Database 30

    Hyperscale 35

Azure SQL Deployment Options 38

    Azure SQL Database Managed Instances 38

    Azure SQL Database Elastic Pools 39

    Azure SQL Database V-Core Tiers 39

Azure Synapse Analytics vs. Azure SQL Database 40

    The Right Type of Data 41

    The Size of the Data 41

    The Frequency of the Data 42

    The Availability of the Data 42

    The Integration of Data 43

Chapter 3: The Integration Engine 45

Introduction to Azure Data Factory 45

The Data Factory Building Blocks 47

    Linked Services 47

    Integration Runtimes 49

    Self-Hosted Integration Runtime 50

    Azure SSIS Integration Runtime 50

    Triggers 52

    Datasets 54

    Pipelines and Activities 55

Activity Types 55

    External Compute Activities 56

    Internal Activities 57

    Iteration and Conditional Activities 58

    Web Activities 60

    Output Constraints 61

Implementing Azure Data Factory 61

    Security in Azure Data Factory 62

    Using the Managed Service Identity 62

    Source Control of Azure Data Factory 63

Templates 63

Solution Structure.. 63

Getting Started with Azure Data Factory... 64

Create Linked Services.. 65

Creating Datasets 72

Creating Pipelines.. 74

Debugging Your Pipelines 78

Monitoring Your Pipelines 78

Parameter-Driven Pipelines 79

Getting Started with Parameters 80

Using the Lookup Activity 82

Getting Started with the Lookup Activity 84

Additional Azure Data Factory Elements.. 85

Additional Invocation Methods 85

Mapping Data Flows... 87

Execute Mapping Data Flows 89

Azure Data Factory Processing Patterns.. 95

Linear Pipelines... 96

Parent-Child Processing 96

Iterative Parent-Child Processing 97

Dynamic Column Mappings.. 99

Partitioning Datasets 102

Chapter 4: The Ingestion Architecture.. 105

Layers of Curation... 105

The Raw Layer.. 106

The Clean Layer.. 107

The Transformed Layer... 107

Understanding Ingestion Architecture.. 108

Batch Ingestion 108

The Risks and Opportunities of Batch Ingestion.. 109

Event Ingestion 117

    The Risks and Opportunities of Event-Based Ingestion................................. 118

    Implementing Event Ingestion 119

Stream Ingestion... 125

    The Risks and Opportunities of Stream Ingestion 126

    Implementing Stream Ingestion 127

The Lambda Architecture.. 129

    Blending Streams and Batches 130

    The Serving Layer... 130

Assessing the Approach.. 132

Chapter 5: The Role of the Data Lake... 133

The Modern Enterprise and Its Data Lake... 134

Azure Data Lake Technology 135

    Azure Data Lake Gen 1 136

    Azure Blob Storage... 136

    Azure Data Lake Gen 2 137

Planning the Enterprise Data Lake.. 138

    Storing Raw Data.. 138

    Storing Cleaned Data.. 139

    Storing Transformed Data... 141

    Facilitating Experimentation... 142

Implementing the Enterprise Data Lake.. 143

    Security Configuration in Azure Data Lake 144

    Implementing a Raw Directory.. 149

    Implementing a Clean Directory.. 151

    Implementing a Transformed Directory 155

Example Polyglot Architectures 157

    Example One... 157

    Example Two... 158

    Example Three.. 159

    Example Four.. 160

Chapter 6: The Role of the Data Contract **163**

What Is a Data Contract? 164

Working with Data Contracts 165

Designing Data Contracts 166

Integrating Data Contracts... 170

Chapter 7: Logging, Auditing, and Resilience **181**

Logging the Data Movement Process 181

Basic Logging Requirements... 182

Extended Logging Capabilities 189

Auditing the Data Movement Process 192

Basic Auditing Requirements 193

Incorporating Resilience into the Data Movement Process 199

Basic Resiliency.. 199

Extending Resiliency 214

Monitoring the Data Movement Process.. 216

Chapter 8: Using Scripting and Automation **219**

The Power of PowerShell.. 219

Commonly Used Scripts... 220

Code Generation 220

Invoke Data Factory Pipeline.. 222

Recurse Data Lake Structures... 225

Chapter 9: Beyond the Modern Data Warehouse **229**

Microsoft Power BI... 230

Working with Power BI 230

Building a Power BI Report.. 231

Publish Report to Power BI Service 238

Azure Analysis Services 240

The Basics of Azure Analysis Services 241

Analysis Services as a Semantic Layer 241

Analysis Services Security Model..242

The Vertipaq Engine..243

Creating an Analysis Services Project 245

Create Analysis Objects 249

Deploy Analysis Services to Azure...261

Processing an Azure Analysis Services Model 263

Azure Cosmos DB..267

The Cosmos DB Architecture 267

Index.. 275

About the Author

Matt How is a professional consultant and international conference speaker who is passionate about data, analytics, and automation. Having spoken at several large conferences across the world, he is committed to sharing knowledge and insight to the wider community. Specializing in the design and delivery of modern data warehouse solutions using the Microsoft Azure Platform, Matt focuses on simplicity and resilience above all when designing cloud solutions. With a growing focus on data science, Matt is now researching techniques to integrate artificial intelligence capabilities into the modern data warehouse at scale.

About the Technical Reviewer

 **Carsten Thomsen** is a back-end developer primarily but working with smaller front-end bits as well. He has authored and reviewed a number of books and created numerous Microsoft learning courses, all to do with software development. He works as a freelancer/contractor in various countries in Europe, using Azure, Visual Studio, Azure DevOps, and GitHub as some of the tools. Being an exceptional troubleshooter, asking the right questions, including the less logical ones, in a most logical to least logical fashion, he also enjoys working with architecture, research, analysis, development, testing, and bug fixing. He is a very good communicator with great mentoring and team-lead skills, and great skills researching and presenting new material.

Acknowledgments

Writing a book was much harder than I ever imagined and so I must start by thanking my awesome wife, Amy, for her everlasting encouragement and support. She always kept the big dreams alive while ensuring my aspirations were founded in reality. I also want to thank my children for being the most welcome distraction to advanced modern analytics I could ever have dreamed of.

Thank you to my parents, friends, brothers, and other family members for their continued interest and encouragement. I sincerely hope they all enjoy receiving the same Christmas gift this year.

I want to acknowledge and thank all my colleagues at Adatis, many of whom have been an excellent sounding board for many of the concepts and ideas included in this book. A special thanks to the directors for their support and guidance throughout the process; they have always been exceptionally accommodating of both personal and professional achievements.

Prior to this project, I had never considered authoring a book and so I am sincerely grateful to Jonathan at Apress for reaching out to me and sparking the initial conversation. His continued guidance and patience have been a true blessing. In addition, I want to thank Jill for keeping everything on track and Laura for her sage advice throughout the editing process.

Finally, I want to thank Carsten for an excellent eye for detail and for providing an abundance of helpful comments and tips as part of his edit. I am very glad to have someone of his experience play a part on the production of this book.

Introduction

An enterprise data warehouse (EDW) is a common, business-critical system that benefits from highly mature concepts and design best practices. In the market today, there is a wealth of books on the topic, some of which examine the differences between the two fundamental ideologies behind the warehouse design, those of Ralph Kimball and his drive for denormalized star schemas and Bill Inmon with his preference for a normalized corporate data warehouse. Others may focus on specific patterns or techniques to solve more tricky modeling problems. However, few focus on the platform that is being used for the data warehouse. Taking nothing away from these books, the concepts they discuss are still relevant today; however, very few books speak specifically about a cloud-based implementation of a data warehouse and how the tooling is different, how the patterns change, and how a developer needs to adapt to the new environment.

Gone are the days when a data warehouse project was a slow-moving, inflexible venture that was difficult to maintain and impossible to extend. We now have an impressive set of tools that allow us to surface analytical insight at massive scale and at incredible speed, without the overhead of maintaining a gigantic server. Not only is a cloud platform perfectly tailored for data processing, but the processes to feed that platform can be completely automated and integrated to just about any source system, making maintenance and development simple and enjoyable. Further to all this, we can now fully explore the different ingestion architectures that comprise streaming, event-based, and batch loading, allowing developers to break free of the "Nightly ETL Window" constraint and fully discover how they can populate the warehouse at the rate of the incoming data.

But is there a reason why an entire book needs to be dedicated to data warehousing in the cloud? Doesn't the cloud provide the same technology as on-premises just without the server management? The short answer is no. As you go through this book, the hope is that you will discover the nature by which the cloud completely changes the way a data warehouse is built and why it is important to consider making this move. The core concepts of on-premises data warehousing still very much apply, but the way in which they are implemented has drastically changed. The cloud has revolutionized the way developers can reason about a problem and even eliminated some compromises that had to be made in the years gone by. This is not without cost however; there are new problems to understand and tackle and part of the aim of this book is to talk these issues through and make clear the patterns that solve those issues.

In this book, you will not find much discussion of Online Transaction Processing (OLTP) type systems nor of the wider capabilities of the Microsoft Azure data platform. This book will not discuss why you should implement either Kimball or Inmon or explain how to create a flashy executive level dashboard. Instead this book is a discussion about the key technologies in the Microsoft Azure data platform that lend themselves to data warehousing and how they connect together. I will explain how to choose a SQL engine that is tailored for your analytical requirements, how to create data movement processes that scale, and how to extend your warehouse to become intelligent and modern.

If you are already building SQL data warehouses, you may wonder if you need a book such as this. You know SQL. You know ETL. What can this book tell you that you do not already know? Well, SQL server is changing. And given that Microsoft is a cloud-first company, the newest features and biggest developments are shipped to the Azure versions of SQL months if not years before they hit the box product. Not only this, there are features arriving in the Azure data platform that will NEVER be available in the box product. Things like Accelerated Database Recovery (ADR) simply cannot be implemented on-premises, and if your organization cares about their recovery time objective (RTO) and recovery point objective (RPO), then this is a feature you need to understand. Ultimately there are an increasingly small number of reasons why a company would choose to avoid cloud software and this book hopes to dispel the last of those.

I sincerely hope that this book eradicates any anxiety about making a move to the cloud, and if your organization has embraced the cloud already, then I aim to provide further insight into how the technologies work at a low level and advise on the patterns and architectures that should be utilized to get the most out of them.

Who This Book Is For?

If you are already building on-premises Microsoft SQL Server data warehouses using common tools such as SSIS, then this book will explain how to move that knowledge into the cloud, giving, where possible, comparisons about the way a thing was done in that world and how it should be done in the cloud. If you are already utilizing some of the

Azure data platform, then this book will hopefully provide a better understanding of how each service operates and why it works the way it does. If you are already successfully running and developing data warehouses with Azure Synapse Analytics (formerly Azure SQL Date Warehouse) or Azure SQL Database and Azure Data Factory, then I hope this book will help to solidify your knowledge and perhaps provide some fresh ideas or patterns that you could use in future development.

If you hope to understand the entire Azure data platform, then this book will not be broad enough to answer all your questions. For example, we will not go deeply into Cosmos DB or any of the third-party database offerings in Azure. Additionally, we will not cover off core data modeling concepts other than where this is critical to the implementation of an Azure Synapse Analytics instance. Despite this, a good working knowledge of the other data stores and technologies available in Azure will open up many new avenues for you to explore that can allow for exciting and highly valuable extensions to a traditional data warehouse.

Assumptions About You

The people that will get the most out this book will be already experienced with data warehousing core concepts and the terminology that goes along with it. A good understanding of the common challenges and why they need to be overcome is also a good base to start from. I have made the assumption that you and your company are already fairly comfortable that a cloud-based architecture will suit your business requirements, taking into account security, cost, admin, and so on. As this book is not a full examination of a cloud data platform, often a warehouse sits among many other databases, it has to be assumed that you and your company have the ability to connect to the cloud and create the necessary resources for testing and proof of concept work where needed.

With this in mind, I am aware that readers may arrive at this book from a spectrum of job roles. Some may come from an analysis background looking to develop the back-end of their reports so that they are more scalable, whereas some may be more comfortable with the data engineering concepts and therefore be looking to replicate existing solutions but without the overhead and hassle of server management. Either way this book will certainly help in making clear the concepts that need to be understood in order to create a functioning data warehouse in Azure.

The Scope of This Book

In any IT project, scope is key. You need to know what you are getting, so let me make this abundantly clear what this book is and is not.

This book is

- A guide to cloud data architecture for data warehousing scenarios, implemented using Azure SQL technologies, Azure data lake technologies, and Azure integration technologies

- A guide to ingesting data with Azure Data Factory and developing metadata-driven pipelines

- An introduction to ingestion patterns that can be automated, be driven by metadata, utilize streaming, and make use of data lakes

- A point of reference for good practice around logging, auditing, and resilience regarding the aforementioned technologies

- A guide to developing and using project accelerators to improve the pace of development and ensure consistency across teams

This book is not

- A detailed description of how to conduct automated deployments to an Azure platform.

- A guide to data modeling best practice. There will be some mention of data modeling as this is key to the structure of Azure Synapse Analytics, but this will not be a book on Kimball vs. Inmon modeling.

- A manual for data preparation and cleansing. I will explain where these elements would slot into the process but not give an abundance of material on how to clean and prepare your data.

Throughout this book, there are step-by-step guides to assist you getting to a basic level of usage with a service; however, the book as a whole is not a step-by-step guide to creating a functional modern SQL data warehouse on the Azure platform.

Organization of the Book

This book is laid out so that the most important topics are covered upfront and that the key elements of a cloud data warehouse are well understood before continuing into how the development process can be accelerated and some other more advanced topics. However, at the very start, there are some handy sections that cover initial guidance for using Microsoft Azure such as subscription organization, security, development tools, and a glossary of common terms. For all of the walk-throughs in this book, you will need access to an Azure subscription where you have a relatively high level of permission for things like setting up service principals.

The bulk of the book begins from Chapter 2, "The SQL Engine," and focuses on the choices to be made when designing your modern data warehouse and how that process can be accelerated and improved. The following is a brief summary of the content of each chapter to allow you to skip to the most important discussions if needed:

- **Chapter 2: The SQL Engine.** The goal of this chapter is to make clear the distinction between Azure SQL Database and Azure Synapse Analytics and when one option should be chosen over another. The conclusion of this chapter talks about your type of data and what SQL engine would be best suited.

- **Chapter 3: The Integration Engine.** This chapter introduces Azure Data Factory and explains the key building blocks that make it a first-class cloud integration tool and really the only option for data movement within the Azure platform. Additionally, an example of how to copy data from source to sink is included.

- **Chapter 4: The Ingestion Architecture.** As this will be a modern data warehouse that can cope with a much more varied workload, we can now consider different types of data processing. You will discover how you can capitalize on event-based processing and streaming and the additional complexities these options introduce, as well as the more traditional batch-based loading technique.

- **Chapter 5: The Role of the Data Lake.** A revolution in cloud data storage has been the advent of the data lake. While the data lake is a broad topic, this chapter will relate specifically to its purpose in the data warehousing architecture. Effectively, the data lake is a single access point for an entire organization's varied datasets, be it media, tabular data, backups, and others. This makes it an ideal staging location for the data warehouse and when properly implemented can vastly improve the efficiency of the data warehouse.

- **Chapter 6: The Role of the Data Contract.** A large amount of data warehouse processing can be automated and defined in metadata. Things like file schemas, transformation rules, and processing steps can all be stored as metadata in a database of some kind. Throughout this chapter, you will gain an understanding of how metadata can be used to solve several common problems and how to store, fetch, and implement it.

- **Chapter 7: Logging, Auditing, and Resilience.** A crucial piece of a production warehouse is the monitoring and auditing of the ingestion process and being able to catch and resolve instances of bad or mis-shaped data. The concepts outlined here will likely not be new if you are an experienced data warehouse developer, but the specific implementation covered will tie in closely with the metadata mentioned previously in Chapter 6, "The Role of the Data Contract."

- **Chapter 8: Using Scripting and Automation**. With any Azure resource, scripting and automation can be a great asset to assist with deployment and management. This chapter will expand on some common scripts I often find useful and explain their usage.

- **Chapter 9: Beyond the Modern Data Warehouse**. This chapter will talk about how the modern data warehouse can be extended to support analytical tools and even application data. We will look at integrations with Power BI, Cosmos DB, and Analysis Services, explaining the security and reliability concepts at play and describe best practice and patterns for implementation.

CHAPTER 1

The Rise of the Modern Data Warehouse

A data warehouse is a common and well-understood technology asset that underpins many decision support systems. Whether the warehouse was initially designed to act as a hub for data integration or a base for analytical consistency, many organizations make use of the concepts and technologies that underpin data warehousing.

At one point, the concept of a data warehouse was revolutionary and the two key philosophies on data warehousing, those of Ralph Kimball and Bill Inmon, were new and exciting. However, many decades have passed since this point, and while the philosophies have cross-pollinated, the core design and purpose has stayed very much the same, so much so that many data warehouse developers can move seamlessly from company to company because the data warehouse is such a prevalent design. The only thing that changes is the subject matter. This is very unlike more transactional databases that may be designed very differently to support the specific needs of an application.

As the cloud revolution began, more and more services began to find homes in the cloud and the data warehouse is no exception. A cloud-based environment eliminates many common issues with data warehousing and also offers many new opportunities. First of which is the serverless nature of cloud-based databases. By not having to manage the server environment, patching, the operating system (OS) or upgrades, and others, the development team can really focus just on the data processing that needs to be undertaken. In addition, the architecture itself can be scaled so that businesses pay for what they actually use and not for a service that offers growth room for the next five years. Instead, the size of the system can be tailed and charged at per hour increments so that aggressive cost optimizations can be achieved.

In times gone by, the on-premises architecture of data warehouses meant that there were hard limits on the amount of data that could be stored and the frequency at which that data could be ingested. Further, the tools used to populate an on-premises data

© Matt How 2020
M. How, *The Modern Data Warehouse in Azure*, https://doi.org/10.1007/978-1-4842-5823-1_1

warehouse had limited ability to deal with complex data types or streaming datasets, concepts that are now prevalent in the application landscape that feed data warehouses. Businesses now require these sources to be included in their reports, and so the data warehouse must modernize in order to keep up. At present, Azure provides many tools and services to help overcome these problems, many of which can be integrated directly into what would now be known as a modern data warehouse.

In addition to modernizing the database, the tools that operate, automate, and populate the data warehouse also need to keep up in order for the solution to feel cohesive. This is why Azure offers excellent integration and automation services that can be used in conjunction with the SQL database technologies. These tools mean that more can be achieved with less code and confusion, by creating standard patterns that can be applied generically to a variety of data processing problems. Common menial tasks such as database backups can be completely automated, making the issue of disaster recovery much less of a worry. With the latest features of Azure SQL Database, artificial intelligence is used to recommend and apply tuning alterations and index adjustments to ensure database performance is at its absolute best. This works alongside advanced threat detection which ensures databases hosted in Azure are safer than ever.

Finally, businesses are increasingly interested in big data and data science, concepts that both require processing huge amounts of data at scale and maintaining a good degree of performance. For this reason, data lakes have become more popular and, rather than being seen as an isolated service, should be seen as an excellent companion to the modern data warehouse. Data lakes offer the flexibility to process varied data types at a variety of frequencies, distilling value at every stage, which can then be passed into the modern data warehouse and analyzed by the end users alongside the more traditional measures and stats.

In recent years, many organizations have been struggling with the issues associated with on-premises data warehousing and are now looking to modernize. The rise of the modern data warehouse has already begun, and the goal of this book is to ensure every reader can reap the full benefit.

Getting Started

Microsoft Azure is a comprehensive cloud platform that provides the ability to build Platform as a Service (PaaS), Software as a Service (SaaS), and Infrastructure as a Service (IaaS) components on both Microsoft-specific services and also third-party and open source technologies. Free trials are available for Microsoft Azure that provide 30-day access and roughly £150/$200 worth of Azure credit. This should allow you to explore most if not all services in this book and gather more of a practical understanding of their implementation. There are also free tiers available for many services that provide sufficient amounts of features for reviewing. Alternatively, you or your company may already have an existing Azure subscription which could then be used to experiment with the technologies listed in this book.

Multi-region Support

A core element of Azure is its multi-region support. As you may know, the cloud is really just someone else's computer, and in this case, the computer belongs to Microsoft and it is stored in a massive data center. It is these data centers that comprise an Azure region. If you are based in America, then you can pick from a range of regions, one of which will be your local region and will likely offer you the lowest latency; you could however deploy resources to a European region if you knew you were supporting customers in that part of the world. Most regions have a paired region which is used for disaster recovery scenarios, but on the whole it is best to keep related resources in the same region. This is to avoid data egress fees which are charged of data that has to be moved out of a region and into another. Note, Azure does not charge data ingress fees.

Resource Groups and Tagging

Once an Azure subscription has been set up, there are a few recommendations to help you organize the subscription. First is the resource group. The resource group is the root container for all single resources and allows a logical grouping for different services that relate to a single system. For example, a modern data warehouse may sit within a resource group that contains an Azure Data Factory, an Azure SQL Database, and an Azure Data Lake Gen 2 (ADL Gen2) account. The resource group means that admins can assign permissions to that single level and control permissions for the entire system. As the subscription gets more use, you should begin creating resource groups per project or application, per environment, so for a single data warehouse, you may have a development, test, and production resource group, each with different permissions.

CHAPTER 2

The SQL Engine

The focus of this chapter is to break open the mysteries of each SQL storage engine and understand why a particular flavor of Azure SQL technology suits one scenario over another. We will analyze the underlying architecture of each service so that development choices can be well informed and well reasoned. Once we understand how each implementation of the SQL engine in Azure processes and stores data, we can look at the direction Microsoft is taking that technology and forecast whether the same choice would be made in the future. The knowledge gained in this chapter should provide you with the capability to understand your source data and therefore to choose which SQL engine should be used to store and process that data.

Later in this book, we will move out of the structured SQL world and discuss how we can utilize Azure data lake technology to more efficiently work with our data; however, those services are agnostic to the SQL engine that we decide best suits our use case and therefore can be decided upon later. As a primary focus, we must understand our SQL options, and from there, we can tailor our metadata, preparation routines, and development tools to suit that engine.

The Four Vs

The Microsoft Azure platform has a wealth of data storage options at the user's disposal, each with different features and traits that make them well suited for a given type of data and scenario. Given the flexible and dynamic nature of cloud computing, Microsoft has built a comprehensive platform that ensures all varieties of data can be catered for. The acknowledgment of the need to cater to differing types of data gets neatly distilled into what is known in the data engineering world as "The 3 Vs" – volume, variety, and velocity.

Any combination of volume, variety, and velocity can be solved using a storage solution in the Azure platform. Often people refer to a fourth V being "value" which I think is a worthy addition as the value can often get lost in the volume.

© Matt How 2020
M. How, *The Modern Data Warehouse in Azure*, https://doi.org/10.1007/978-1-4842-5823-1_2

As the volume increases, the curation process to distil value from data becomes more complex, and therefore, specific tools and solutions can be used to help that process, validating the need for a fourth V. When attempting to tackle any one or combination of the four Vs, it is important to understand the full set of options available so that a well-informed decision can be made. Understanding the reasons why a certain technology should be chosen over another is essential to any development process, as this can then inform the code, structure, and integration of that technology.

To use an example, if you needed to store a large amount of enterprise data that was a complete mix of file types and sizes, you would use an Azure Storage account. This would allow you to organize your data into a clear structure and efficiently increase your account size as and when you need. The aspects of that technology help to reduce the complexities of dealing with large-scale data and remove any barriers to entry. Volume, check. Variety, check.

Alternatively, if the requirement was to store JavaScript Object Notation (JSON) documents so that they can be efficiently queried, then the best option would be to utilize Cosmos DB. While there is nothing stopping JSON data being stored in Blob Storage, the ability to index and query JSON data using Cosmos DB make this an obvious choice. The guaranteed latency and throughput options of Cosmos DB mean that high-velocity data is easily ingested. When the volume begins to increase, then Cosmos DB will scale with it. Velocity, check. Volume, check.

Moving to a data warehouse, we know we will have a large amount of well-structured, strongly typed data that needs to rapidly serve up analytical insight. We need a SQL engine. Crucially, this is where the fourth V, "value," comes into play. Datasets being used to feed a data warehouse may contain many attributes that are not especially valuable, and good practice dictates that these attributes are trimmed off before arriving in the data warehouse. The golden rule is that data stored in a data warehouse should be well curated and of utmost value. A SQL engine makes surfacing that valuable data easy, and further to that, no other storage option can facilitate joining of datasets to produce previously uncovered value as effortlessly as a SQL engine can. Value, check.

However, a wrinkle in the decision process is that Azure provides two types of SQL engine to choose from; each can tackle any challenge in the four Vs; however, it is wise to understand which engine solves which "V" best. Understanding the nuances of each flavor of Azure SQL will help developers make informed decisions about how to load, query, and manage the data warehouse.

The first SQL engine we will examine in this chapter is Azure Synapse Analytics (formerly Azure SQL Data Warehouse). This massively parallel processing (MPP) service provides scalability, elasticity, and concurrency, all underpinned by the well-loved Microsoft SQL server engine. The clue is certainly in the former title; this is a good option for data warehousing. However, there are other factors that mean this may not be the right choice in all scenarios. While Azure Synapse Analytics has a wealth of optimizations targeted at data warehousing, there are some reasons why the second SQL option, Azure SQL Database, may be more suitable.

Azure SQL Database is an OLTP type system that is optimized for reads and writes; however, it has some interesting features that make it a great candidate for a data warehouse environment. The recent advent of Azure SQL Database Hyperscale means that Azure SQL Database can scale up to 100 TB and provide additional read-only compute nodes to serve up analytical data. A further advantage is that Azure SQL Database has intelligent query processing and can be highly reactive to changes in runtime conditions allowing for peak performance to be maintained at critical times. Finally, there are multiple deployment options for Azure SQL Database that include managed instances and elastic pools. In essence, a managed instance is a full-blown SQL server instance deployed to the cloud and provides the closest match to an existing on-premises Microsoft SQL server implementation in Azure. Elastic pool databases utilize a single pool of compute resource to allow for a lower total cost of ownership as databases can consume more and less resources from the pool rather than having to be scaled independently.

Azure Synapse Analytics

When implementing an on-premises data warehouse, there are many constraints placed upon the developer. Initially there is the hassle of setting up and configuring the server, and even if this is taken care of already, there is always a maintenance and management overhead that cannot be ignored. Once the server is set up, further thought needs to be applied to file management and growth. In addition, the data warehouse itself is limited to the confines of the physical box, and often large databases have to utilize complex storage solutions to mitigate this issue.

However, if you are reading this book, then it is clear you are no longer interested in this archaic and cumbersome approach to data warehousing. By making the move up to the Azure cloud, you can put the days of server management behind you, safe in the knowledge that Microsoft will take care of all that. And what's more, Azure does not just provide a normal SQL instance that is purely serverless; they have restructured the underlying architecture entirely so that it is tailored for the cloud environment. This is then extended further to the point that Azure Synapse Analytics is not only purpose-built for the cloud but purpose-built for large-scale data warehousing.

Understanding Distributions

A key factor that needs to be understood when working with Azure Synapse Analytics is that of distributions. In a standard SQL server implementation, you are working in a symmetric multi-processing (SMP) environment which means there is a single storage point coupled to a set of CPUs and queries are parallelized across those CPUs using a service bus. The main problem here is that all the CPUs need to access the same storage and this can become a bottleneck, especially when running large analytical queries.

When you begin using Azure Synapse Analytics, you are now in a massively parallel processing (MPP) environment.

There are a number of key differences between SMP and MPP environments, and they are illustrated in Figure 2-1. The most important is that storage is now widely distributed and coupled to a specific amount of compute. The benefit here is that each node of the engine is essentially a separate SQL database and can access its own storage separately from all the other nodes without causing contention.

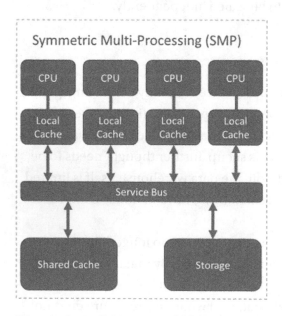
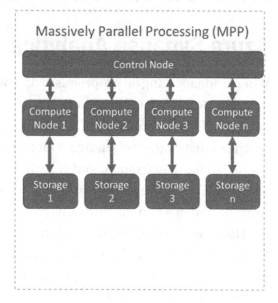

Figure 2-1. *Diagram of SMP vs. MPP*

Figure 2-1 shows how in an SMP environment, there can be contention for storage resources due to the single point of access; however, this problem is alleviated in the MPP environment as each compute node is coupled to its own storage.

In an MPP environment, when a query gets executed, the control node sends a copy of the query to each compute node in the engine. From here the compute node can access its allotted storage, perform the query, and return the results back to control node to be aggregated with the other result sets.

The First Problem

The concept of separating compute and storage is fundamental to Azure Synapse Analytics, and while this produces an ideal platform to run blazing fast analytical queries, it can also begin to pose problems. As the service is built to run in the cloud, the notion of scaling the resource to meet needs comes into play, and while it is simple enough to add and subtract computation resource, scaling up distributed data storage is trickier.

Let's imagine we have ten glasses of water – these are our storage distributions. Now let's add two athletes that need that water as fast as possible – these are our compute nodes. An essential consideration here is that we are only as fast as our slowest athlete; if the water is poorly distributed and contains skew, then one athlete will have to become idle and wait for the other to finish. Now, it would be easy for us to introduce two additional athletes and clearly the water would be consumed twice as fast. However, as the glasses get more and more full, we decide that we actually need 20 glasses to hold all the water to avoid any overflow and so place 10 more glasses on the table. To avoid skew and unbalanced consumption, we would now need to completely redistribute our water across all 20 glasses, and this action becomes very inefficient when we want to do this regularly.

Bringing this back to the warehouse scenario, you can see why scaling storage can become problematic when the data needs to be evenly distributed. To get around the issue, Microsoft has fixed the number of distributions at 60. Whatever the size your data is, you will have to distribute it over 60 storage nodes. This ensures that the compute can be scaled up to further parallelize the processing, but the storage layer does not need to change at all. It is worth mentioning here that distributed tables are presented as a single table, as if they were stored in an SMP type system.

However, now that we know our data will be distributed 60 ways regardless of the compute size, we are faced with the next question. How do we distribute our data? The key thing to remember is that we want to minimize skew. To define skew more clearly, it is the imbalance of data being stored on one storage node vs. another. Thankfully Microsoft has made it easy for us to monitor skew with some handy Data Management Views (DMVs), but I will introduce these fully, later. First let's understand how we can mitigate skew.

ROUND ROBIN Distribution

The first way to mitigate skew is to use the *ROUND ROBIN* approach. At the point of ingesting your data, Azure Synapse Analytics will assign each row to the next available storage node in the system. Figure 2-2 shows how each new incoming row is distributed to each compute node sequentially.

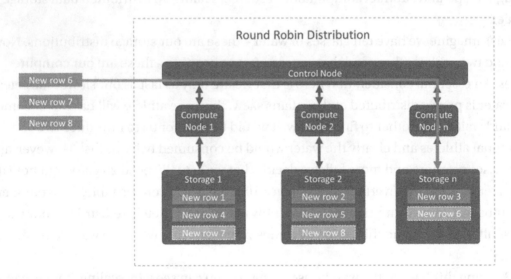

Figure 2-2. *Diagram of data begin distributed row by row onto each distribution*

The syntax to write an Azure Synapse Analytics table that uses Round Robin distribution is documented in Listing 2-1.

Listing 2-1. Data definition language (DDL) statement to create a table with Round Robin distribution

```
CREATE TABLE myTable
  (
    id int NOT NULL,
    firstName varchar(20),
    lastName varchar(20)
  )
WITH (
    DISTRIBUTION = ROUND_ROBIN,
    CLUSTERED COLUMNSTORE INDEX
      );
```

This approach eliminates skew as it is completely removed from the context of your data. You guarantee an even distribution. A simple sum of a column grouped by another column would perform fine because each node can determine its result and pass it back to the control node to be aggregated. However, at some point the data will need to be joined back together, only now your data is spread far and wide across the warehouse and importantly the server does not know which storage node holds each record.

To analyze the problem further, we can use the scenario of joining a fact table to a dimension table. To perform the join, each node needs to obtain the dimension rows from the other nodes in the warehouse and store that data on its own storage. Once it has those rows, it can perform the join and return the result. This process is called data movement and is a large cost on the query plan. Further, this movement is conducted at query runtime, and therefore you must wait for these additional steps to take place before any results can be obtained. Unfortunately, this movement is performed for each query that requires it, and the result is removed once the query completes.

HASH Distribution

If we are to avoid the problems of data movement, we need to distribute our data more intelligently. The method for this is to use *HASH* distribution, which will create a hash of a columns value and locate matching values on the same node. As shown in Figure 2-3, when Hash distribution is used, each row is hashed using a set key and then grouped with other rows that have the same hashed value.

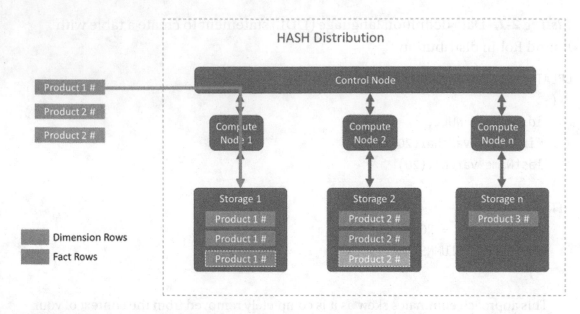

Figure 2-3. *Diagram of data being distributed using Hash keys*

The syntax to write an Azure Synapse Analytics table that uses Hash distribution is shown in Listing 2-2.

Listing 2-2. DDL code to create a table with HASH distribution on the "id" column

```
CREATE TABLE myTable
  (
    id int NOT NULL,
    firstName varchar(20),
    lastName varchar(20)
  )
WITH (
    DISTRIBUTION = HASH (id),
    CLUSTERED COLUMNSTORE INDEX
    );
```

To use the fact and dimension scenario again, if all the dimension and fact rows are stored on the same storage node, then no data movement is required. All the joining can be performed in isolation. For this to work, however, the following things need to be considered:

- Which column to distribute on?

- What is the cardinality of that column?

The Distribution Column

If we are to use the Hash distribution approach, then we must plan which column we will use to distribute our data. For a column to be considered as a Hash distribution column, it should contain the following properties:

- Low cardinality

- Even distribution

- Often used in joins

- Not used in filters

To expand on each of these points, a column with a very low cardinality (less than 60 unique values) will not use our entire storage allocation as the server will not have enough values to distribute the data on. To avoid this and maximize performance, an ideal number would be over 600, but really the more the better. Secondly, an even distribution means that we can still eliminate the problem of skew. It is unlikely to be as smooth as a Round Robin distribution, but by analyzing the data upfront, we should get an idea of whether there is a strong favor for some particular values over others, and if there is, then it would not be a good distribution column. If the chosen hash column is often used in joins, for example, customer or product, then the likelihood of the server being able to avoid data movement increases dramatically. Finally, if the column is commonly used as a search predicate, then you will be limiting the opportunity for parallelism as the filter could remove the need to run the query on certain nodes of the warehouse.

If none of your columns have more than 60 unique values, then you should explore the possibility of creating a new column that can be a composite of several columns in the table, thereby gaining a higher cardinality. To remove the need for data movement, you should use this column in the join arguments. You may also notice that in order to understand the joins and filters that will be commonly used, you will need to establish the types of queries being run on the warehouse by your users. Once you have this knowledge, then you can plan your distribution accordingly.

How to Check if You Have the Right Column

Ultimately, if you are designing your warehouse with Hash distribution in mind, you will choose a column to distribute on. Once you have this and have loaded your data, you will need to determine if the distribution played out like you expected or whether some unforeseen aspect of the data has made it not a good column for distribution. To check your skew and distribution, there are Data Management Views (DMVs). These are system views put together by Microsoft that provide easy insight into the inner workings of your server. The following SQL code can be used to show one of these DMVs:

```
DBCC PDW_SHOWSPACEUSED('dbo.myTable');
```

From the information returned, you may determine that the designated column is not the most appropriate, and in that case, you can easily redistribute the data by redefining your table with a CREATE TABLE AS SELECT (CTAS) statement.

REPLICATED Distribution

A third option for data distribution is to utilize the *REPLICATED* distribution. Rather than distributing data across the server, a full copy of the table is placed on each compute node of the engine, not storage node. When a query is executed that requires joining to that table, data movement can be spared as the data is already in the right place. In the context of a warehouse, replicated tables can be very effective when used for smaller dimension tables (less than 2 GB on disk – more on how to determine this later). When designing the warehouse, there is likely to be some tables that will be joined using a column that is not used for distribution. In these instances, data movement would be required unless one of the tables was replicated, in which case the data is already accessible to the compute node. The syntax to write an Azure Synapse Analytics table that uses Replicated Distribution is as shown in Listing 2-3.

Listing 2-3. DDL statement to create a table using replicate distribution

```
CREATE TABLE myTable
  (
    id int NOT NULL,
    firstName varchar(20),
    lastName varchar(20)
  )
```

```
WITH (
    DISTRIBUTION = REPLICATE,
    CLUSTERED INDEX (lastName)
    );
```

Note that in the preceding DDL statement, a clustered index is chosen over a clustered column store index. This is because a clustered index is more performant than a heap; however, a table that is being replicated is not likely to have enough rows to gain any real benefit from the clustered column store index used for the HASH and ROUND_ROBIN tables.

As with all design decisions, however, there are considerations that need to be made. In the case of replicated tables, it is important to consider the logistics of replicating data across each compute node. The goal is to reduce the number of rebuilds for that table, and the operations that cause rebuilds are the following:

- Data is inserted, deleted, or updated.

- The warehouse is scaled up or down.

- The definition of the table is changed.

The rebuild itself is twofold. When the data is first updated, then the table is copied to a master version of the table. This ensures that the insert, delete, or update operation can be completed most efficiently. Only once the replicated table is selected from will the data be further copied onto the compute nodes in the server. On the first read of the data, the query will run against the master table while the data is copied asynchronously to the compute nodes. After this, any subsequent queries will run against the replicated copy of the data.

Hopefully this explanation of the different distribution types available through Azure Synapse Analytics offers some insight into the benefits of massively parallel processing and some of the challenges that need to be overcome. Without doubt, one of the benefits of the cloud computing model is the separation of compute and storage and the flexibility this can provide.

Resource Management

Understanding how to manage the resources allocated to an Azure Synapse Analytics instance is vital to ensuring the engine performs well for the users it serves but also does not cost the Earth to run. Ultimately the amount of compute assigned to your server is determined by the number of Compute Data Warehouse Units (cDWUs). This setting is a blended metric that comprises CPU, memory, and I/O into a normalized figure that can be used to determine performance and is also known as the *service objective*. As a starter, the smallest cDWU setting for an Azure Synapse Analytics instance is cDWU 100. This equates to one compute node with 60 GB of memory and is therefore responsible for all 60 storage distributions. This could be scaled up to a cDWU 500, meaning that you still have a single compute node in charge of 60 storage distributions but now has 300 GB of memory. As you get past cDWU 500, you begin to increase the number of compute nodes, for example, a cDWU 5000 is 10x more powerful than the 500, meaning you would have 10 compute nodes aligned with 6 storage nodes, each with 300 GB of memory. The highest setting is cDWU 30000, meaning that each of your 60 compute nodes is attached to a single storage node with 18,000 GB of memory available.

Resource Classes

Given the amount of resource allocated by the service objective, it is up to you to further tweak how this is utilized in the server to ensure maximum performance. The first concept to grasp is that of resource classes. The purpose of resource classes is to pre-assign the amount of compute that is assigned to each query so that you can plan the load on your server more accurately. The two levers that are controlled by resource classes are that of concurrency and resource utilization, and the interaction between the two is such that a larger resource class will increase the resource utilization per query but limit the amount of concurrency available to the server. A smaller resource class does the opposite and will limit the amount of resource provided to a query but will increase the concurrency, meaning more queries can be run at the same time. Concurrency slots is the name given to the amount of concurrency available to the server, and this is explained later in the chapter.

The implementation of resource classes is done though user security roles which have been preconfigured on the server for you to use. In practice there are two types of resource class:

- Static resource classes
- Dynamic resource classes

Static Resource Classes

A static resource class provides a fixed amount of compute to a query regardless of the service objective, meaning that as an Azure Synapse Analytics Cluster scales up, the amount of concurrency available to run queries is directly increased. There is a range of sizes to choose from ranging from staticrc10 up to staticrc80, and each level assigns an increasing amount of concurrency slots to a query. Note that the amount of concurrency slots assigned to a query does change as you scale up an Azure Synapse Analytics. Within Azure Synapse Analytics, concurrency slots are akin to reserving seats at a busy restaurant. Each query "books" a determined amount of concurrency slots, and that number directly affects the number of other queries that can be run at the same time. As soon as that query completes, the concurrency slot goes back in the pool. The static type of resource class is tailored for scenarios where the data volumes are well understood and consistent. Let's look at a few scenarios.

If you are using an Azure Synapse Analytics that is scaled to cDWU1000c, you will have 40 total concurrency slots. This means your maximum number of queries run at any one time is 32. This could be 32 analyst type users running queries under the staticrc10 resource class which, at DWU1000c level, assigns 1 concurrency slot per staticrc10 query. However, not all of your users will be analysts, and some may be "load" users – specific user accounts configured to run batch loads within the warehouse. These loads may be large, and for the query to execute in good time, you can assign your load user to a larger static resource class so that more memory is assigned for the query. If we use a staticrc60, then our query will be gifted 32 concurrency slots, taking up a lot more of the available resources. While this query is running, all queries that require more than eight concurrency slots will be queued until the query completes.

Now let's say you have a second load that needs to be processed regularly and efficiently alongside your first load. To allow this to happen, you must scale the warehouse up. If we were to choose a DWU3000c setting, then we now a have 100 concurrency slots to play with, and because a staticrc60 query consistently assigns 32 concurrency slots, we know we can safely run two of these queries side by side with some additional head room for user queries on top.

Dynamic Resource Classes

Dynamic resource classes work very differently, and rather than assigning the same amount of concurrency regardless of the service objective, they actually increase the amount of concurrency per resource class as the Azure Synapse Analytics instance scales. As a result, there are only four dynamic resource classes:

- **smallrc**: 3% of available concurrency (the default for all users)

- **mediumrc**: 10% of available concurrency

- **largerc**: 22% of available concurrency

- **xlargerc**: 70% of available concurrency

To use the same example, an Azure Synapse Analytics scaled to DWU1000c will allow 22% of concurrency slots to a largerc workload. Given that there are 40 available slots, this equates to 8 being assigned to the query. However, if we found that the queries being run under the largerc were becoming slow, we could again increase the service objective to DWU3000c and now our query will be granted over 3x the amount of resource with 26 concurrency slots. While this will ensure our query completes faster, it does not mean that more queries can run at the same time.

Obviously in a full implementation of an Azure Synapse Analytics, you would expect to see a mix of both types of resource class being used – some static for predictable and consistent workloads and perhaps some dynamic for less routine, occasional workloads.

Pausing and Resuming the Warehouse

Because the compute and storage resources of the warehouse are not tightly coupled, it means that you can have full control over the scale and even status of the warehouse. As a user, you can scale the data warehouse at peak times to ensure maximum processing power and then scale the server back down when processing is completed. You can then turn the server off completely at night and weekends if required so that the cost of your warehouse can be dramatically reduced. Bear in mind that while compute can be paused, storage cannot, and this will be charged for regardless of compute scale. As mentioned previously in this chapter, scale operations can have side effects and so should be planned for in advance and not done on a whim. Additionally, pausing and resuming the warehouse can take time, and this should be planned for when designing the warehouse.

The operation itself can be performed either through the Azure portal or by using a REST API call from Azure Data Factory. Figure 2-4 points out the Pause/Resume button.

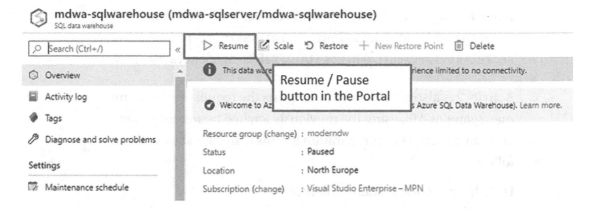

Figure 2-4. *Diagram of portal button to pause and resume warehouse*

The Data Factory pipeline shown in Figure 2-5 demonstrates a method to pause or resume an Azure Synapse Analytics instance using Data Factory orchestration of REST API calls.

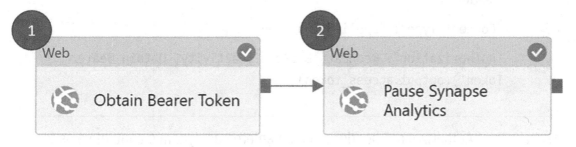

Figure 2-5. *A Data Factory pipeline showing how to pause a Synapse Analytics instance*

1. Activity one is a Web activity that obtains a bearer token. This is required in order to authenticate the request to pause or resume the warehouse. The configuration of this activity is shown as follows:

    URL: `https://login.microsoftonline.com/<tenant-id>/oauth2/token`

Method: POST

Headers:

```
"Content-Type": "application/x-www-form-urlencoded"
```

Body: grant_type=client_credentials&client_id=<service-principal-client-id>&client_secret=<service-principal-secret-key>&resource=https%3A%2F%2Fmanagement.azure.com

2. Activity 2 is also a Web activity and posts the request to the Azure management API, using the previously fetched bearer token for authentication. The configuration for this activity is shown as follows:

URL: https://management.azure.com/subscriptions/<*subscription-id*>/resourceGroups/<*resource-group-name*>/providers/Microsoft.Sql/servers/<*sql-server-name (without .database.windows.net)*>/databases/<*database-name*>/pause?api-version=2017-10-01-preview

Method: POST

Headers:

```
"Content-Type": "application/json"
```

```
"Authorization": @concat('Bearer ', activity('Obtain Bearer
Token').output.access_token)
```

Note   The "Authorization" header must be entered as dynamic content so as to use the value from the previous activity. You can access this pane using "Alt + P".

Body: {} (A valid body is needed to validate Data Factory but not for the actual request.)

This pipeline could then be triggered using a wall clock type schedule or even by a custom invocation. These types of invocations will be discussed later in the book.

A further option for scaling your Azure Synapse Analytics instance is to use Azure Automation. This provides a service that allows you to execute run books – read PowerShell scripts, on a schedule or using a web hook API. It is important to consider that the warehouse can take a short while to come back online, and while it is paused, no queries can be run against the data, nor can you access the data by other means.

Workload Management

Another feature of Azure Synapse Analytics is that of workload management and importance. Importance is a feature that allows specific users to be tagged as higher priority, and therefore this affects the order in which the server processes queries. As mentioned earlier, if there are no concurrency slots remaining, then queries enter into a queue and this queue is built up in a first in, first out (FIFO) manner, meaning that the first query to queue will ordinarily be the first query to be processed.

However, let's imagine a scenario where you have two users querying your busy warehouse and are waiting in the queue. Let's say one user is an analyst and the other is the CEO who has been tagged with high importance. In this scenario, even if the analyst submitted their query before the CEO, the CEO's query will be pulled off the queue and executed first.

Additionally, this importance feature can affect how the server handles locking. Locking is used throughout the warehouse to ensure consistent reads and is a fundamental concept in any database engine. If we have a table that is regularly updated, then there will often be a lock in place on this table, thereby blocking other processes until the lock is released. Without importance in place, queries will be handed the lock in a chronological order. However, this can be changed with importance, ensuring that the important queries obtain the lock prior to the normal queries, thereby ensuring the important queries complete quicker.

Finally, importance will even permeate into the optimizer, as this is the part of the Azure Synapse Analytics instance that estimates the size of each job and decides when to execute them. Usually the optimizer prioritizes throughput and will therefore execute jobs as soon as a sufficient amount of resource is available; however, in some scenarios, this can cause big delays for larger processes. If there are a number of small queries running and some further small queries in the queue, then as the small queries complete, the small queued queries will be executed because the required resources match up. If a large query enters the queue, it will have to wait until enough resource is available at any given time before it can execute. However, if the query is tagged with importance, then the optimizer is aware that it needs to make room for the larger query and will avoid continually pulling smaller jobs off the queue. This ensures that required amount of resource is available quicker.

PolyBase

PolyBase is a technology that provides a seamless interface between your data lake platform and your Azure Synapse Analytics instance. The data in your data lake can be exposed to your Azure Synapse Analytics instance as an external table, meaning the data within the file or files can be operated on as if it were a table in the database.

To do this, there are a couple of additional components required which are

- Database scoped credential
- External data source
- File format

The database scoped credential is used to authenticate the Azure Synapse Analytics instance into the data lake. The permissions here should be tightly controlled and well planned out. Multiple versions of these credentials may be needed to ensure the correct granularity. The pieces of required information are the service principal id (and its accompanying authentication end point) and the secret or key that is created for that service principal. The syntax for the credential creation is shown in Listing 2-4.

Listing 2-4. The syntax used to create a database scoped credential

```
CREATE DATABASE SCOPED CREDENTIAL DataLakeCredential
  WITH
    IDENTITY = {service principal id}{OAuth End Point},
    SECRET = {service principal secret key};
```

The next requirement is the external data source. This now makes the connection to your data lake and is used to describe the type of external source, as data lake is one of a number of options, while also supplying the root path of the data. It is important that the path specified here only goes as far as the top level required as further directory navigation can be added on when using the data source from a query. This data source also references the database scoped credential, so it is important to ensure that the service principal you use has the access that is required for the external data source. The syntax for the external data source is shown in Listing 2-5.

Listing 2-5. The syntax used to create an external data source for the data lake

```
CREATE EXTERNAL DATA SOURCE [DataLakeSource]
    WITH (
        TYPE = HADOOP,
        LOCATION = N'abfss://{container name}@{account name}.dfs.core.
                    windows.net',
        CREDENTIAL = [DataLakeCredential])
```

Finally, we need to specify a file format so that our Azure Synapse Analytics understands how to read the data it finds in the lake. Here we can set a number of options about the files we want to read. A key point to bear in mind here is that the file format cannot be parameterized, so it is important to read from a standardized layer in your data lake so that you can reduce the number of file formats needed. The syntax for creating the file format is shown in Listing 2-6.

Listing 2-6. The syntax used to create a file format that reads pipe delimited data and formats dates into the UK standard format

```
CREATE EXTERNAL FILE FORMAT PipeDelimitedText
WITH (
    FORMAT_TYPE = DELIMITEDTEXT,
    FORMAT_OPTIONS (
        FIELD_TERMINATOR = '|',
        DATE_FORMAT = 'dd/MM/yyyy',
        STRING_DELIMITER = '"'
    )
);
```

We can now very easily ingest data into our warehouse by using these components to access data in the lake in a secure and robust way. Given these three elements, we can utilize external tables to expose the data in the lake as if it were a standard SQL table. Alongside this external table, we can also determine what happens to rows that do not fit the definition of our external table and where they should be landed. The feature allows us to easily handle bad rows, whether they be caused by data type violation or additional columns. Listing 2-7 shows how you can define the external table so that it uses the previous three components to access data in the lake.

Listing 2-7. The syntax to define an external table that reads from the "Read_directory" which is a subfolder of the root defined in the external data source. Additionally, we have specified that PolyBase should fail the ingestion if 100 or more rows are invalid, writing the bad rows into the "Reject_directory."

```
CREATE EXTERNAL TABLE [dbo].[ExternalTable]
(
    [Col_one]   TINYINT        NULL,
    [Col_two]   VARCHAR(100)   NULL,
    [Col_three] NUMERIC(2,2)   NULL
)
WITH
(
    DATA_SOURCE = DataLakeSource
    ,LOCATION = '/Read_directory'
    ,FILE_FORMAT = PipeDelimitedText
    ,REJECT_TYPE = VALUE
    ,REJECT_VALUE = 100
    ,REJECTED_ROW_LOCATION= '/Reject_directory'
)
```

The preceding REJECT_TYPE argument can be defined as "VALUE" or "PERCENTAGE." The *value* reject type means that PolyBase will fail reads from this table if the absolute number of rows specified in the REJECT_VALUE argument is exceeded. Alternatively, if the type is set to *percentage,* then the read will fail if the percentage of rows set are invalid. Additionally, you must set the REJECT_SAMPLE_VALUE which tells Azure Synapse Analytics how many rows to attempt to read as a batch before moving on to the next batch. If the batch size is set at 1000 and the reject value is 10 (note, not 0.1), then Azure Synapse Analytics will read in the first 1000 rows, and if more than 100 of those rows fail, the batch will be failed. If less than 100 rows fail, then Azure Synapse Analytics will complete the batch and begin reading the next 1000 rows.

In order to finally persist this data into the warehouse, we need to land the data in an internal table. An internal table can be treated exactly the same as a regular SQL table; however, the data is of course distributed across the 60 storage nodes as defined in the table definition. The way to do this is to utilize the CREATE TABLE AS SELECT statement which allows you to create a table as the output of a select statement. The syntax in Listing 2-8 shows how you can select the contents of the external table defined previously (this is a file in the data lake) and land it in an internal table.

Listing 2-8. The CTAS syntax to read data from the external table

```
CREATE TABLE dbo.InternalTable
      WITH
      (
          DISTRIBUTION = ROUND_ROBIN
      )
      AS
      SELECT
            Col_one
            ,Col_two
            ,Col_three
      FROM dbo.ExternalTable
```

An important point to emphasize here is that this method to ingest data into the warehouse is the only to load data in bulk in a minimally logged manner. All other methods, such as SSIS, Data Factory, and others, push data through the control node which thereby causes a bottleneck. As a result, this route for loading data should be used before all others to ensure data is processed as efficiently as possible.

Azure SQL Database

Azure SQL Database (Azure SQL DB) is a major cloud-hosted database technology offering from Microsoft and can be thought of as a Platform as a Service version of a traditional on-premises SQL database. There are of course major alterations to the way the service is deployed so that as a user, you get the much beloved SQL engine combined with the benefits of it being cloud hosted. The point to make clear upfront is that an Azure SQL DB is a single database ONLY, there is no server instance surrounding the database, and this means no access to the SQL Agent, PolyBase, cross database queries, and others; however, there are alternative deployment options that make some of those things available. When creating an Azure SQL Database, you will see a logical server will be created; however, this is a namespace only and holds none of the items mentioned previously. This book is focusing on cloud data warehousing, and it may seem confusing why a developer would not just choose Azure Synapse Analytics when designing their architecture. This section will outline the reasons why an Azure SQL DB may be a better fit for some scenarios and speak about the features that make it so.

The Cloud-Based OLTP Engine

Many data warehouse developers will be familiar with the difference between online transactional processing (OLTP) systems and online analytical processing (OLAP) systems and when to use which system. Generally speaking, an OLAP engine would be preferable for a SQL data warehouse, particularly one used for decision support, because most queries will be using aggregations and grouping to compute large-scale calculations, and therefore the engine is tuned for enhanced query performance over transactional inserts and updates. An OLTP type database would be more commonly used as a source of data for a warehouse and may be the focal point of a great number of transactions, often at very large scale and volume. That said, beneath a threshold, there is no reason why a standard OLTP type system cannot handle the analytical queries presented by a user; in fact for smaller data warehouses, this may be a more appropriate option.

The Benefits of Azure SQL Database

When designing a data platform solution, there are several points that need to be considered, and, in a number of categories, Azure Synapse Analytics falls short when compared to Azure SQL Database. This is not to say that workarounds cannot be created; however, some of the following benefits may be a really critical requirement. The rest of this section discusses those concepts that may nudge Azure SQL DB in front of Azure Synapse Analytics when designing a data platform for analytics.

Improved Concurrency

One element that is perhaps taken for granted in an on-premises SQL server implementation is that of a high level of concurrency. Having the ability to process a great number of queries at any given time is often essential, given the nature of a database. However, Azure Synapse Analytics has a limit on the number of concurrent requests, and even at the highest service objectives, this limit is 128 queries at one time. Just to be clear, this means that no more than 128 queries can be run at the same time on Azure Synapse Analytics and often this number is smaller, for example, a DWU1000c data warehouse has a concurrency limit of 32! If there is a large analytical community looking to use the warehouse alongside a host of report and load users, these concurrency slots will quickly run out and processes will be throttled unless you can afford to scale up. Alternatively, you could review the option of using Azure SQL DB which, due to the nature of being a write optimized OLTP engine, is designed to process a high level of transactions concurrently. Because the engine is built using a traditional SMP architecture, the processing route for queries is much simpler; they are evaluated by the optimizer and then passed to the execution service instead of, as in the case of Azure Synapse Analytics, being distributed across a network of compute nodes to then be aggregated back together once all nodes have completed.

Trickle-Fed Data Warehouses

Before embarking on any data warehouse project, it is important to understand the data that will be loaded and the queries that will be performed. Once you have a good understanding of this, you can begin to make justified decisions about how you will load and process the data in your warehouse. In some cases, there may be the need to ingest very large files regularly and blend this with equally if not larger tables of existing data; this is where Azure Synapse Analytics comes in handy. However, there can also be instances where smaller more frequent files are common, and this is where an Azure SQL DB may become a more desired option.

In Azure Synapse Analytics, the CREATE TABLE AS SELECT (CTAS) statement is the go-to method for loading tables. This approach means that you literally recreate the table every time using the result of a SELECT statement. To produce the effect of UPDATES and INSERTS, you produce the data in multiple SELECT statements and union them together to create the entire table in one query. While this is very efficient for blending large datasets, it becomes very inefficient if you only need to add a few records – a simple INSERT and UPDATE would suffice. While an INSERT and UPDATE both exist in Azure Synapse Analytics, they do not automatically create statistics and therefore any stored procedures using these need to do that manually and this additional complexity makes the pattern cumbersome and difficult to maintain. In the case of Azure SQL DB, we can easily reuse existing logic if it exists or create procedures using common patterns and well-understood processes such as upserts or merges.

Further to this, data warehousing is no longer just about processing regular, batched up source files; a warehouse should be able to accept event-driven or streaming data and often these records can arrive in micro batches (one or so records at a time). Were we to use an Azure Synapse Analytics, this would mean rebuilding the entire table every few seconds or so just to incorporate a handful of records. Obviously, this approach is completely inefficient; however, an Azure SQL DB would handle these micro batches easily and allow for a wider variety of data ingestions patterns.

Managing Slowly Changing Dimensions

Often the issue of slowly changing dimensions is one to be tackled prior to ingesting any data because it is important to document which dimensions will have slowly changing elements and what type is needed. To allow for conformed understanding, the three main types are

- **Type 0**: Data is not affected at all and no updates are made. The dimension is append only.

- **Type 1**: Data is simply overwritten so that the latest state of the record is maintained in the dimension table.

- **Type 2**: The latest version of the record is inserted into the dimension table and the historical record is marked to indicate it is no longer current. This can either be with a set of data bounds or an "is current" flag.

While there are additional types that can be implemented, the logic can be derived from one of the preceding three options. When using Azure SQL DB, the implementation logic of slowly changing dimensions becomes simple because very often we can write a single statement that can take care of the update in the case of Type 1 or a collection of insert and updates to cover off Type 2. Conversely, in Azure Synapse Analytics, the statement needs to be comprised of a number of SELECT statements that then get unioned together to form a final result which is the entire table. This means that even records that are not changing need to form part of the SELECT statement. Additionally, this becomes more awkward to debug and report on as part of a warehouse processing routine because the logic is not broken out into steps as is the case in Azure SQL DB.

Intelligent Query Processing and Tuning

Another feature of Azure SQL DB that makes this technology stand head and shoulders above others is that artificial intelligence has been integrated directly into the SQL engine to allow for adaptive query processing and automated performance tuning. The primary reason for this feature is to compensate for poor statistics in the database and ensure that a query is as performant as can be, even once the plan has been sized and handed off to the executer. Given a warehouse implementation is all about the ability to query and read data, this feature helps to compensate for the fact that there are no multiple compute nodes processing the query and instead allows for the warehouse to be proactively pursuing the best possible performance. The intelligent query processing and tuning is manifested in a number of features of the SQL engine which are available in all deployments of Azure SQL DB.

Automatic Tuning

The first feature is automatic tuning, which learns from the collective pool of Azure SQL Databases and feeds the insights gathered back into your target databases at times of low activity. The feature itself can be turned off entirely or applied to a level where recommendations are generated but not applied. However, in the full implementation of automatic tuning, the service will generate tuning suggestions and automatically apply them for you with the additional benefit that the engine will verify the benefit of the recommendation and, if there is no discernible improvement, will roll back the change. The recommendations will be made up of CREATE and DROP INDEX suggestions and FORCE LAST GOOD PLAN suggestions. The CREATE INDEX element will identify missing indexes and create them while also verifying the improvement to the workload, whereas DROP INDEX will actively remove surplus or duplicate indexes. The FORCE LAST GOOD PLAN element will identify queries that are using a query plan that is not as performant as a previous plan and will query using the better plan instead of the more recent one.

Adaptive Query Processing

Adaptive query processing is a major change to the way a query is executed in SQL server. In a usual query process, the plans are produced and sized with the smallest one being chosen and executed; however, there can be times when poor statistics mean that the query was incorrectly sized and is therefore not the most efficient. Despite this, the optimizer continues to run the query based on the plan. Adaptive query processing allows for the engine to adjust the subsequent plan based on the row counts that are accumulated throughout execution and becomes effective through a number of individual features which are

- Batch mode memory grant feedback

- Row mode memory grant feedback

- Batch mode adaptive join

- Interleaved execution

Batch Mode Memory Grant Feedback

The memory grant controls the amount of memory that is given to a query to process and is estimated prior to the execution of the query by the optimizer. The reason for this is to ensure that the query has enough memory to execute efficiently but not too much to drastically reduce concurrency within the database. The value is then stored alongside the plan in the plan cache. However, if the memory grant has not been correctly estimated, then the performance hit to your query can be devastating. A grant that is too low will cause spills onto disk which becomes very expensive compared to reading directly from memory. Alternatively, an oversized estimate will unnecessarily reduce the amount of parallelism and resource available to other activities in the database.

With this feature enabled, the SQL engine will review the estimated memory grant vs. the actual required to read all rows into memory and update the number attached to the plan in the cache. This means that subsequent queries will use the updated estimate rather than the initial one that was incorrect.

The same feature is also available for row mode queries; however, at the time of writing, this is in preview.

Adaptive Joins

The adaptive join feature allows the SQL engine to choose a join mode after the first input has been scanned, meaning that there is a realistic evaluation of rows before deciding on the type of join to be performed. The types in question are Hash mode, which is the default, and Nested loop mode. With this feature enabled, a threshold is put in place to determine whether the number of rows is small enough to be executed better by a Nested loop type join or whether the plan should continue to use Hash mode. If the process does in fact switch from Hash mode to Nested loops but has already read in rows from the input, then these rows are preserved and do not have to be read again; although there is still a slight overhead in the use of adaptive joins, this is still a very useful feature for workloads that often vary in size.

Interleaved Execution

As mentioned previously, a standard query plan will be produced by the optimizer and then run by the executor; however, this linear mode of planning and running queries can cause performance issues when the estimates are not correct. Currently, without interleaved execution, Multi-statement Table-Valued Functions would always use a fixed cardinality estimate of 100, regardless of the actual number. This often means there can be large discrepancies between that estimate and the actual number of rows; however, interleaved execution allows for the optimization process to be paused, a better estimate to be gathered and then resumed with that estimate in hand, thereby informing the optimizer of how to write the subsequent plan in the best way. This means that subsequent join algorithms are more efficient and memory spills are far less likely to occur.

Hyperscale

By this point, I am sure you can see that there are many reasons why an Azure SQL Database may provide a richer feature set than Azure Synapse Analytics and certainly an on-premises solution. However, a standard deployment of Azure SQL DB does have an upper limit on the size of your database which is currently set at 4 TB, not tiny, but not enough by many standards, and that is why Microsoft has completely redesigned the architecture from the ground up to be entirely tailored to the cloud. The new approach is termed Azure SQL Database Hyperscale and is the latest addition to the V-Core purchasing tier. The technology has been tested with databases up to 100 TB although this is not a technical limitation and Microsoft actively encourages customers with larger databases to push that limit further, claiming confidently that the Hyperscale technology will cope with it.

The reason that Hyperscale databases can scale to such large capacities is because the entire architecture of the resource has been adapted to exploit the cheap storage and flexible compute resources that are made available when working in a cloud-based platform. In much the same way that Azure Synapse Analytics separates storage from compute, Azure SQL DB Hyperscale does the same. This means that storage can scale linearly, but the compute power used to process that data can grow and shrink as required. Despite this similarity, the data in Azure SQL DB Hyperscale is not distributed like in Azure Synapse Analytics. The architecture still facilitates an SMP approach to data access which means that storage is essentially held in one place and only written to using a single master compute node.

The Hyperscale Architecture

To start from the top of the Hyperscale stack, we have the compute nodes. The compute nodes house the relational engine, SQL server, and control all interaction with the rest of the Hyperscale service. There will always be a single primary compute node that handles read and write transactions for the database; however, this can be supported by multiple read-only secondaries that can be used as hot secondaries for failover functionality but can also handle read-only workloads – such as hefty analytical queries. Additionally, these compute nodes utilize SSD caches, named Resilient Buffer Pool Extensions (RBPEX), so that the time to fetch page data can be minimized. A key point of interest relating to the purpose of this book is the concept of read-only secondaries. These can be utilized by specifying the **Application Intent** parameter as true in the connection string, indicating to the service that this is a read-only query and can therefore be routed to the read-only secondary nodes rather than the read-write master node.

Supporting the compute nodes is a set of page servers, which are really what allow Hyperscale to reach the scale that it does because there is no finite number of page servers in a given Hyperscale implementation. As the database continues to grow, more page servers are allocated to the service. Each page server handles a 1 TB subset of the data pages and delivers them to the compute nodes on demand, additionally making use of the RBPEX caching to avoid network round trips and support the low latency guarantees made by Microsoft. Importantly, the page servers are allocated 1 TB at a time, so each time a new page server is created, it will handle the next 1 TB of data; however, the service itself is billed in 1 GB increments so you do not pay for excessive storage although it is allocated to your service anyway. The other role of the page servers is to ensure the pages are kept up-to-date by replaying log transactions from the log service.

At the lowest level is remote storage, which is updated by the page servers and is the final place for data storage and is therefore used to support the snapshots that are created for backups and to enable Accelerated Disaster Recovery.

The final piece of the Hyperscale puzzle is the log service which again is implemented very differently to an on-premises transaction log. In an on-premises implementation of SQL server, the server itself will maintain a log file that continues to populate until it reaches a certain threshold and then begins to overwrite the previous log items, giving the impression that the log is circular. With Hyperscale, this is not the case. Because cloud storage is cheap, the log can easily be portioned off and stored in long-term cold storage, meaning that the log storage is practically infinite. The other key role of the log service is to accept transactions from the primary compute node and apply those changes to the secondary compute nodes and the pages stored on the page servers. As you can imagine, having to wait for the log service to complete that level of activity would add significant latency to a query response so the log service is designed so that there is essentially a landing area that persists the transaction record into a cache. Once persisted, the transaction is considered to be logged and then the replication of the transaction to compute nodes and page servers is done in the background, without delaying the query response.

With this architecture in mind, the flow of data through the Hyperscale service can be somewhat convoluted. In the first instance, data would be stored in an RBPEX cache on the compute nodes and therefore accessed very quickly. Alternatively, if the data is not on the compute node, then the read may have to go back to the page servers to fetch the data from there. When doing writes, the transaction is passed from the primary compute node to the log service. It is then the role of the log service to apply the transaction to the secondary compute nodes and the page servers; finally the page servers apply the change to the remote Azure Storage files.

Accelerated Disaster Recovery

A key concern for anyone managing a large database is "how long will it take to restore were it to go offline." In Hyperscale, this operation can be done very efficiently regardless of the size of data. It makes no difference to the restore activity whether the data is 1 TB or 100 TB which is an incredible level of comfort to provide for whoever must answer that question. Were the database to go offline and require a restore, the only activity that is needed is to repopulate the page servers with the data stored in Azure remote storage. Given that this operation can be scaled out by the number of page servers in the instance, it means that only a single TB must be restored onto any given page server regardless of the size of the database. To put this into perspective, a restore operation of a 50 TB Hyperscale database would mean that 50 page servers are created and populated with a TB of data from the remote storage; Microsoft has demoed this 50 TB restore completing in just 8 minutes.

While it is of course possible to manage a large, multi-terabyte database on-premises, a restore of that database would take considerably longer than 8 minutes. These kinds of disaster recovery options simply could not be achieved with the box version of SQL server because of the scale out operations required to facilitate them.

Azure SQL Deployment Options

When assessing the features that set Azure SQL Database and Azure Synapse Analytics apart, a key consideration is the deployment options. Often this can drive a number of conversations, that of cost, maintainability, management overhead, and alike. As both are cloud native solutions, scalability and compute size can be tailored with ease. Even if an initial deployment is very small and lightweight, a production scale up can easily be planned and implemented. Further to this, the size and scale of each solution can then be further tailored to meet the needs of users/processes throughout the day or week using Azure Automation scripts.

Both Azure SQL DB and Azure Synapse Analytics have support from Visual Studio SQL Server Data Tools (although Azure Synapse Analytics is in preview currently) allowing for seamless deployment and schema compare via Visual Studio. This means that from a development perspective, there should be little change between current on-premises practices and cloud practices; both are maintained and source controlled through Visual Studio.

Even though the development experience may be roughly the same between the two Azure SQL options, the target deployment platforms can vary greatly. Azure Synapse Analytics has a single deployment option as a stand-alone resource managed through the Azure portal. The deployment can be automated through the use of ARM templates; however, this only makes the deployment of that single Azure Synapse Analytics instance more efficient. Conversely, Azure SQL DB has a variety of options that can make the move to the cloud easier due to the flexibility of the platform.

Azure SQL Database Managed Instances

A managed instance is the closest cloud alternative to a traditional on-premises deployment of SQL server. Without a managed instance, you would create a logical SQL server that is no more than a namespace to group individual databases; however, with a managed instance, there is a real SQL server instance that hosts the databases and therefore access to the SQL Agent, Database Mail, Linked Servers, cross database queries, change data capture, and others. While this offers a level of comfort and the ability to reduce the amount of application rework, you also benefit from the Platform as a Service gains that Azure has to offer. Features such as automatic patching, automated backups, and v-nets are all configured out of the box without any management overhead for the business. For users looking to simply migrate to Azure with minimal disruption, this can be a very useful deployment option; however, significant cost optimizations are available if the stand-alone database deployment option can be used.

Azure SQL Database Elastic Pools

A second deployment option is that of elastic pools. Here, a pool of resources is created and shared between a multitude a single databases so that there is a single cost to pay and also a lot more ability to deal with sporadic spiking in database usage. Elastic pools work well when multiple databases need occasional high levels of performance but generally average at quite a low eDTU setting especially when the peaks are at varying times. In the scenario that you are supporting multiple databases that occasionally require high performance, without elastic pools, you would need to trade off between scaling to a tier that can handle peak usage and overpay the rest of the time and scaling to a lower tier and sacrificing performance, particularly at peak times. When designing an Azure SQL DB deployment, if elastic pools seem like a good option, then it is important to plan the size of the pool, the service tier of the contained databases, and the times at which those databases peak. You will need to know how many databases can spike at any given time while still remaining within your elastic pool size but also how you ensure that you have enough activity in the pool to make it more cost efficient than scaling the databases separately.

Azure SQL Database V-Core Tiers

When Azure SQL Database first arrived, the scale, and therefore pricing, of your database was configured using DTUs (Database Transaction Units). A single DTU is an abstracted metric that comprises storage, memory, and CPU to provide an easy single figure that is directly related to the overall performance of the database. However, the arrival of the V-Core option allows you to scale storage and compute separately, meaning the database can be completely tailored to your individual needs. When creating the database, you would choose the number of V-Cores to instantiate and then set a max storage size. The V-Core purchasing model is also available at different tiers, offering different performance characteristics and high availability/disaster recovery options.

- The lowest tier is General Purpose, being the standard for most business workloads.

- Next is Hyperscale which offers compatibility for databases above 4 TB while also guaranteeing high performance even at very high scale.

- Last is the Business Critical tier that offers the highest level of performance and reliability although still limited to a 4 TB maximum.

A point worth mentioning is that Hyperscale databases use the V-Core purchasing model but vacillate between the General Purpose and Business Critical tiers in terms of performance. When data is stored directly on the compute node's local RBPEX, then the performance will be at Business Critical scale without the cost overhead. Only when the Hyperscale service gets a cache miss on the compute node's local RBPEX would it have to go back to the page server, and this performance would replicate that of a General Purpose tier.

Inside of the V-Core tier is the ability to choose a "provisioned" deployment and a "serverless" deployment. The provisioned deployed means that the deployed resource is always active and therefore chargeable. Alternatively, a serverless deployment allows the service to be paused and resumed as needed, meaning you would only pay for what you actively use. This can provide a huge cost saving in development and test environments but may not be suitable for a production deployment. The base reason for this is that once the database is paused, the first query issued to the service will resume it but not complete successfully. Once resumed, all other queries will complete as expected unless the specified inactivity threshold is reached, and the service will pause again automatically. If this deployment option is of interest, it is possible to orchestrate a dummy query as an early part of the ETL process so that the service is running when needed.

Azure Synapse Analytics vs. Azure SQL Database

Now that the fundamentals of each technology option have been outlined, it is important to understand the attributes about your data that may drive you to use a particular Azure SQL engine over another.

The Right Type of Data

The first thing to confirm in this design process is that your data is going to be structured in a tabular format. These two SQL options only support tabular data and therefore should not be used to store non-/semi-structured data such as documents, JSON data, or multimedia files directly, unless stored as text in a tabular column. For JSON data, you could consider Azure Cosmos DB, and non-structured data and multimedia can be stored in the data lake. Of course, there may be scenarios where you need to process JSON from a source system into the data warehouse in which case you can load the JSON into a NVARCHAR (MAX) column and then read it using the OPENJSON table-valued function. If the data you need to store cannot be loaded and queried using a SQL database engine, then neither of these options are for you.

The Size of the Data

When choosing your SQL engine, the size of data plays a key role. If your database is less than 1 TB and not likely to increase beyond that point, then Azure Synapse Analytics is not a good option and you should look to use Azure SQL DB. Conversely, if the database is already 1 TB or bigger and is expected to grow, then Azure Synapse Analytics is firmly back on the table. If your data volumes are between 1 and 4 TB, then the cheaper option sits with Azure SQL Database – here we see a 2 TB database costing roughly £1.3k per month vs. an Azure Synapse Analytics at the same size costing £3.9k. When we scale this up to 100 TB, then there are a number of changes to be aware of. Firstly, only an Azure Hyperscale SQL Database can support a database that large, so your options are limited to using Hyperscale if you want to use an Azure SQL Database. Alternatively, you could swap to using an Azure Synapse Analytics as at 100 TB; you are able to really benefit from the massively parallel nature of the architecture. Full disclosure, the Azure Synapse Analytics instance is still more expensive but importantly will likely perform large-scale analytical queries better than a Hyperscale database due to the distributed nature of the database, especially when the data is correctly spread across distributions ensuring that common joins are heavily optimized given that the Hyperscale database cannot store data in this way. Ultimately, an Azure SQL Database will always be cheaper than Azure Synapse Analytics instance; however, it is also not optimized for analytical loads and does not contain features such as PolyBase, and so at small scales of data, a SQL DB will almost always be a better option. However, as the volumes increase, performance becomes more critical and this is where Azure Synapse Analytics earns its place.

The Frequency of the Data

Given this book is focused around data warehousing, I am discounting the need for traditional OLTP workloads; however, there are very often scenarios where a data warehouse needs to be trickle fed. In these scenarios, the patterns that are often used in Azure Synapse Analytics become inefficient and cumbersome; however, when the opposite is true, and data arrives at massive scale at more regular intervals, then the PolyBase and CTAS pattern make Azure Synapse Analytics a much more efficient processing option. When planning the ingestion process for your warehouse, it is essential to understand the needs of your users and the availability of your data. If you need to have rapidly refreshing dashboards that can be loaded from an event-based source system, micro transactions are needed and therefore an Azure SQL Database is likely a better option. Should you only need to refresh a dashboard once or twice a day with data that arrives with row counts in the billions, Azure Synapse Analytics will be able to ingest and process that data much faster. Should you need to combine approaches, then you could experiment with a SQL DB that processes your micro transactions into batches and loads them in Azure Synapse Analytics or explore the lambda architecture that is detailed later in this book.

The Availability of the Data

Any data warehouse project comes with a bunch of nonfunctional requirements, things that are required to satisfy the brief but don't necessarily deliver a functional advantage to the solution. Often these requirements include the recovery point objective (RPO), the amount of data lost after an incident, and the recovery time objective (RTO), the time it takes to get a system back up and operational. In Azure Synapse Analytics, regular automatic restore points are taken throughout the day and kept for a default of 7 days; however, you can also manually create restore points after significant events in the warehouse to ensure the maximum granularity of restore options and therefore minimal RPO. Conversely, Azure SQL Database also has very good options for RPO and RTO, and particularly within Hyperscale, giant databases (e.g., 50 TB+) can be restored in under 10 minutes with a 0-minute RPO due to the limitless page servers that simply need to be populated from the snapshots in Azure Storage. In addition to the RPO and RTO requirements, concurrency can heavily affect the availability of your data, and in Azure Synapse Analytics, availability is limited depending on the cDWU setting you have configured, whereas Azure SQL DB has a much higher concurrency given that it is an SMP system. If there are a very large number of concurrent users looking to query the warehouse, then an Azure Synapse Analytics may struggle to cope with this requirement without the use of Azure Analysis Services or another database on top.

The Integration of Data

Both flavors of Azure SQL integrate seamlessly with Azure Data Factory – the cloud integration tool of choice when working in Azure. However, Azure Synapse Analytics can make use of PolyBase providing a seamless layer between the data lake and the data warehouse.

In summary, Azure SQL Database is a cheaper option and potentially more flexible to a number of scenarios; however, there are specific features of Azure Synapse Analytics that make it a candidate for any data warehousing scenario assuming the data volumes are larger than 1 TB. When designing the warehouse, a worthwhile exercise is to write down all the pooled knowledge of the incoming data, incoming queries, ingestion patterns, and others and determine where each one of those attributes would be served better. From there, you can begin to discuss the features that mean the most to you and your organization and ignore those that are not essential. A final point to touch upon, and a pretty fundamental one, is that while the core concepts of each technology remain consistent, the features do change and improve over time, and it is important to keep up with each technology in case a really key feature comes about that changes the way you think about a particular technology.

The Integration Engine

The concept of data integration often sparks a lengthy and convoluted debate as to the best approach and technology for the given sources and destinations. In addition to the out-the-box products such as SQL Server Integration Services (SSIS), there is also a wealth of open source tools to consider, not forgetting the third-party connectors and bespoke, source system–specific integration tools that all help to muddy the water.

When operating on the Azure platform, the established convention is to use Azure Data Factory (ADF) V2. This is the primary integration and orchestration engine for any data movement in to or out of Azure, and the goal of this chapter is to remove the need for any upfront debate about tooling by justifying why Azure Data Factory is a one-stop shop for data integration.

Introduction to Azure Data Factory

Within Azure, there is really only one option for cloud scale data integration and this is Azure Data Factory (ADF). No other engines exist within the Azure service itself, and while this may seem limiting, it is actually refreshing because there is no real debate to be had; if you want to remain on the Azure platform, you use ADF.

Some developers may be warned off Data Factory and there may be good reason for this. In its first carnation, Azure Data Factory V1, many developers were expecting SSIS in the cloud and unfortunately this service fell well short of that mark. While the concept had promise, the service itself had some initial limitations. In this first iteration, the concept of parameters was not realized, and the only authoring option was to manually write JSON into the portal or in a local editor to be deployed using PowerShell. Far from the orchestration capabilities on offer today, in ADF V1, dummy datasets would have to be created, not to produce any kind of output but just to be used as an interface between daisy-chained activities. The limitations also extended to the triggering of Azure Data Factory which was based around tumbling windows. With these triggers, you could set up a start and end date and Data Factory would divide that time span into specified

© Matt How 2020
M. How, *The Modern Data Warehouse in Azure*, https://doi.org/10.1007/978-1-4842-5823-1_3

chunks, for example, days. ADF would then pre-populate these chunks in its execution queue and run the Data Factory every time a new window came into scope. However, there were no other triggering options to speak of.

As a user of ADF V1, easily the biggest pain point was the total lack parameters and variables; everything had to be hard coded upfront and could not then adapt to changes in the runtime environment, nor could you pass information between chained activities. Often when performing data integration, indeed in any programming task, you look to build generic elements that can be reused efficiently when supplied with varying parameters and this simply was not possible. Ultimately, Azure Data Factory V1 was difficult to work with and offered little to the developers looking to replace an on-premises SSIS implementation with a cloud alternative.

Luckily, Microsoft had many improvements up their sleeve, and Azure Data Factory V2 quickly became a much more exciting prospect. From a user's perspective, it appears as though the learnings gained from developing a well-matured integration tool such as SSIS had been blended with the recognized need for a cloud-based alternative as the software itself now does a lot more out of the box and has options for implementing many common programming routines. At first the focus was not on traditional ETL (extract, transform, load) but more on an ELT (extract, load, transform) approach which meant that data could be moved from source to sink and then transformed using the compute power of the destination, but some of the newer features of ADF V2 mean that either ETL or ELT can be implemented, depending on the scenario.

Initially there was a small step back – the only way to work with ADF V2 for the first few months was by writing JSON locally and deploying it to the ADF service using PowerShell. There was no way to visualize the objects that had been created, nor could you monitor the run of a pipeline. However, this did give users a great way of understanding the key concepts that underpin Data Factory, and even though there is now a full UI, the underlying JSON is still accessible and often is the easiest way to debug an issue. This inconvenience was forgivable though as we now had parameters to play with, and flexible, parameter-driven data processes that make use of reusable generic routines were now an option. In addition to this, we also began to receive other forms of activities such as the "If" activity and "Execute Pipeline" allowing developers to operate conditional logic and execute different pipelines depending on the result. With more and more features regularly arriving, we now have an integration engine that can live up to the demand, and what's more, it is fully integrated with Git and can even execute SSIS packages in the cloud. This chapter will focus solely on ADF V2 and the features that make it an all-round integration engine.

The Data Factory Building Blocks

When starting out with Azure Data Factory V2, it is important to understand the different elements that give it the ability to move data and orchestrate activities in a disparate cloud environment. Those key elements are

- Linked services
- Triggers
- Datasets
- Pipelines
- Activities

Each of these elements can be configured from within the Azure portal or scripted locally and deployed to the service using PowerShell or via source control (Git is the only source control option for ADF currently).

Linked Services

To begin with, the Data Factory needs to be able to make connections to the services it will copy data between or orchestrate jobs for. These connections are made through linked services, and these objects hold all the required parameters such as connection strings and credentials. Any credentials being used by Azure Data Factory should be stored in key vault as this ensures that your passwords and connection strings can easily be managed and updated in one place rather than having to track down every instance of a password that needs changing. To make use of Azure Key Vault, you would first need to create a key vault resource within the subscription and set up your secrets there. Once your key vault resource is in place, you can create a linked service connecting to that key vault account and your secrets will be automatically pulled from there when they are referenced through your Data Factory Linked Services. The steps to create a key vault and link it to your Data Factory instance via a linked service are described in the section "Getting Started with Azure Data Factory."

Typically, a data store linked service would connect to a service at a very high level. For example, if we use a linked service to connect to an Azure SQL Database, then it does only that; any logic to access a certain table with a certain query is routed through a dataset which sits on top of the linked service, more on this later in the chapter.

From within the UI, you can create a linked service connection to over 80 different data stores, some of which are Azure native such as Azure SQL Database and Azure Data Lake, while some are totally outside of Azure and even Microsoft such as Salesforce, Amazon S3, HDFS (Hadoop distributed file system), and local file systems on virtual machines (VM). As each of these data stores have different connection protocols you will find that you will need different pieces of information for each linked service option. Again, another reason why key vault is a preferable option over the native Data Factory credential management is because all these disparate pieces of information can be stored and maintained through one resource.

Data store linked services allow you to fetch data or deposit data; however, you can also create Compute Linked Services that allow you to execute jobs on Azure-based compute resources such as Azure Databricks, Azure Functions, and Azure Synapse Analytics, to name a few. This capability means that you can create processes and solutions outside of Data Factory that can then easily be executed as you run your Data Factory pipeline. Some examples of how this may work could include creating an Azure Databricks notebook that cleans and standardizes the data within a cloud data store before it is processed into your warehouse. Alternatively, you could utilize the Azure Batch compute service to create a scalable C# application that handles a particularly tricky or bespoke piece of logic that may have been implemented using an SSIS custom activity in an on-premises solution. This added flexibility makes Azure Data Factory more than just a service to copy data between storage locations but an orchestrator of cloud integration patterns executing jobs across your Azure subscription at scale!

A fundamental part of any linked service is the connection credentials, and there are several options supported here depending on the service you are connecting to although, as always, there are some best practices to be aware of. Most organizations prefer to administer permissions across an Azure subscription using Azure Active Directory groups as this allows for a single configuration of the permissions and then the group can just be populated as new users join or need that permission set. Additionally, this means that both service accounts and individual users can be added to a group ensuring that service accounts are not secret backdoors to a higher level of permission than was intended.

When applying this to a linked service connection, it means that we can use a service principal to authenticate our Data Factory and then just ensure that the service principal is added to a group that has access to the resource we want to connect to. In most cases, a service principal is an option for the connection credentials and needs only to be supplied with the service principal app id and the authentication key which could be supplied via key vault. In some cases, you may decide that you need a single connection that can read data from a given source but then only write into a particular folder in your cloud data store and then a second connection that can only read and write to different folders within the data store. This configuration means that writing into your data store is tightly controlled, as data can only arrive in one place due to permissions, and that data cannot leave the data store without explicitly creating a third connection or modifying an existing one. To support this scenario, you would need to create two linked services specifying the different service principal connection details on each.

Another option that is commonly available is to utilize the Azure Data Factory Managed Service Identity (MSI), which is essentially a service principal that represents the Azure Data Factory instance. This can be a useful option as it allows you to grant permissions explicitly to your Data Factory, knowing that you are not inadvertently granting permission to a different service you were not aware of. Also, the MSI is managed by the Data Factory service, so you do not need to manage the credentials of the identity through key vault or any other method – you simply tell the linked service to authenticate using the MSI. Of course, you still must provide the MSI with permission onto the service you want to connect to, and you can locate the MSI application id by following the setup instructions later in this chapter.

Integration Runtimes

Underpinning all activity in Azure Data Factory is the integration runtime (IR). This is the scalable, cloud compute resource that actually does the heavy lifting when copying data from one place to another or routing jobs to the required external compute resources. In most cases, you can default to using the Azure Integration Runtime which leaves the provision of the compute resource up to Azure itself and requires no further thought on the part of the developer. When executing jobs in external compute resources, there is no need to scale the compute as the process is simply to route the job to the correct resource. However, when doing data movement, you may want to kick the compute up a notch in order to get the job running quickly. The number of data integration units and degree of parallelism can easily be configured in the settings of the Copy Data activity within your Data Factory pipeline. Examples of how to do this are later in the chapter.

Self-Hosted Integration Runtime

When connecting to an on-premises data store, the connection must go via a Self-Hosted Integration Runtime (SHIR), which is a special gateway that is configured on the machine you are connecting to. For clarification, an Azure Virtual Machine (VM) falls under the bracket of on-premises even though it is technically IaaS. The reason a Self-Hosted Integration Runtime is needed is primarily focused around security. The Azure Data Factory service is exposed through a set of public IP addresses, and therefore without the Integration Runtime, you would have to configure an inbound connection to your network, undermining many security best practices. The SHIR means that the Azure Data Factory service simply needs to post a request to the Integration Runtime queue, which is then responded to as an outgoing connection from the machine. This is now far more secure as no inbound traffic is required. When connecting to the on-premises server, you will need to create the standard username and password credentials and these should be stored in key vault to ease administration.

There are some considerations to bear in mind when configuring the SHIR. The first is that only a single SHIR can be installed on a given machine; however, you do not need to install the SHIR on to the machine that holds the data. In the scenario that two Data Factories need to access the same dataset separately, you can create a second SHIR on a different machine in the same network and allow it access to the dataset. Consider that the second SHIR is further away from the data source and therefore may incur some degree of latency over the SHIR that is on the same machine as the data source. Alternatively, you can configure the sharing feature of the first SHIR so that it can be shared between Data Factories. Another point to consider is that a single SHIR can access multiple on-premises data sources, meaning that, in most cases, a single SHIR within your network is enough to cover off most scenarios. The recommendation from Microsoft is to install the SHIR on a separate VM than those that host the data source as this removes the risk of resource contention. In most implementations, a separate VM is created solely to support the SHIR.

Azure SSIS Integration Runtime

In some cases, there is a need to simply migrate existing SSIS packages from their on-premises environment into the cloud. This enables the cloud first approach but can avoid the need to rebuild logic and processing steps that are perhaps well tested and mature already. In an ideal world, these packages would get rebuilt eventually using pure Azure Data Factory components, but if time is of the essence, then this is certainly a worthwhile option.

In response to this need, Data Factory has the ability to execute SSIS packages using its cloud-based architecture so that you get the PaaS benefit but can also reuse your existing code base if needed. In order to make use of this, you will need to create the Azure SSIS Integration Runtime (IR) and also maintain a separate Azure SQL Database that will host your SSIS DB Catalogue. When creating the Azure SSIS IR, Data Factory will create the SSIS DB Catalogue for you on the nominated database. When configuring the Azure SSIS IR, you can specify the node size and the node number which allows you to configure your scale up/scale out requirements. For example, to run large, compute heavy packages, then you should choose a large node size, and if you want to be able to run many of these in parallel, you should choose a large node number. Of course, if you want to run many small packages in parallel, then you can choose a small node size and a large node number. At later stages in the process, you will also be asked to specify connection strings for your SQL database and the degree of parallelism to use when running the packages.

In order to deploy and run packages using Data Factory, you will need to create a connection to the Azure SQL Database that is running the SSIS DB Catalogue and deploy the SSIS project using the deployment wizard that can be accessed by right-clicking the project and choosing "Deploy Project…."

Finally, to run and monitor the SSIS package execution, you can simply choose to execute using the SSMS dialog, passing in any parameters or settings for connection managers as needed. Once the package is running, the overall status can be monitored using the Azure Data Factory UI which can also report back the SSIS DB Operation ID to allow for a more detailed view to be surfaced using the SSMS execution report.

As you can see, this method does allow a fairly painless adoption of a PaaS-based architecture while maintaining the same processes and tools that would be used were this to be running in an on-premises solution. It is worth remembering however that while this approach does allow for backward compatibility, the goal should be to make the move into the cloud a decisive one and rebuild the existing functionality using the native Data Factory tools. The result of this will be a drastic reduction in maintenance overheads as no SSIS IR or SSIS DB Catalogue is required, but also your developers will have a much fresher, cleaner development experience that thrives in a big data scenario where sources and sinks are widely distributed.

Triggers

Triggers are the method by which pipelines are invoked and allow ADF to support a variety of types of automation. When developing a Data Factory pipeline, you can test the pipeline in debug mode which allows the pipeline to execute fully only on a debug cluster and does not require a publish action. You can monitor your pipeline from within the authoring UI and check the input and output of each activity as execution occurs. Additionally, any activities that are configured to run in parallel will be run sequentially so that you can easily step into any activity in the pipeline. An alternative to the debug method that can be used once the development process is completed is to publish the Data Factory definition to the service and trigger the pipeline from the UI, effectively testing the pipeline against runtime conditions. This is called a manual trigger and can be monitored not from the authoring UI but from the Azure Monitor UI. The reason for this is that ADF understands that this invocation is no longer just for testing and therefore fully logs the pipeline execution while also honoring the parallel configuration of activities. Once you are satisfied that development is complete and that appropriate testing has been completed using a manual invocation, automatic triggers can be established so that processing can occur at defined intervals or at acknowledgment of a specific event. The automatic triggers cater for a wide variety of automation options and fall under three categories which are listed here:

- Schedule triggers
- Tumbling window triggers
- Event triggers

The first of these, the schedule trigger, will execute the specified pipeline based on a given recurrence and can be set to run on a regular interval based on minutes, hours, days, weeks, or months. The start time is the root of the schedule, and so it is important to set this correctly when building the trigger as the intervals that are defined are then based as an offset of that date and time. For example, to set a schedule that would run twice a day, you would set the interval to be "hours" and the recurrence to be 12. Assuming the trigger was started at 12:00, you would get two executions of your pipeline in a 24-hour window, once at midday and once at midnight. A common requirement however is to run pipelines multiple times in a day but not on a symmetric schedule like the preceding example but perhaps on a workday schedule such as at 08:00 and 17:00. To support this scenario, you would have to create two triggers, each set to run once a day, that start at the desired times.

The tumbling window trigger is maintained in Data Factory from version 1 and works in some ways similar to the schedule trigger but does have some key differences. To make use of this trigger, it is important to know at what intervals your source data is refreshed because the upshot of the tumbling window is that it will automatically create slices of data based on its configuration. For example, if you know that the source data is refreshed daily, then you can create a trigger that has an interval of daily and recurrence of one, and then Data Factory will create a daily slice of data for each day from the start date up to the current date. As soon as the next day comes around, and therefore the next slice of data, then Data Factory creates a new data slice and execute the Data Factory pipeline to process it. This type of processing can be really useful when loading historical data into a cloud data store as you often want to maintain some sort of date/time-based partitioning even though the data is historical. If you need data from 5 years ago to be loaded and partitioned by day, then you simply set your start date to be 5 years in the past, set the recurrence to be once daily, and then Data Factory will churn through each of those 1825 data slices sequentially. Furthermore, you can configure the concurrency of this type of execution to ensure the Data Factory does not consume too many resources while it runs.

The issue with both of these types of triggers is that they do not understand what is going on in the source data, and so if the data is held up for any reason, they will still execute the pipeline and potentially process old data if the proper precautions have now been put in place. What is more, the triggers do not actually filter any source queries you may have configured in the dataset, so while Data Factory may know when the window of data you are interested in starts and ends, it does not actually enforce that onto the data source. This must be done by the developer by accessing the trigger properties using notation such as `@trigger().outputs.windowStartTime` and passing the dates/times of that trigger into your query.

To get around this, there is a final type of trigger which utilizes events to invoke the Data Factory rather than a clock. Events in this instance are constrained only to when blobs are created or deleted in a Blob Storage account, and while ideally this would be slightly less constrained, this method of invoking Data Factory does allow the process to be run once the source data is ready to be processed and not before. When configuring this type of trigger, you can optionally specify filters that ensure you are only listening for events created by blobs in a particular container or folder or alternatively blobs that have a certain name of extension.

Datasets

With a linked service, you have a connection, but you now need to add a layer on top of that to implement logic that allows you to access specific tables, files, directories, and others. This layer is known as the dataset and you can specify as many of these as needed that utilize the linked service. A common usage of a dataset is to specify a specific folder location in a cloud data store that you may want to load data from or copy data to. At the time of data movement, the dataset is used to reference a specific file to copy or write to and passes its configuration via the linked service to the data store and either fetches the file or writes to the specific location.

Further to this, datasets can be used to compress or decompress files after a Copy Data activity and even understand the metadata of the file so that it can be fully accessed by Data Factory. With this capability, you can configure the elements such as the file format, column delimiter, and row terminator to be used when reading the file and then specify different metadata to write the file using. With this capability, you can easily read text files from the raw source but then drop them into a cloud data store in an optimized format such as Parquet or Optimized Row Columnar (ORC). Conversely you could unzip a collection of files and either flatten their hierarchy to give you a single level of files in your copy destination or preserve the hierarchy to ensure consistency between your source and destination. A final option is the use of binary copy which removes the complexity of trying to read the file and simply copies the file as is into your destination. This is particularly useful if you want to copy totally unstructured data across your subscription.

As this book is focused around data warehousing, I will make the assumption that the majority of loading done through Data Factory is with structured source files that are either in a raw text-based format such as CSV or already in an optimized format such as ORC or Parquet. Depending on which stage of your data processing pipeline you are building in Data Factory, you may wish to enforce a schema on your file to ensure consistency is maintained. Of course this is optional, as often when reading files from a source system, you may want to disregard the fact that some rows may not conform to your schema because ultimately you would rather have the data in a domain that is accessible to you as a developer. When creating schemas in Data Factory, you first need to input the schema for each dataset. This is where heavy parameterization of your datasets can become problematic as you will need to import the schema for each file it will read, but assuming a dataset aligns to a table, then this should be pretty simple. Data Factory even offers an "Import Schemas" option that reads the metadata of your database and creates the schema for you. Once you have a schema for both your source and your sink, you can then provide those to the Copy Data activity. In the Copy Data activity configuration there is a "Mapping" tab which allows you to do just that – map each source column to a sink column. Here you can either choose to map an incoming column directly or utilize an expression to populate the sink column. Also you can remove a sink column if you do not wish to map a value to it.

Pipelines and Activities

Azure Data Factory Pipelines are the heart of engine. They define the routine of activities that are to be executed and can be roughly likened to the control flow concept in SQL Server Integration Services. Underneath the covers, every object in Data Factory is just a JSON definition that is interpreted by the service, and while both linked services and datasets are stand-alone objects, a pipeline definition contains multiple JSON objects called activities. In addition, the pipeline also holds the definition of any parameters and variables that may be utilized throughout the pipeline as part of an activity. Without pipelines, a Data Factory is really a collection of data source connections and pointers to specific locations within those sources. It is the pipelines that make sense of these connections and define how one source feeds data into another while also providing a parameter-driven interface so that these connections and pointers can be dynamic and reusable depending on the specific runtime environment. Additionally, pipelines allow for interconnectivity across the Data Factory by having the ability to pass parameters into subsequent pipelines and receive parameters from prior pipelines. We can go a level deeper, however, and reveal that pipelines are more of a canvas for you to distribute activities on, applying an operating scope for parameters and variables to interact within. Activities themselves can take many shapes and forms depending on the type of activity and what the activity is doing; these are examined in the next section.

Activity Types

Activities are highly specialized JSON objects and provide the ability to do just one action. If you want to use the Databricks activity, then you must specify which Notebook or Python job to execute as well as the cluster linked service. Alternatively, if you want to call a web service, then you must provide the web URL of the service, the header and body values, as well as any authentication parameters that are needed. For that reason, it is worth the time and effort before development begins to plan and structure the activities you need in your pipeline so that you can define patterns upfront to avoid creating unnecessary activities that require further maintenance and understanding. Additionally, some activities execute compute jobs, some perform data movement, some run nested activities, while others implement control logic and looping. This huge amount of variety is what makes ADF so flexible but also requires prior thought to ensure the right activities are used.

Broadly speaking, the activities within Data Factory can be bucketed up into four groups. These are

- External compute activities
- Internal copy activities
- Iteration and conditional activities
- Web activities

External Compute Activities

As previously mentioned, Azure Data Factory is heavily used to orchestrate external resources and can efficiently execute, monitor, and report the result of jobs being run outside of Data Factory. The activities that fall into this category include

- **Custom**: Scalable C# activities that are executed using Azure Batch compute.

- **Databricks**: Notebooks, Python Scripts, or compiled .jar files executed on a Databricks job cluster.

- **Data Lake Analytics**: Jobs written in U-SQL executed using the Data Lake Analytics service.

- **HDInsight**: Spark, Pig, MapReduce, and Hive job executed against an HDInsight cluster.

- **Machine Learning**: Execute machine learning tasks such as batch scoring against an Azure Machine Learning resource.

- **Stored Procedure**: Call a stored procedure on a linked SQL service. Be aware that this is a non-query execution and will not return a result set to Data Factory even if one is generated by the stored proc. Of course, you can pass parameters into the stored procedure which can even be derived by Data Factory parameters or variables.

For each of these resources, you would need to create a linked service to store the authentication and connection details; however, a dataset is not required as you are not referencing a dataset. An additional consideration with the external services is that of the timeout and retry policies. As these services are not directly controlled by Data Factory, there can be scenarios where the first attempt at the connection fails but the second will succeed, so be sure to specify a retry attempt number and interval.

Internal Activities

Probably one of the most used activities in Data Factory is the Copy Data activity. This is because it allows you to move data, at scale, from one disparate data store to another with very little complexity. To make use of this activity, you will need both a linked service and at least one dataset although assuming you are moving data from one place to another, you would have two for each. The nomenclature of the Copy Data activity describes the origin of your data as the "source" and the destination as the "sink," and you can also specify configuration properties about the Copy Data activity such as

- The number of integration units to use (the scale of the job).

- The degree of parallelism to utilize.

- The fault tolerance setting: When you make use of the copy schemas, you can either set this to fail on first incompatible row, skip incompatible rows, or log and skip incompatible rows. Rows commonly fail if the data type is not supported by the .NET type system or if the source type is not compatible with the destination type; however, it can also conduct primary key validation.

Another option in the internal activities is the Delete activity, allowing you to use a dataset to define files for deletion; again you can fully utilize parameters to make this highly dynamic. In this activity, you also have the option to log the deleted file names to a storage account.

A relatively recent addition to these internal activities is that of data flows which allow for proper data transformation activities to be applied to your datasets. The data flows are authored and configured separately to the pipelines and can then be executed, monitored, and daisy chained just like any other activity in your pipeline. Under the covers, the information about how to perform the data transformation is packaged up and executed using Databricks clusters which allows for configurable scaling and compute type selection. However, the management of the Databricks cluster abstracted from you, the developer, does not incur the need for an additional linked service. To give a flavor of some of the transformations that a data flow can perform, there are four main categories of transformation which are listed here with some examples included:

- **Multiple inputs/outputs**: Branching, joining, and lookups – break up datasets into multiple processing flows and look up data from sources using a lookup key

- **Schema modifier**: Derived columns, aggregations, windowing, and pivoting – transform the schema of the file by computing new columns or performing aggregations and grouping

- **Row modifier**: Select, filter, and sort data with the additional capability to apply updates, inserts, and deletes to individual rows in the dataset

- **Destination**: Add an output destination to land the transformed dataset into one of the supported sinks

In addition to these transformations, data flow also supports options for allowing schema drift and validating that incoming data meets the specified schema before processing in the data flow to allow flexibility or enforce consistency depending on the scenario.

Iteration and Conditional Activities

One major piece of functionality that was missing from the first version of Azure Data Factory was the ability to implement some very common programming concepts such as looping and conditional logic. With version 2, we can now use activities that allow us to write these kinds of procedures into the control flow. The activities that fall into this bucket are

- **Set and Append variable**: Two separate activities that allow developers to create variables that exist with the scope of the pipeline and optionally append further values to an array variable. Note that parameters can be passed between pipelines, however variables cannot.

- **Execute Pipeline**: Using this activity, parent and child pipelines can be created that allow for layers of logic to be built up rather than have single gargantuan pipelines. This also facilitates passing parameters into the executed pipeline and can be very easily called from within a loop. For example, iterate a list of file location and execute a copy pipeline for each one.

- **Get Metadata**: Returns a configurable list of metadata attributes about the target file or directory.

- **Lookup**: This is a useful activity that allows the developer to access a data store, retrieve values, and then assign them into variables or pass them into subsequent activities as parameters. Importantly this activity can be run against SQL datasets using queries or stored procedures but also cloud data stores such as Blob Storage meaning configuration metadata can be stored in JSON format and read in at runtime using the Lookup activity.

- **Wait**: Implements a delay in the pipeline of a specified interval.

- **For Each Loop**: This is one of the major developments in ADF V2 that allows developers to really make their pipelines more than just many repeated activities. You can pass an array of items into this activity and then execute a nested activity for each item in the array. What is more, you can access the items inside your array using the `@item().{arrayitem}` notation, meaning you can very simply Lookup a list of files to process and then pass their locations into Copy Data activity nested within a For Each loop, accessing the file location as an attribute of the list on each iteration. Finally, this activity can be run either sequentially or in parallel. If parallel is chosen, then a batch limit can optionally be specified to control the amount of concurrent executions.

- **If Condition**: As described in the name, you can use the If Condition activity to assert conditional logic on your pipeline. By first writing an expression that evaluates to either true or false, you then nest the various activities to be called in each scenario. Be aware that the subsequent activities do have to be nested within the activity definition, so the best practice when having many activities following an If Condition is to utilize an Execute Pipeline activity based on the output of the expression. Additionally, there is a restriction on the activities you can call when you are working within a nested activity already. For example, you cannot call another If Condition, For Each loop, or Until Loop when you are defined the set of actions to be nested within one of these activities. The reason is to prevent infinite looping that can occur when nested activities continually call further nested activities.

- **Until Loop**: This loop executes the nested activities until the specified expression evaluates to true. Here the developer could utilize variables to control the number of iterations from within Data Factory or make use of the Lookup activity and parameters to control the iteration from outside of Data Factory.

With the exception of the Lookup and Get Metadata activities, none of these activities require datasets or linked services as they execute internally to Data Factory, but they may require a good working knowledge of the expression builder as many of these require the ability to access array items using expressions or determine a valid Boolean result using an expression.

Web Activities

The final category of activities are the web activities, and the reason for these being separate and not considered as external compute is that these are not for heavy lifting of data. These are designed to be "chatty" rather than chunky and are great for facilitating lightweight messaging and alike. In truth, they are simply a way to call a REST API, so they are generally very flexible, but any large-scale data processing that needs to use C# or another programming language should be written using Azure Batch and the custom activity. The Web activity can make generic HTTP calls to any web service when provided with a URL and the required headers, body, and authentication, while an Azure Function does essentially the same but means that you can simply create the linked service and then call the function by name, rather than having to specify the full URL.

Output Constraints

It is worth making the point that all Data Factory activities will report on their completion status, and so if an activity does fail, you can create a separate branch of your pipeline that handles the failure in the appropriate way. Further to this, you can create multiple output constraints on any given activity that allow for several branches to be created depending on the job's outcome. The possible configurations for these output constraints are

- **Success**: Execute subsequent activities only if the job succeeds

- **Failure**: Execute subsequent activities only if the job fails

- **Completion**: Execute subsequent activities whether the job fails or succeeds but is run

- **Skipped**: Execute subsequent activities even if this activity is skipped

At this time, the output constraints are *AND* only, meaning that all constraints must be met in order to execute the subsequent activity. This is not generally an issue but does make handling errors perhaps slightly more cumbersome than it needs to be. The approach for any pipeline should be a standard error handling routine that logs the error and alerts an individual at the very least. Once a routine has been built, this can be hooked into each one of your activities so that they can all benefit from this method; however, if you use multiple failure outputs, then all of the connected activates MUST fail in order to execute your error handling process. Unfortunately, the best alternative is to abstract the logic into a separate pipeline and connect an "Execute Pipeline" task to every activity that you want to handle errors for.

Implementing Azure Data Factory

With any technology decision, there should always be a discussion beyond the theoretical benefits of using a given tool. This discussion should look at the real-world usage of the item in question and examine it through a number of lenses, for example, security, developer productivity, and source control. This next section unpacks these topics to offer assurances about how Azure Data Factory can be used in the real world by real developers.

Security in Azure Data Factory

The essential feature of Azure Data Factory is being able to connect up to a wide variety of data sources and either read data from them or write data into them. Of course nearly all of these sources have some form of security in place, and, depending on the number of sources, there is a high likelihood that you will need to store a good number of credentials. As discussed earlier in this chapter, best practice dictates that any credentials are stored in key vault and referenced with your linked service definition. This means that the security of these sources is transparent to ADF and allows for administrators to update passwords and details without making any changes to ADF. Often credentials are not only usernames and passwords but may also be service principal details, which are Azure service accounts used for interacting with Azure native services, and this too can be configured as an option on your linked service. Using either of these options means that Data Factory will execute as the given service principal or user when interacting with a connected service.

Using the Managed Service Identity

An alternative option for authentication in Azure Data Factory is to use the managed service identity (MSI), which is essentially a service principal that represents the Data Factory instance. All Azure Data Factories are created with an MSI and the details of this can be collected from the Azure portal. Providing these details are then granted the appropriate permissions, you will be able to utilize the MSI when running Data Factory jobs by choosing the "Managed Service Identity" options when configuring the linked service. To locate the MSI details, you can follow these steps:

1. Navigate to the Azure Data Factory resource from within the Azure portal – you cannot use the Azure Data Factory UI for this guide.

2. Choose "Properties" and locate the "Service Identity Application ID." You can copy this ID and configure permissions for it as you would a usual service principal.

3. Navigate to your data lake and grant permissions to access the data needed for the Service Identity Application ID.

4. Once you have set the appropriate permissions, then you can choose the "Managed Identity" option in the "Authentication type" drop-down.

Source Control of Azure Data Factory

As with any ETL tool that is used in a production system, source control is crucial. In Data Factories' formative years, there was no integrated source control and the only option was to store the JSON definition files in a source-controlled folder. This meant that developers had to go through several manual steps in order to protect their work and remember to do those steps in the first place! Nowadays, Data Factory can be integrated directly into a Git repository hosted either on GitHub or within an Azure DevOps workspace, thus ensuring changes are automatically detected and committed when working in the Azure Data Factory UI. By default, the Data Factory instance will not be connected to source control of course, and therefore changes are made to the single Data Factory version. If left unchanged, changes can easily be overwritten and lost as there is no option for branching or merging. When specifying your source control option, you can define the account and project to associate your ADF instance to and then easily choose from any branch in the repo to begin updating. What you will notice when working in this way is that you can save and run your Data Factory in debug mode; however, you will need to create a pull request in order to publish code back to the master Data Factory instance and trigger the process in a non-debug way.

Templates

Templates allow developers to define a pipeline and then save it into the template repository. For this feature to work, your Data Factory instance must be connected to a source control option. Once created, all developers can benefit from the templates by pulling the definition into their workspace, thereby removing the need to create any objects that might be considered standard throughout the solution.

Solution Structure

When creating a Data Factory solution, indeed any ETL solution, the structure is very important as this dictates how the objects are organized. A well-defined and logical structure here ensures that even as your Data Factory instance grows, the essential items are no more difficult to find. To maintain a good solution structure, the following points should be considered:

- **Use folders**: Folders allow you to group similar objects together within the scope of pipelines, datasets, and data flows. As Data Factory often deals with source systems, it is good practice to create a folder for each source system and place the relevant objects within it. Additionally, if some pipelines deal with ingestion from source and some deal with data cleaning, then a hierarchy of folders can be used to further partition the objects.

- **Use a clear naming convention**: A strong and consistent naming convention means that items are easily identified without developers having to review any code to understand what the object is for. Source system names, source and sink references, pipeline purpose, and others are all useful attributes to highlight in the object name.

- **Use templates**: Templates ensure that developers can easily pick from agreed patterns when building a Data Factory, therefore increasing efficiency standardization. This is particularly useful when addressing common requirements such as logging mechanisms.

Getting Started with Azure Data Factory

In order to create the Azure Data Factory V2 resource, you will need access to an Azure subscription and resource group with contributor or owner access. With these permissions in place you can use the "Add" button within the resource group and search for "Data Factory" to create the resource. Once you have this, you can start to work through the subsequent configuration steps to perform an initial Copy Data activity. The following steps provide a basic starting point from which to further develop your use of Data Factory. The first piece of configuration to prepare is that of the linked service. In the example here, we will be performing a common data movement task that is required in almost all data warehousing scenarios by copying a file from a cloud data store into an Azure SQL Database, and to complete this action, we will need two linked services, one for the data store and one for Azure SQL Database.

Create Linked Services

The following steps will explain how to create a linked service in Azure Data Factory. This particular walk-through will use Azure Data Lake Gen 2 as the source connection but will also make use of a key vault linked service to ensure security best practice.

1. Navigate to the resource group containing your resources and click add in the top left corner. Search for "key vault" and choose the "Azure Key Vault" resource. Navigate through the wizard and use the form to supply a name, region, and pricing tier (standard is all that is needed here). Figure 3-1 shows a completed form.

Basics   Access policy   Networking   Tags   Review + create

Azure Key Vault is a cloud service used to manage keys, secrets, and certificates. Key Vault eliminates the need for developers to store security information in their code. It allows you to centralize the storage of your application secrets which greatly reduces the chances that secrets may be leaked. Key Vault also allows you to securely store secrets and keys backed by Hardware Security Modules or HSMs. The HSMs used are Federal Information Processing Standards (FIPS) 140-2 Level 2 validated. In addition, key vault provides logs of all access and usage attempts of your secrets so you have a complete audit trail for compliance. Learn more

Project details

Select the subscription to manage deployed resources and costs. Use resource groups like folders to organize and manage all your resources.

Subscription *	Visual Studio Enterprise – MPN (d6c9085f-1bef-4f0b-85e8-a30400cbbd0c) ⌄
Resource group *	moderndw ⌄
	Create new

Instance details

Key vault name * ⓘ	ModernDWKeyVault ✓
Region *	North Europe ⌄
Pricing tier * ⓘ	Standard ⌄
Soft-delete ⓘ	(Enable Disable)
Retention period (days) * ⓘ	90
Purge protection ⓘ	(Enable Disable)

Figure 3-1. *A completed form to create an Azure Key Vault*

2.   Click "Next: Access Policy" and click "Add access policy." Use
     the form to choose the "Secret Management" access policy
     template. By clicking the "Select principal" field, a new blade
     will appear on the right where you can select which principal
     is attached to this access policy. Type the name of your Data
     Factory and this will automatically select the Managed Service
     Identity. See Figure 3-2.

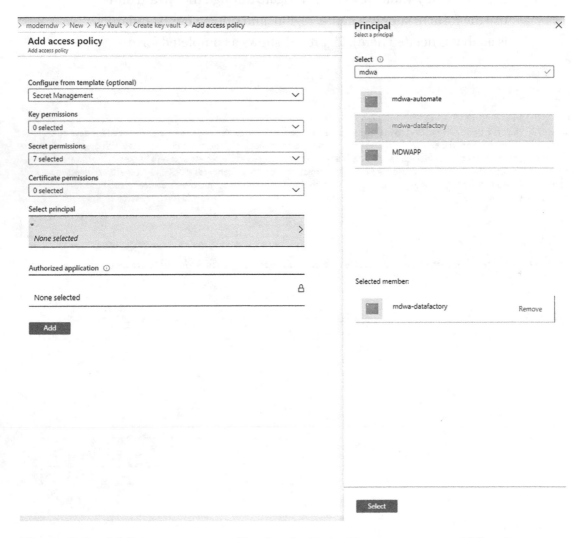

Figure 3-2. *Adding an access policy for the Data Factory managed identity*

3. Once selected, click "Add" to get back to the main key vault wizard shown in Figure 3-3.

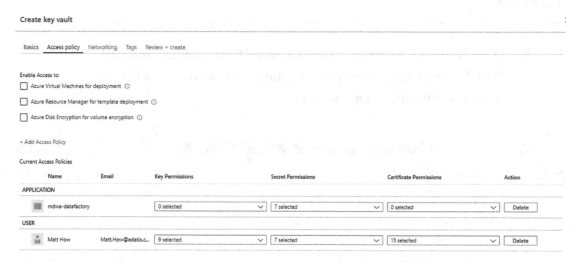

Figure 3-3. Access policies created for the key vault

4. Click "Review + create" to complete the setup and validate the deployment by opening the resource once finished.

5. To create the linked services, navigate to the Data Factory resource and click the "Author & Monitor" button. This will open the Azure Data Factory UI. Figure 3-4 highlights this button.

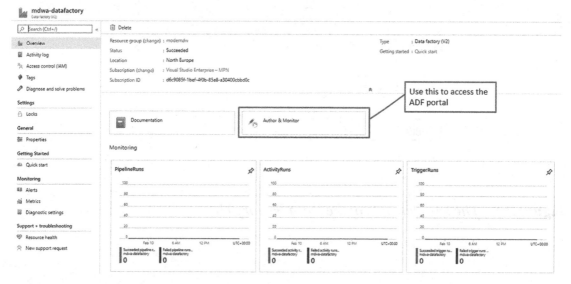

Figure 3-4. The Author & Monitor button

> **Tip**   Use the link `https://adf.azure.com` to navigate straight to the Data Factory UI

6. In the bottom left corner, you can choose "Connections" and click "New" in the connections pane. Figure 3-5 shows the Data Factory UI and points out the key elements.

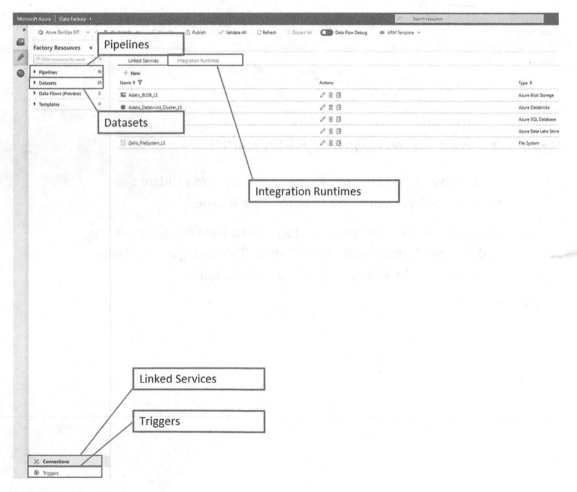

Figure 3-5. *The key elements of the Data Factory UI*

7. From the menu, choose "Azure Key Vault." Using the form that pops up, supply a name and choose the key vault resource as shown in Figure 3-6.

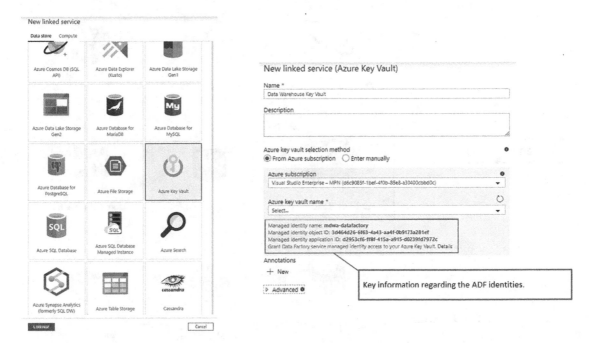

Figure 3-6. *Creating the key vault linked service in Data Factory*

Now that you have the key linked service, you can utilize this with all other linked services.

8. Add a new connection, and from the menu that opens on the right, select "Azure Data Lake Storage Gen2" and hit "Continue." See Figure 3-7 for an example.

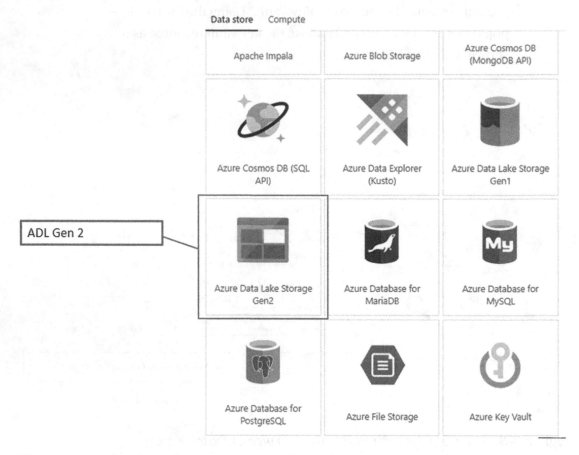

Figure 3-7. *Choosing the Azure Data Lake Storage Gen2 option for a linked service*

9. Here you can now provide the following:

    - **Name and description**: Use a name and aim to conform to a
      standard naming convention like the one included in Chapter 1,
      "The Rise of the Modern Data Warehouse".

    - **Integration runtime**: You can use the Azure IR by default as this
      leaves the resource negotiation to the Azure platform.

    - **Authentication method**: There are a few options here to choose
      from. The first being Account key which allows you to simply
      specify the key for your Blob Storage account. Other methods
      include using a service principal or using the ADF MSI as
      mentioned previously.

- For the **Account selection method**, choose "Enter manually" and then select "Azure Key Vault." You can now choose your key vault linked service and specify the secret name. Leave the Secret version field blank to ensure the latest version of the secret is always fetched.

- Finally, test the connection and ensure you have successfully set up the linked service via key vault as per Figure 3-8.

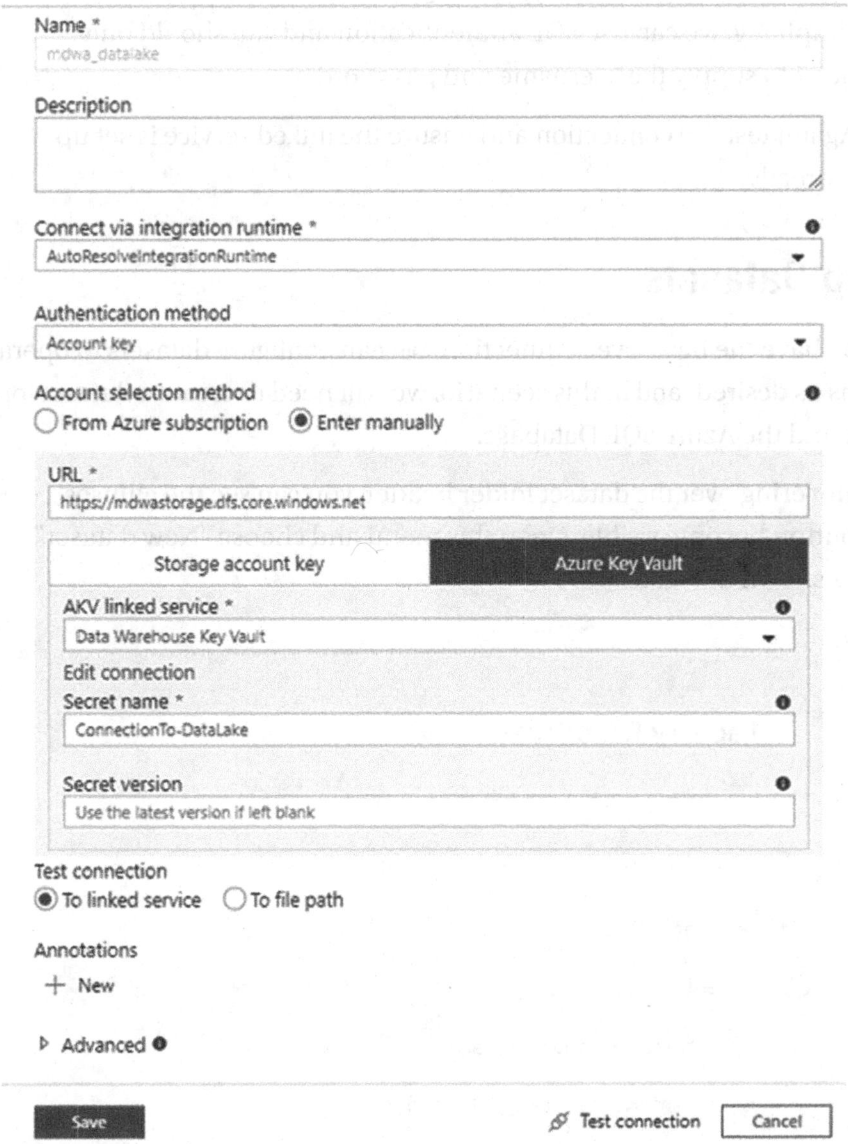

Figure 3-8. *A completed Azure Data Lake Gen2 linked service, utilizing key vault secret*

10. Once you have navigated back to the main linked services pane, click "New" again to begin setting up the Azure SQL Database Linked Service.

11. From the list that opens on the right, choose "Azure SQL Database" and supply the name, subscription, server name, and database name to the linked service.

12. You can now choose the type of SQL authentication. For simplicity, we can use SQL authentication and you should only need to supply the username and password.

13. Again, test the connection and ensure the linked service is set up correctly.

Creating Datasets

Now that we have the base level connection, we can configure datasets to operate these connections as desired, and in this scenario, we will need to create a dataset for the Data Lake Gen 2 and the Azure SQL Database.

1. Hovering over the dataset folder header, you can see the ellipses button become visible. Open this menu and choose "New dataset" as shown in Figure 3-9.

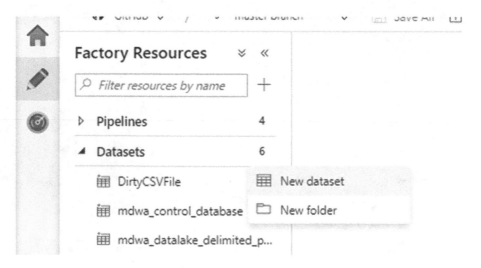

Figure 3-9. *Creating a new dataset in Data Factory*

2. Choose "Azure Data Lake Storage Gen2" and then "DelimitedText." Click "Continue" to navigate to the next form. Figure 3-10 shows the selection of data lake storage and delimited text.

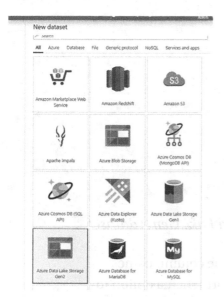 

Figure 3-10. *Choosing a delimited text option for Azure Data Lake Storage Gen2*

3. Supply a name and choose your existing Data Lake Gen 2 linked service in the "Linked service" drop-down and then enter the following details:

   FilePath: File system = "datalake", Folder = "RAW", File = "DemoSales.csv". See Figure 3-11 for an example.

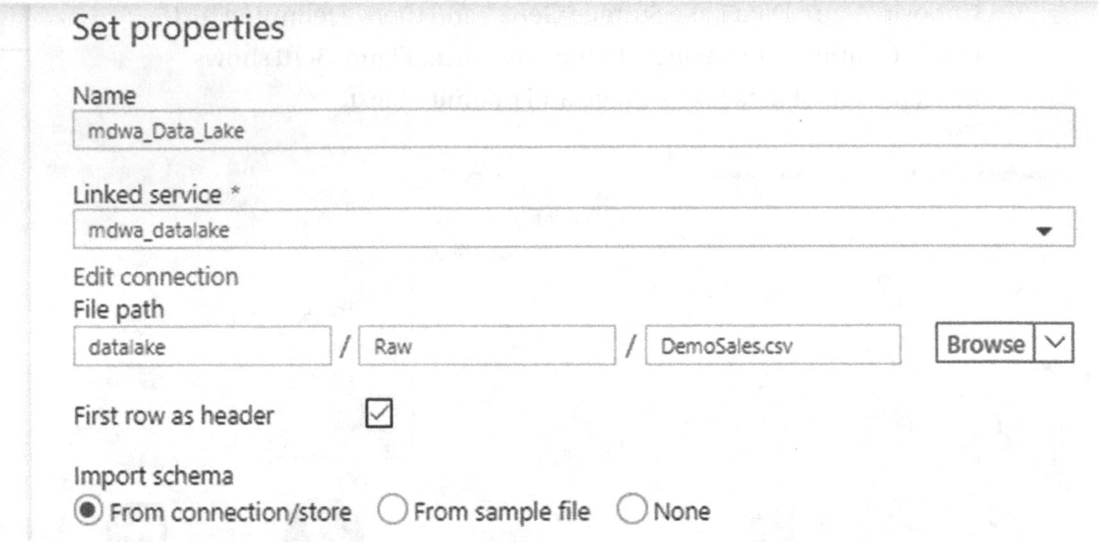

Set properties

Name

mdwa_Data_Lake

Linked service *

mdwa_datalake ▼

Edit connection
File path

| datalake | / | Raw | / | DemoSales.csv | Browse ∨ |

First row as header ☑

Import schema
◉ From connection/store   ○ From sample file   ○ None

Figure 3-11. *Entering the directory details for Data Lake Gen 2 dataset*

4. Tick the "First row as header" box to ensure the column names
    are removed from the data. Also, set the Import schema option to
    None for the time being.

5. Click "Continue" and you will see your new dataset appear on the
    left of the authoring view. Select the "Connection" tab and review
    the settings, noting the different parameters that can be supplied
    to help ADF read your file.

6. To create the second dataset for your SQL database, you can
    follow the same logical steps as before, only instead of choosing
    Data Lake Gen 2, you should choose Azure SQL Database.

7. Once chosen, you will be prompted for a name and a linked
    service and can then choose a table from the database to be
    attached to the dataset.

Creating Pipelines

Finally, we can use the pipeline to execute a set of activities that utilize the datasets and
linked services that have been previously created:

1. Hover over the Pipelines header and open the ellipsis menu, choosing "Add Pipeline" from the list of options as shown in Figure 3-12.

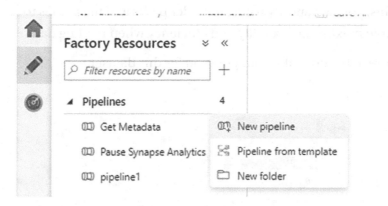

Figure 3-12. *Creating a new pipeline*

2. In the "Activities" tool bar on the right, expand the "Move & transform" node and drag the "Copy Data" activity onto the design surface. Provide a name to the activity. See Figure 3-13 for an example.

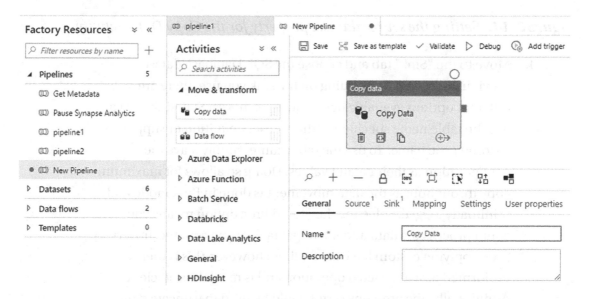

Figure 3-13. *An example of a copy data activity*

3. Move to the "Source" tab. Here you can choose your Azure Data
    Lake Gen 2 dataset. Note the tick box "Recursively" which allows
    you to specify a folder to the dataset and allow Data Factory to
    copy each file as it navigates through the subfolders. Further
    to this, you can specify wildcard folder paths and file names to
    enable maximum flexibility and efficiency when reading data.

    Figure 3-14 shows the configuration for this dataset.

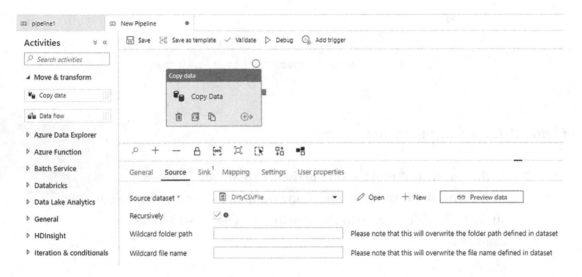

Figure 3-14. *Setting the source dataset property for the Copy Data activity*

4. Move to the "Sink" tab and choose the SQL Database dataset
    previously created. Depending on the sink you use, there are
    different options available here, and as we have a SQL sink, we can
    use the table name specified in the dataset definition or supply
    a stored proc name. To use the table name, simply leave the
    configuration as their default values. Doing so allows for maximum
    copy throughput as the data movement is done in Bulk mode and
    minimally logged. Selecting the Stored Proc option means you
    could process the data into the target table using a merge/upsert
    proc applying custom logic as required; however, this is then
    performed as a transacted operation and is much less efficient.
    Additionally, the pre-copy script could be used to truncate data or
    other cleanup activities prior to the Copy Data activity starting.

Figure 3-15 shows the configuration for this activity.

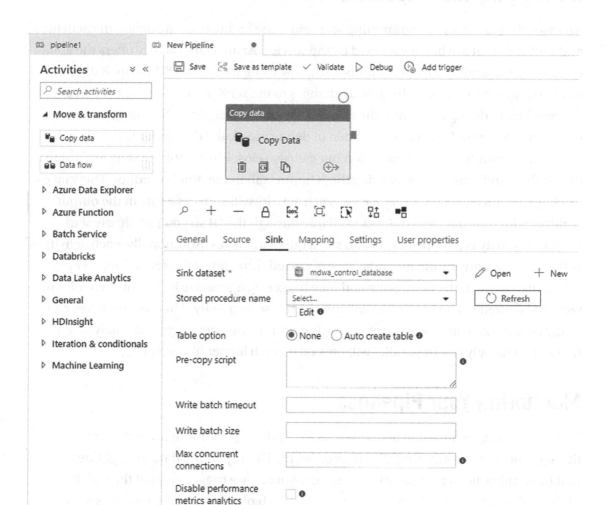

Figure 3-15. *Configuring the sink dataset for the copy data activity*

5. You now have a configured pipeline that can copy data between
    two systems and you can optionally debug the pipeline in place,
    which will execute the process on a debug cluster and allow you to
    watch the activities progress or trigger the pipeline manually and
    observe the pipeline execution through the monitor window.

The JSON definition of all of these objects can be found alongside all of the other
artifacts at the following GitHub repo: `https://github.com/MattTheHow/Modern-Data-`
`Warehouse-In-Azure`

Debugging Your Pipelines

An essential part of any programming scenario is the ability to easily debug the activities and methods that are being executed by the service. Azure Data Factory offers the ability to debug your pipelines from the author window using the "Debug" button. Rather than needing to save and publish your changes to the service, you can simply execute the pipeline in debug mode and the Data Factory service deploys the configuration to a debug environment for execution. When in debug mode, the developer is free to make use of break points to pause execution but can also closely monitor the state and values of variables and parameters by using the "Output" tab in the pipeline editor. This makes tracking the lineage of data very easy as each activity will show as a row in the output window with its inputs and outputs available through the UI so you can clearly see what the activity is passing across into subsequent activities. Additionally, each activity will report back any errors that may have occurred throughout the execution. A key difference between the debugging and fully triggering a pipeline is that any activities that were configured to run in parallel will now be run sequentially. This is so that they can easily be analyzed one by one, but bear this in mind when debugging, as many activities that would usually run in parallel will now take much longer to execute.

Monitoring Your Pipelines

In debug mode, the pipeline only executes in the debug environment and is not logged through the main monitoring UI. The monitoring UI only shows data for pipelines that have either been manually triggered or invoked by a trigger created through the "Triggers" panel. Inside the monitoring portal, each pipeline is represented as a row in the table which can be filtered by the final status of the pipeline and also the execution start date. From this view, you can see some useful metrics such as the start time, duration, and resulting status of the pipeline, and you can also access the parameters that were specified at the time of pipeline invocation as well as any errors that occur within the pipeline. As each pipeline is a collection of activities, you can use the [ ] button to retrieve the detail of each activity that was executed as part of the pipeline. In the activity view, you see a similar table as that in the debug mode, therefore giving access to inputs, outputs, and errors. Additionally, you can rerun the entire pipeline from this view or choose a specific activity to rerun the pipeline from. This means that lengthy pipelines are much easier to fix and maintain. See Figure 3-16 pointing out the aforementioned features.

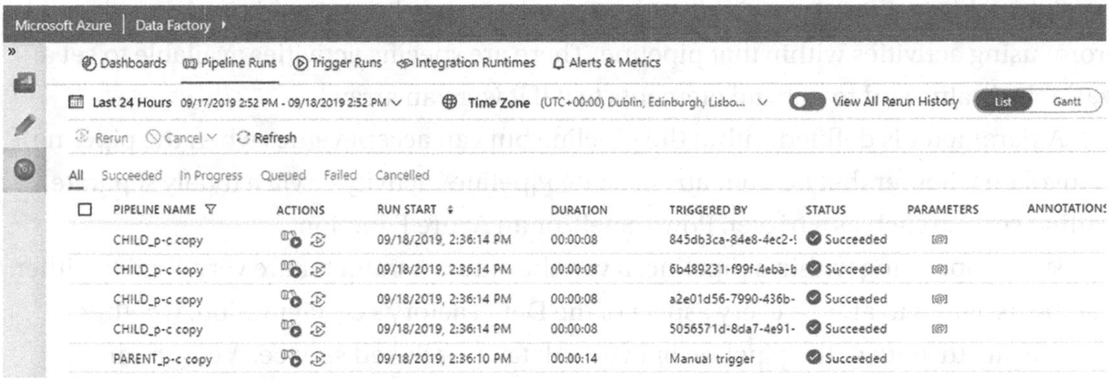

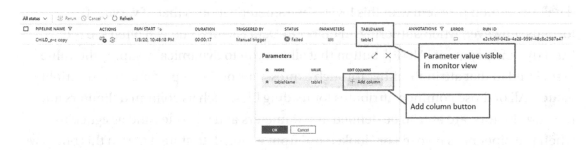

Figure 3-16. *An example of Data Factory monitor view*

In this view, the parameters dialog can be expanded and the parameter values shown can be added to the main monitor view above by clicking "Add column," as demonstrated in Figure 3-17.

Figure 3-17. *Adding input parameters to the monitor view*

Finally, there is also a dashboard view that uses log analytics data to show the number of successful pipelines, activities, and trigger runs in the last 24 hours although the time period is configurable.

Parameter-Driven Pipelines

In almost all data integration scenarios, there is a high level of repeatable code and reusable connections, and the role of a good data integration engine is to allow the developer to efficiently manage these common elements so that the resulting code is clean, easy to maintain, and efficient. Azure Data Factory uses parameters and variables to enable these concepts in much the same way that SSIS did before. A definition of the difference between an ADF variable and a parameter is the following.

A variable is scoped to a single pipeline and can only be assigned to, and read from, using activities within that pipeline. There are specific activities available to set a variables' value and to append elements to it if it were an array.

A parameter is defined within the pipeline but can accept values when the pipeline is invoked whether that be from an "Execute Pipeline" activity or via a totally separate calling service such as a trigger, PowerShell, or an Azure Function.

When operating within a pipeline, a variable and a parameter are very similar. Either can be assigned to almost every aspect of the Data Factory's configuration, whether that be an attribute of the pipeline or even a dataset or linked service. A common use is to configure the specific file or location that the dataset refers to at runtime by either passing in the directory path when it is called or deriving the value by using an expression (such as if you were to need today's date as part of the file path). To use an example, we could create datasets that are at a 1:1 ratio to linked services where the linked service expresses the connection and the dataset is parameterized to the point that it can access every conceivable location within the linked service that stores the data. A common problem with this level of parameterization is that of varying file formats; however, when authoring an object in Data Factory, you will often see the "Add dynamic content [Alt+P]" button that allows you to dynamically supply the value associated to that attribute either through expressions or direct parameter and variable values. All of those common attributes for reading files, such as column delimiters and row terminators, are able to be defined as parameters and variables and assigned to when the pipeline is invoked or "looked up" from a metadata store. Later in this book, we will utilize a metadata-driven approach to allow us to make full use of these parameters to define the reading attributes for each file at runtime.

Getting Started with Parameters

Extending on the previous guide, we can now utilize parameters to make the process more flexible. To achieve this, you should follow these steps:

1. Create a new pipeline and name it something similar to your original pipeline but with some text that distinguishes it as a parameter-driven pipeline.

2. Navigate to the parameter tab and click "New." You will now be able to create the following three parameters:

    a. SchemaName

    b. TableName

    c. FileName

3. Now create replicas of your original datasets; only rename them to denote them as parameter driven.

Tip Use the "Clone" feature to quickly recreate your existing datasets and pipelines.

---

4. Once you have created both of the new datasets, navigate to the SQL database dataset and choose the "Parameters" tab. Here you create the TableName and SchemaName parameters.

   It may seem confusing to have to create these parameters twice; however, they are needed for two different objects. The pipeline needs them so that they can be passed in from the service that invokes the pipeline and the dataset needs them so that the values can be passed in from the pipeline and then applied to the dataset.

5. Now navigate to the data lake dataset and create a TableName parameter.

6. Once you have these parameters created, you can navigate to the connection tab for each dataset and specify the connection to use your parameter values instead of the hard-coded ones provided before.

   a. For the SQL dataset, check the "Edit" box and click the first empty text field. Hit Alt+P to enter edit mode and then you should see a "SchemaName" parameter available at the bottom of the "Add Dynamic Content" pane. You can repeat this process for the TableName parameter.

   b. For the data lake dataset, click the third box under the "File path" header and use Alt+P to enter the dynamic content window. You can then supply the "FileName" parameter to this dataset.

7. If you now save and debug your pipeline, you will notice that you are prompted to provide values for your three parameters. This is because they are defined on the pipeline.

All of the code for this guide can be found using the following GitHub link: `https://github.com/MattTheHow/Modern-Data-Warehouse-In-Azure`

In the next guide, we will extend this further by looking up the parameter values from the control database, thereby replicating the movement of metadata throughout the ETL system.

Using the Lookup Activity

The Lookup activity in Azure Data Factory allows for the developer to call out to a remote service and retrieve some values to be utilized later in the data processing pipeline. Most of the data store connections can be used as a lookup source, but some common examples include

- **Cosmos DB**: JSON data stored in a document database

- **Azure SQL Database**: Structured tabular data accessed with a query

- **File system**: JSON files stored locally or on a remote VM

- **Blob Storage/data lake**: Files stored in cloud storage

- **HTTP**: Web endpoints

- **Third-party sources**: Salesforce, ServiceNow, Jira, and others

To utilize the lookup, you simply need a dataset that is associated to a linked service for the given source of data, and then this can be referenced in the Lookup activity configuration pane. There is a limitation on the amount of data returned by the Lookup activity which is 5000 rows or 2 MB depending on the source. However, whatever the source, the data arrives back at Data Factory in JSON format, so in order to access a value in the first item of the array (or the first row), you can use the following syntax: `@activity('Lookup').output.value[0].AttributeName`

Using this expression, you can assign a given value to a parameter or a variable or even assign the entire set of rows to an array so that it can be used at any point in the pipeline.

To explore some examples, a Lookup activity can be particularly useful when implementing logging in your data processing. If we create a stored proc in an Azure SQL Database that logs a record for each run of an ADF pipeline and returns the unique id of that record after creating the row, then we can call this stored procedure from the Lookup activity. The stored procedure code may look something like the code shown in Listing 3-1.

Listing 3-1. A stored procedure used to log a pipeline run and return the unique id

```
CREATE PROC logging.logPipelineRun (
    @pipelineName VARCHAR(50) NOT NULL
)
BEGIN

    INSERT INTO logging.PipelineRun
    VALUES (@pipelineName, GETDATE())

    SELECT @@Identity AS loadId

END
```

To use this proc in conjunction with the Lookup activity, we can create a linked service and dataset that reference that proc. When you configure the lookup, you just need to select the dataset from the drop-down. If you created a parameter in the pipeline called loadId, then you easily assign the unique id of the pipeline run returned by the SQL proc by using the following expression:

```
@activity('Lookup').output.value.loadId
```

Additionally, because we know that our proc returns only a single value, we can check the "Return first row only" box that signals to Data Factory that it will be a single record or scalar value returned and not an array. Once the value of the loadId is stored in a parameter, you can pass that into any child executions or even pass that load id back to the SQL source when the pipeline completes to log whether the pipeline was successful or not. As you can see, using this method allows lightweight pieces of data to be traded between sources and Data Factory to enable logging or other granular transactions. An alternative scenario is using the Lookup activity to retrieve an array of values, such as a list of tables to load or files to process. These can then be passed into a For Each Loop activity, executing a child pipeline for each file or proc in the array in parallel. Once you are operating inside of the array, you could pass each file location or proc name into a single dataset that is parameterized to receive an input. Of course you could use both approaches in parallel by fetching a load id at the top of the pipeline and passing that into each child pipeline so that the child executions are logged against the parent.

We will go into more depth about these scenarios later in Chapter 7, "Logging, Auditing, and Resilience."

Getting Started with the Lookup Activity

This guide will extend the previous guide to utilize the Lookup activity to fetch the required values from a control database:

1. Create a new pipeline – this could be a clone of your parameter-driven pipeline – and specify its new name.

2. For this guide, we will only need to change the pipeline definition and not the datasets or linked services.

3. Add a new "Lookup" activity to the pipeline which is located under the general node of the activities menu. Give the activity a sensible name.

4. From this new activity, you can now create a new linked service and dataset that is linked to the Demo Control Db. This database can be created using the script located using this link: `https://github.com/MattTheHow/Modern-Data-Warehouse-In-Azure/blob/master/SQL/Control%20Database/Scripts/CreateDatabase.sql`. Once created, use the "Settings" tab of the new Lookup activity, you can optionally choose a Table, Query, or Stored Procedure. By choosing "Stored Procedure," you can see the Guide.ObtainSampleValues proc that should be used here. You can leave "First row only" ticked.

   Now that we have the Lookup activity, we can plumb the returned values into the subsequent Copy Data activity. In order to access the returned values from the Lookup activity, you should use the syntax: `@activity('Lookup Metadata').output`. This snippet can also be acquired by using Alt + P to open the dynamic content window and choosing the appropriate value under the "Activity Outputs" section. This snippet only gets you some of the way; however, you still need to specify the required attribute from the *output* object. Because the "First row only" option was left ticked, the object immediately beneath the *output* object is named "firstRow." Inside the *firstRow* object are the named attributes returned by the SQL database, using the column names, and so if we are to obtain the file name value, we would extend the preceding snippet to resemble the following: `@activity('Lookup Metadata').output.firstRow.FileName`.

5. In order to complete the pipeline, you should replace the FileName, TableName, and SchemaName parameter placeholders with the following values:

   a. FileName: @activity('Lookup Metadata').output.firstRow.FileName

   b. TableName: @activity('Lookup Metadata').output.firstRow.TableName

   c. SchemaName: @activity('Lookup Metadata').output.firstRow.SchemaName

6. Finally, you can debug your pipeline to see how Data Factory retrieves the data from the SQL database and passes the values into the Copy Data activity.

Additional Azure Data Factory Elements

This section advances on the essential elements of Azure Data Factory and discusses some of the additional concepts that can influence design choice and developer practice.

Additional Invocation Methods

In addition to the manual and automated triggers mentioned previously, you can also create a new execution of the pipeline using either PowerShell or the REST API. A PowerShell execution of Data Factory means that ADF pipelines can easily be scripted and gives developers a flexible method of calling pipelines based on events and processes outside of Data Factory. For example, if you wanted to do a one off copy of 100 sequentially incremented files from a folder into a SQL server instance, you could easily create a loop within PowerShell and invoke a single pipeline containing a Copy Data activity on each iteration of the loop. The alternative, using an ADF-only approach, would mean creating an exterior pipeline to look up the 100 tables to process and then creating several activities to increment variables and execute interior pipelines. For a one-off exercise, this is perhaps a little excessive, although this depends on how familiar you are with PowerShell. Additionally, many database professionals use PowerShell to automate any number of menial administration tasks, and given that ADF can be triggered from PowerShell, they can now trigger Data Factory pipelines at appropriate times in their scripts – for example, after a backup/restore.

Listing 3-2 gives an example of how to call a Data Factory pipeline using PowerShell.

Listing 3-2. Invoking Data Factory pipelines using PowerShell

```
$paramObj = @{
    InstanceName = "MDWA-Instance"
}

Invoke-AzDataFactoryV2Pipeline `
    -DataFactoryName "mdwa-datafactory" `
    -PipelineName "Pause Synapse Analytics" `
    -ResourceGroupName "moderndw" `
    -Parameter $paramObj
```

As mentioned before, pipelines can accept parameters, and so when invoking pipelines from PowerShell, you can declare a parameter object containing each value and pass that into ADF. This method is shown in the preceding code listing, passing in the parameter name "InstanceName" with the value "MDWA-Instance."

Another invocation approach outside of Azure Data Factory is to use Azure Functions. Azure Functions are serverless pieces of C# code that allow developers to hook into HTTP events and triggers without having to go through the lengthy configuration process of servers. When coupled with Azure Data Factory, they act as an extension to the already existing trigger schedule option. Currently, the trigger schedule option only listens to events arising from Blob Storage; however, Azure Functions provide a much broader interface and, once triggered, can call the Azure Data Factory invocation API so that essentially your Data Factory can be invoked from a much wider variety of sources. A similar approach in terms of execution is to use Azure Logic Apps; however, this approach allows for a no code solution to much the same problem. Logic Apps are heavily integrated across Azure and beyond, having many useful third-party triggers straight out of the box, and also have the ability to call Data Factory with a simple activity.

All of the preceding invocation methods extend the ability to integrate Data Factory with existing or new processes that are not accessible to Data Factory out the box.

Mapping Data Flows

Azure Data Factory Mapping Data Flows provide a graphical interface to enable detailed data manipulation in a step-by-step, left-to-right format. Without this feature, you could copy data and transform its storage format, but any actual manipulation would have to be performed within an external compute service. Passing data around external services requires a degree of orchestration to ensure the jobs are executed correctly and that the outputs are then properly passed further down the pipeline. With Mapping Data Flows, this process can be built directly into the pipeline so that debugging becomes much more seamless and external compute resources are not required. In fact, the computation itself occurs on a Databricks cluster that is managed by the Data Factory service, and there is no need for the developer to configure or understand any aspect of Databricks. However, the developer should be familiar with the idea of ETL vs. ELT as Mapping Data Flows mean that data can actually be transformed in flight akin to tools such as SQL Server Integration Services.

An advantage of Mapping Data Flows is that they have some useful options for analyzing the source data before it progresses into the flow itself. Primarily the developer can choose to "Allow schema Drift," meaning that data will always be accepted into the data flow and passed through to the sink. This is very useful when the source data changes frequently. Alternatively, Mapping Data Flows can validate the schema of the source data and fail if any columns do not match what is set out in the dataset. These options mean that the developer can cater for a much wider array of scenarios with a minimum degree of effort. In any data integration process, there will always be an element of schema drift, and while sometimes it is best to reject this, there are definitely times when it is preferable to capture the data as it arrives and handle the schema changes later in the pipeline. Alternatively, this could be used to raise a detailed alert to a developer that schema drift has occurred. Even if it does not progress further through the pipeline, being able to capture the data in its new schema rather than it being rejected with an error is likely to be a better solution.

The transformations that are available closely resemble those that were available through SSIS and fall into several categories which are

- Multiple Inputs and Outputs

- Schema Modifier

- Row Modifier

Multiple Inputs and Outputs

This collection of transformations allows for data to be joined, split, unioned, and looked up. It is good to point here that the lookup transformation is not the same as the Lookup activity in the Data Factory pipeline editor. Rather than returning single values or an array that can be used in processing, this uses a column value to join to another table and retrieve an associated value, such as providing a business key to a dimension table to retrieve its surrogate key.

Schema Modifier

This collection of transformations provides the ability to modify the actual shape of the data that is passing through the data flow. This includes activities such as derived columns to create additional columns using calculated values or expressions, aggregations to summarize data, and also pivoting, windowing, and the ability to create surrogate keys. In particular the ability to summarize data within the data flow and apply surrogate keys can be very useful in a warehousing scenario as this means that logic can be removed from being implemented with stored procs in the SQL engine and placed in the Data Factory. While this approach may not be ideal in all scenarios, it does provide the ability to implement these concepts in a low or no-code fashion.

Row Modifier

The final collection of transformations provides the ability to change the number of rows that flow through the data flow. This implements filtering, sorting, and exists concepts as well as selecting a set of columns to be passed through to the next transformation step. Additionally, this set of transformations contains the "Alter Row" transform which allows the developer to specify one to many Boolean expressions that when evaluating to true can execute different activities for each row of the dataset. These can be one of the following:

- Update
- Insert
- Delete
- Upsert

These activities can only operate on databases sinks (destinations), and each type of activity must be explicitly enabled on the sink itself.

Execute Mapping Data Flows

To use a Mapping Data Flow as part of your pipeline, you simply choose the activity from the "Move & transform" segment of the activity list. Here you can configure the activity name, the data flow name, and the runtime to utilize for the execution. Additionally, you can specify the compute type and core count of the Databricks cluster that will execute the data flow through the settings tab of the activity. Figure 3-18 shows how the pipeline can be configured to invoke a Mapping Data Flow.

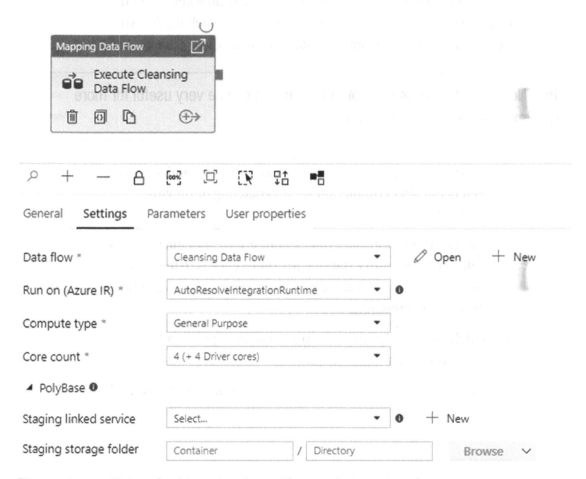

Figure 3-18. Using the Mapping Data Flow activity to invoke a Mapping Data Flow

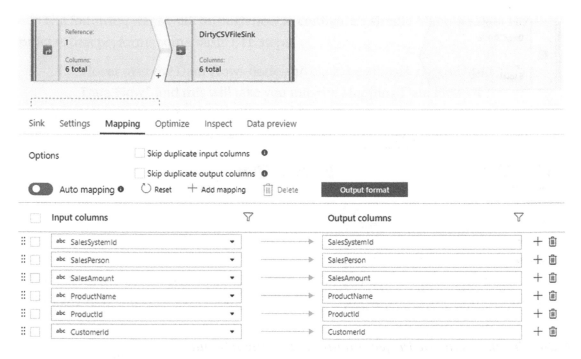

Figure 3-20.   *Mapping fields from source to sink in Mapping Data Flow*

At this point, Mapping Data Flow is performing a basic copy; however, we can begin doing the actual transformation.

4. The first transformation will *trim* whitespace from columns.
    Click the + icon and choose *"Derived column's settings."* Within
    the "Derived column's settings" tab, you should add each of the
    columns in your source dataset and then enter the following
    expression for each one in the expressions editor: trim({column
    name}). This expression will remove any whitespace from the
    column value ensuring the database receives a clean value.
    Figure 3-21 shows how this should look once completed.

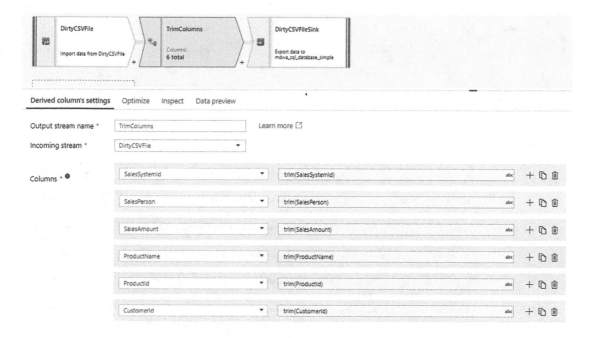

Figure 3-21. *Applying a trim function to incoming columns*

5. The next transformation step will standardize any NULL-Like
    values into true NULL values.

    •   Click the + icon again and choose "Derived column's settings."
        Similar to the preceding step, add an entry in the "Derived
        column's settings" tab for each column, and use this expression
        to replace empty and "Unknown" values with database NULLs:
        `replace(replace({column name}, " ',"),'Unknown',").`

    •   In some cases, there may be the need to cast string values as
        other datatypes such as ints or decimals. To do so, the preceding
        expression can be wrapped in a `toInteger()` or `toDecimal()`
        function as shown in Figure 3-22.

Figure 3-22. Adding data types to column values

6. A final check should be done on the sink activity to ensure that the casted data types have been pulled through. By navigating to the sink activity and choosing the "Mapping" tab, you can ensure the correct columns are selected from the drop-down menu. Figure 3-23 shows how the mapping is configured for the sink activity.

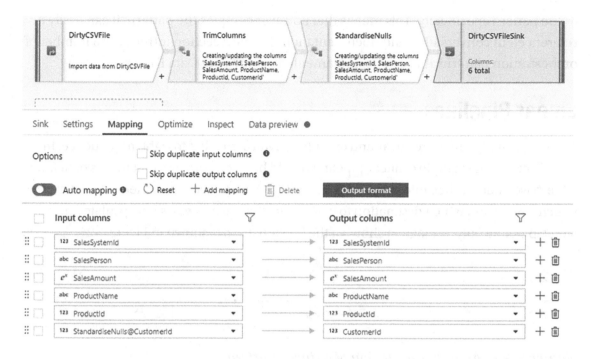

Figure 3-23. *Mapping the columns into the sink dataset*

At this point, the data flow should consist of four steps that resemble the preceding screenshot. Once your Data Flow debug session is online, you can debug the data flow and see the cleaned values load into the database. While completing these steps, I recommend reviewing the Inspect and Data preview tabs. The Inspect tab gives a bit more information about what steps are taking place on the data in that activity and the Data preview will show you how the data will look, although the Debug session needs to be active for this to work. Finally, the Optimize tab allows you to set the partitioning of the data using techniques such as Round Robin, HASH, and range distribution.

Azure Data Factory Processing Patterns

When designing your Data Factory instance, it is essential to consider the methods and configurations used for loading data in certain scenarios. These methods are known as *patterns* and can be used to reference a whole collection of activities or perhaps just a single configuration option. In my experience, the best way to remove confusion in any debate about a Data Factory implementation is to define the pattern used and then refer to the pattern specifically. This means that however complex the pattern, it can easily be referenced in conversation and documentation. The next section introduces a number of orchestration patterns that can be implemented using Azure Data Factory.

Linear Pipelines

The simplest pipelines are linear and execute activities from left to right, in sequence. In Data Factory, an example of linear pipelines could be a copy process that moves data from a file-based data source into a database. The pipeline may accept parameters to determine which source and which destination to connect to, but the process is encapsulated into a single pipeline only. A diagram showing the linear pattern is shown in Figure 3-24.

Figure 3-24. *An implementation of a linear pattern*

Parent-Child Processing

The parent-child pattern in its simplest form describes a two-level process; however, any number of tiers could exist to implement the pattern much like grandparents having children who then produce grandchildren and so on. At any level, there will be the concept of an exterior pipeline, the parent, and an interior pipeline, the child. The parent pipeline is responsible for initiating a process using an Execute Pipeline activity and then optionally awaiting the result of that pipeline or continuing to move through the rest of the activities. The child is then in charge of accepting the values passed from the parent, executing the "heavy lifting" of data, and then passing execution back to the parent when complete.

The benefits of this pattern are several:

- **Simpler error handling**: Handling multiple errors in a single pipeline requires the need for the same error handling activity to be copied for each activity that needs to be covered. This is cumbersome and difficult to maintain, whereas with a parent-child pattern, a single error handling activity can be placed on the "On Failure" output of the Execute Pipeline activity, thereby catching any error that happens in the child pipeline. See Figure 3-25 for an example.

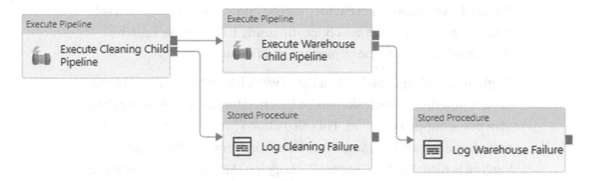

Figure 3-25. *An image of single error handling activities being hooked to the "On Failure" outputs of Execute Pipeline activities, avoiding the need for duplicated error activities*

- **The ability to await a child process**: Data processing pipelines are often comprised of different tiers of activities and there is usually at least one or two that must complete before anything else can continue. Conversely there may also be some long running processes that do not need to be awaited. By using the Execute Pipeline activity with the "Wait on completion" box ticked, Data Factory will ensure no further processing is started before the child activity begins. This is useful when orchestrating sequential segments of a larger pipeline, for example, data acquisition or ingestion. With the "Wait on completion" box unticked, Data Factory will fire and forget the child pipeline, meaning that process is not depended on at all and processing will continue immediately. This is useful for running logging activities or error handling routines.

Iterative Parent-Child Processing

A slight extension to the parent-child process can be achieved by preceding it with a Lookup activity. The Lookup activity can be used to collect a list of items to be processed from the metadata database, and this list can then be iterated by a For Each Loop activity, executing the child pipeline for each element in the list and passing in the necessary information at the point of invocation. This pattern has a few benefits over the linear pipeline:

- **Parallel execution**: Data Factory can be configured to execute a set number of child pipelines at once, meaning ETL windows can be shortened as data can be copied more efficiently.

- **Logical batching of tasks**: As a list of work has to be obtained by the parent pipeline, these tasks can be batched together to ensure related processes happen together. This also allows for better options around error handling and logging. More detail on error handling and logging is discussed in Chapter 7, "Logging, Auditing, and Resilience."

Figure 3-26 describes a basic implementation of the iterative parent-child pattern.

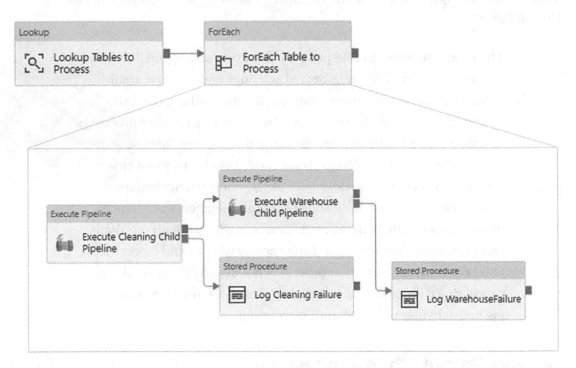

Figure 3-26. *An implementation of the iterative parent-child pattern. The boxed activities sit within the For Each Loop activity*

In practice the parent-child pattern is implemented very simply in Azure Data Factory with the key elements being a For Each Loop activity and an Execute Pipeline activity. The For Each Loop activity accepts an array of JSON objects; this is essentially the list of jobs to complete. Then, nested within the For Each Loop activity is the

Execute Pipeline activity which should accept a set of values passed in by the iteration context (the "row" the For Each Loop activity is on at that time) and execute the specified pipeline with the aforementioned values as parameters. This ensures that the pattern is very flexible, as the array passed to the For Each Loop activity can easily be extended to include any values as required and then the receiving pipeline just needs to have a parameter configured to accept those values. An added benefit of this pattern is Azure Data Factory's ability to parallelize items in a For Each Loop activity. While sequential execution can be chosen, and is sometimes appropriate, more often than not developers can maximize processing efficiency by starting multiple child pipelines at a single time. If the array happens to contain a large number of items, then a maximum batch count can be set to limit the number of jobs that are executed at any one time.

Dynamic Column Mappings

A key component of data movement technologies is the ability to map source columns to destination columns. In Data Factory this is available through the "Mapping" tab, but in order for this to be done visually, you have to import the schemas into the source and sink datasets. In doing so, you fix these datasets for that single table or file structure and not exploiting the full dynamic nature of Data Factory. A further issue is the ability to handle files without header rows. Of course you can derive the schema from the file and create a mapping; however, this again locks the schema to the dataset, crippling your flexibility.

The recommended approach is to use a column mapping JSON object which is supplied to the mapping tab by way of a parameter. This method allows the developer to create a JSON mapping object at runtime and use that to define how Data Factory routes the columns, instead of having to pre-populate the mapping object. The required JSON object is built using an array of mapping objects, and each mapping object has a source and sink attribute, making it very clear which columns are to be used where. By using the metadata stored as part of the data contract, a query such as the following can be used to create a stored procedure that can generate these mapping objects as required. This stored procedure is documented in Listing 3-3.

Listing 3-3. Stored procedure code to create a dynamic mapping object

```
DECLARE @EntityName VARCHAR(100)
SELECT (
    SELECT
        'TabularTranslator' AS 'type',
        JSON_QUERY(
            (   SELECT
                    SourceColumnName AS 'source.name',
                    'String' AS 'source.type',
                    ColumnName AS 'sink.name'
                FROM [Metadata].[EntityColumn]
                WHERE EntityCode = @EntityName
                FOR JSON PATH
            ), '$') mappings
    FOR JSON PATH, WITHOUT_ARRAY_WRAPPER
) AS JsonMapping
```

The preceding code generates a mapping object like the one shown in Listing 3-4.

Listing 3-4. The output JSON from stored procedure shown in Listing 3-3

```
{
    "type": "TabularTranslator",
    "mappings": [
        {
            "source": {
                "name": "UserId",
                "type": "Guid"
            },
            "sink": {
                "name": "MyUserId"
            }
        },
        {
            "source": {
                "name": "Name",
                "type": "String"
```

```
        },
        "sink": {
            "name": "MyName"
        }
    },
    {
        "source": {
            "name": "Group",
            "type": "String"
        },
        "sink": {
            "name": "MyGroup"
        }
    }
    ]
}
```

This object could be fetched from the SQL database using a Lookup activity and pushed into the dynamic mapping object value using the Mapping tab in the Data Factory portal as per Figure 3-27.

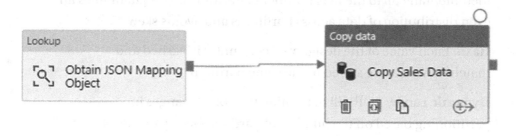

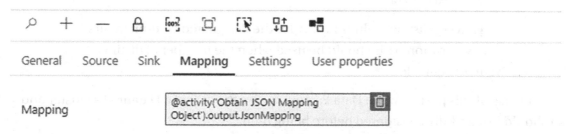

Figure 3-27. *An image of the dynamic mapping setup in Azure Data Factory*

With this approach, the source and sink columns both need to exist in the database; however, a similar but slightly different approach could be taken if the mapping needs to be derived each time a file is loaded. By using a Get Metadata activity prior to the Copy Data activity, the columns in a file could be detected and mapped as needed at runtime.

Partitioning Datasets

When working with large amounts of data or highly volatile data, it is important to utilize partitioning to either maximize parallelism or eliminate parts of the larger dataset that are not relevant to the query. SQL tables often get intelligently partitioned, by year, for example, to facilitate data warehousing performance, and this is handled by the SQL engine. Unfortunately, using a CETAS pattern to write data back into the lake from SQL (as described in Chapter 4, "The Ingestion Architecture") will only create a non-partitioned table, even if the source table is partitioned. This same issue is apparent even if you decide to use the Azure Data Factory native Copy Data activity.

In order to write data out of the database with intelligent partitioning, Azure Data Factory Mapping Data Flows can be used. This technology has the ability to partition datasets in a number of different ways:

- **Round Robin**: Each row is handed to a different partition incrementally up to the max number of partitions. This guarantees an even distribution of data across partitions and avoids skew.

- **Hash**: Each value of the designated column(s) is hashed and matching values are stored in the same partition.

- **Dynamic range**: ADF will determine the correct ranges for partitioning based on the number of partitions set by the developer and the column designated for partitioning on.

- **Fixed range**: The developer can set the ranges used for partitioning with an expression.

- **Key**: Every distinct column value for the designated column incurs a new partition. This should be used when the number of distinct values is fairly low.

The use of this part of Azure Data Factory incurs the cost of a Databricks cluster and so should be carefully considered before being built.

The following steps describe the process of loading a file from a source database and landing that in a data lake, partitioned by year and company name:

1. Following a similar set of steps as the Mapping Data Flow guide mentioned previously, create a pipeline and add a Mapping Data Flow activity. Once in the UI, create a source activity and choose a SQL dataset that needs to be stored in the data lake with intelligent partitioning.

2. Add a sink activity and ensure the connection string of the sink does not have a specified file name; it must be just a path. Be aware that the partitioned files will be deposited using a GUID for their name.

3. Open the "Optimize" tab of the sink and choose a partition strategy. By selecting "Key," the Mapping Data Flow will create a folder for each unique value of the specified column and place the partitioned data inside. Figure 3-28 contains an image of the optimize options in a Mapping Data Flow.

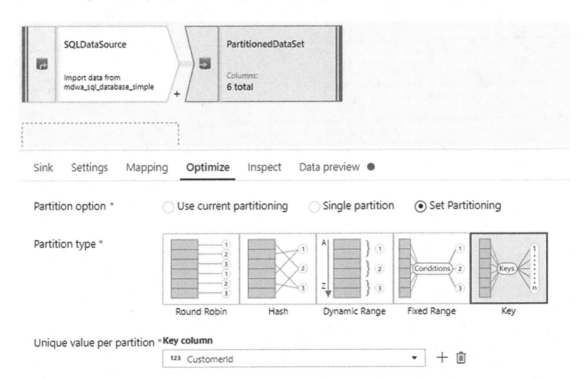

Figure 3-28. Choosing the "Key" partitioning option in a Mapping Data Flow

The configuration shown in Figure 3-28 produces the folder structure in the data lake that is shown in Figure 3-29.

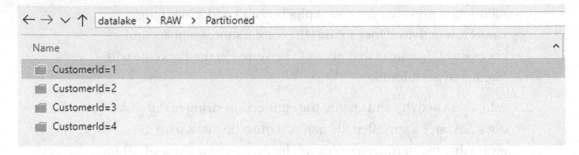

Figure 3-29. *A portioned dataset in Azure Data Lake Gen 2*

CHAPTER 4

The Ingestion Architecture

Data does not stand still. As data warehouse developers, this is a known fact on which our careers are based. For data to have value, it has to be reliably moved to a place where that value can be realized and the method by which we move data should depend on the needs of our users and the frequency of the data, not on the physical or technological limits of the system. As this book examines a *modern* data warehouse, we need to research beyond the traditional defaults such as batch-based ingestion and simple lift and shift extract, transform, and load (ETL) patterns and explore how we offer more flexibility to the end users. This chapter outlines an approach for warehouse loading that promotes efficiency and resilience, moving on to describe three ingestion modes. By defining the risks and benefits of batch-based, event-based, and streaming modes, you will know how to implement each approach while also being aware of the additional complexities of each, ensuring a successful implementation.

Layers of Curation

ETL describes the process of lifting and changing data so that it can be used in an analytical data warehouse. Often this process requires many complex steps involving data cleaning, data transformation, and data integration, and in some systems, there is an attempt to negotiate all of these steps in once single process. Arguments are made regarding the efficiency or compact nature of such an approach, but ultimately, these ETL designs nearly always become slow, difficult to maintain, and a primary reason for rebuilding ETL pipelines.

For these reasons, it is crucial to partition the ETL work up into clearly defined layers that separate loading and cleaning concerns from transformation and integration concerns.

© Matt How 2020
M. How, *The Modern Data Warehouse in Azure*, https://doi.org/10.1007/978-1-4842-5823-1_4

The Raw Layer

The initial layer in your data warehouse loading process should hold your source data in its rawest format. No cleaning, no filtering, just data exactly as it arrives from your source provider. This convention should be followed even in the instances where you collect data directly from a database yourself. Even though that data could go directly into another database, having the forethought to snapshoot the data in a raw layer will have numerous benefits downstream. Additionally, data in this area should be truly immutable (never deleted or updated). By storing data in this way, you ensure that in the worst possible case, your warehouse can be truncated and rehydrated from data that exactly matches how it arrived in the first place - an ultimate rollback option from any given point in time. Additionally, if your source datasets need to be consumed and integrated by other areas of the business, you can easily provide access to this consistent raw layer without the need to make any changes to your ETL processing pipeline.

Because of the demands of this layer, the most fitting technology is a data lake. Primarily, data lakes have the ability to scale to limitless capacity and can store files of any type and size without the need for a set column structure or data types, as would be the case in a database environment. In order to make your data lake as efficient as possible, it should be a developer lead initiative that promotes clear organization and, while allowing datasets to be easily ingested, should also enforce a rigorous convention for placing datasets in a well-defined, logical directory structure. In almost all cases, this structure should have an initial layer that is divided by source system. This is so that cleaning and sensitivity concerns can be considered separately and ensures that changes to one source systems processing should not have any knock-on effects to other source systems. Beneath this source system–driven layer, you should then split data by individual dataset with further year, month, and day partitioning below that. This instills a degree of metadata into the lake directory itself but also helps to derive chronology and lineage in a very intuitive way. An example of this structure is shown in Figure 4-1.

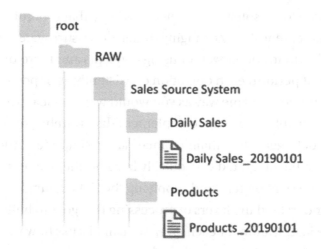

Figure 4-1. *A folder hierarchy showing the RAW directory with one source system and two datasets*

The Clean Layer

The first step in moving data from its raw source format into a curated, data warehouse-ready format is to clean and standardize that data. By cleaning your data, you ensure that bad records are not processed into the warehouse and the standardization allows you to integrate data consistently across your platform. Depending on the quality of data that arrives from your source systems, you may find that cleaning rules can become very complex, hence why they should be performed in their own layer so as not to interfere with your immutable source but also so that value adding business logic is not hindered by complex cleaning rules.

The output of the clean layer should be stand-alone datasets that are primed and ready to be integrated, and this could mean that data has been filtered, columns have been removed, or that values have been transformed in some way so that they will align better with similar type values from different systems.

The Transformed Layer

The final movement of data in this layered system is from its clean location into an analytical data warehouse. The demands of this layer require data to be joined, aggregated, and integrated, and again the processing logic can get very complex. Of course, this is made simpler because you know you are only working with clean, valid data and can therefore focus solely on the business logic that is required. Ultimately this layer will have to implement slowly changing dimensions, surrogate keys, conformed dimensions, as well as many other warehousing concepts and therefore should attempt to utilize patterns that perform each operation consistently as opposed to designing each flow per dataset. In much the same way as you would want to clean strings consistently across all inputs, you would also want to implement data warehouse concepts consistently so that debugging and maintenance can be simplified. Additionally, new feeds of data can then be integrated very quickly because the patterns exist; it is simply a matter of choosing the right pattern and supplying the right columns.

Now that you understand the layers of processing that go into building the warehouse, and the justification for each layer, we can discuss how the differing processing architectures can interact with each layer.

Understanding Ingestion Architecture

At the start of a modern data warehousing project, there should always be a phase of planning and discovery. Part of this phase should be spent understanding the methods by which data arrives and then using this knowledge to plan how that data will be fed into the warehouse. For example, if a source provider delivers datasets at a single point on a daily basis, then there is no need to ingest that data into the warehouse more than once a day. Streaming this data constantly would provide no benefit to the users as nothing would change. Conversely, if a source provider has the ability to stream data into your environment, then this opportunity should be realized. There should be no reason why the users cannot see the data in near real time. By understanding each of the potential ingestion scenarios, you can begin to plan how your data warehouse might handle each of these.

Batch Ingestion

By far the most tried and tested method of populating a data warehouse is to use batch ingestion, a process where data is loaded from raw through clean and into the warehouse in regular, predefined, scheduled increments. The reason for this method being so popular is that it promotes resilience and stability above all other attributes. Optimizations can be made for speed and efficiency, but the batch is still a batch, with a start and an end and a relatively stable amount of processing in the middle. Were the batch to fail, then we can safely say that the entire batch failed and that it would need to be processed again. Additionally, batch loads often have to conform to a fixed window and so users can easily grasp the schedule by which their data arrives and know when to refresh reports and dashboards. For a long time, batch ingestion suited nearly all scenarios; however, there are of course increasing needs to have data arrive more frequently or perhaps not based on a schedule but on the occurrence of an event.

The Risks and Opportunities of Batch Ingestion

The term "risks" is applied loosely here as batch ingestion is by far the most stable ingestion method; however, there are certainly things it cannot do, the risk being you may need to do those exact things some other way.

The ETL Window

In nearly every batch-based scenario, there is an allowable start and end time. This window is known as the ETL window, and it is the role of the developers to ensure that the entire end-to-end processing occurs within these times to avoid disruption to the business. Generally, these times are set to ensure the processing starts a safe amount of time after the last daily transaction and then to complete a safe amount of time before the next day begins. Often between midnight and 5am are peak processing times for ETL solutions. The rigid nature of this scheduled window gives developers key metrics to work toward, and its simplicity comes from being analogous to a calendar date. All being well, report users can rely on their data being no more than one day out of date and can live in certainty that no numbers will change between the first glance at a dashboard in the morning and a last check before going home.

However, as data feeds increase, it is not long before what may have seemed like a generous ETL window begins to feel constricting. More and more pressure will be placed on performance, but ultimately, things can only go so fast, and while speed is a focus, reliability is likely to suffer. Of course, you can explore options around splitting batches, prioritizing certain workloads, or beefing up servers; however, these are only kicking the can down the road. Ultimately, there is the risk that your batch can become too big for your ETL window. Of course there is always the risk that a user may require data to be processed outside of the ETL window; now you have to handle the fact that transactions are happening throughout your batch load, greatly increasing the chance for error.

A final issue with the ETL window is that there can be times when data arrives late. How can you process a critical dimension if the data of the required day has not yet arrived? What is more, your batch is only aware of schedules, so unless this delay is pre-arranged, there is a high chance of failure or worse, success, but with the wrong data! Ensuring that scenarios such as this are handled is critical to a batch processing architecture, and often the ability to programmatically decide to halt or postpone a batch using a series of checks saves a large amount of headache further down the line.

The ETL Anti-window

Given that a batch process happens within a set window, it means therefore there is an anti-window, the passage of time that is not considered critical for processing. This regular ETL anti-window means that the development teams have a prime opportunity to deploy new code or data feeds into the batch process without the risk of immediately creating problems. New solutions can be deployed and tested safely with the knowledge that if the tests fail, the deployment is rolled back, and the batch continues as normal, again, reiterating the point that batch equals resilience and stability.

Failure Investigation and Troubleshooting

Continuing from the idea of the anti-window, this also provides the development team a chance to investigate and resolve any issues that occurred in a nightly batch. Knowing that the system does not need to operate again for several hours allows team members free reign to investigate issues without the risk of accidentally interfering with some ongoing process. Once an issue is determined and a fix implemented, this can be tested and then promoted into the production environment all within the relative safety of the anti-window.

However, while this activity is going on, there are potentially two problems that are unfolding in the background. The first is that an analyst or C level exec is waiting for a report to arrive. Because the issue happened overnight, often issues are not discovered until the next morning, and even if an on-call service is provided, there needs to be significant investigation to determine if the whole batch is bad or if only part of the batch needs rerunning.

The second problem is that regardless of whether you must completely restart a batch or can operate on a subset, you will likely still have some amount of processing time ahead once the issue is resolved. The point of a batch is that it is a larger amount of data processed at a *convenient* time. However, in this occasion, you could be dealing with a large amount of data that needs to be processed at a very *inconvenient* time.

The Batch Ingestion Tools

An implementation of batch ingestion could be stood up using a variety of tools. Most SQL engines lend themselves nicely to batch-based tasks, and I imagine most developers reading this will have tools in mind to perform such a solution. To elaborate, Azure Synapse Analytics can connect directly to several cloud data stores and utilize PolyBase and external tables to read data straight from a file, into an internal SQL table. This approach requires only that Azure Synapse Analytics is running and that it has a connection to the relevant data store; no other tools would be required.

However, the more common scenario is that a database does not have PolyBase technology, for example, Azure SQL Database, and will need to be fed using some kind of integration engine. In this case, Azure Data Factory is by far the best tool as it supports a multitude of connectivity options and has specialized activities for the task of loading databases. Of course, SQL Server Integration Services (SSIS) is an alternative option here; however, it cannot scale to the realms of big data as easily as Azure Data Factory can.

Finally, there may be times when files are simply too large or too complex to be read using SQL engines, and therefore, extended processing to a data lake–based tool may be required. One such tool is Azure Databricks, a PaaS implementation of Spark, which will be discussed later in this book as a potential alternative when data exceeds the reasonable limits of Azure SQL engines.

Batch Ingestion for Azure Synapse Analytics

Reading large batch files efficiently is something Azure Synapse Analytics does very well, and when reading from a data lake, there is a huge efficiency gained from using the PolyBase engine. A common pattern is to define an external table root location that is the starting point for a partitioned set of data made up of any number of files, for example:

```
/Raw/Sales System/Daily Sales/...
```

This root location is then the starting point for PolyBase when it begins searching for data in the lake. Underneath the root location, you could create many files and folders; PolyBase will be able to see and read them all. Often you would extend from the table root with a year/month/day structure although you could use other partitions as well such as customer, product, and so on.

Many file types are not type safe, meaning the data within each column may not conform to a set data type. In these cases, it is important to either remove the offending rows using the PolyBase rejected rows functionality, or assuming you do not want to lose data, set each column of the external table to be NVARCHAR(1000). However, a Parquet file type is type safe and therefore the external table can be strongly typed also, removing the need to cast as part of the ETL, and this is a major reason for choosing Parquet files when performing ETL a large scale.

Once the data is visible to Azure Synapse Analytics through the use of an external table, it needs to be read into a persisted table in the database. There are a few ways to do this; however, the CTAS method provides a minimally logged option that also surfaces the most flexibility for the developer.

The Create Table As Select statement is the staple method to move data around in Azure Synapse Analytics. The reason for this is that it works in a parallelized manner but also provides a great deal of control to the developer. With a CTAS statement, many key parts of the DDL can be changed, such as the distribution type, the index type, the partition values, and even the columns data type. These inherent capabilities make the CTAS statement ideal for loading data through a layered processing pipeline because each transformation can be optimized down to the index, distribution, and partitioning level. The following steps show how the CTAS pattern can be used to facilitate ETL through each layer of the warehouse:

1. A raw CSV file in the data lake would be exposed as an external table with NVARCHAR(1000) type columns. By using the Create Table As Select statement, the DDL of the produced internal table will be derived from any casting or transformation implemented by the developer. Additionally, indexing and distribution can be configured intelligently as opposed to relying on the defaults. An example of CTAS for this layer is documented in Listing 4-1.

Listing 4-1. A CTAS statement used to load data into a clean area

```
IF OBJECT_ID('Clean.DirtyCSVFile') IS NOT NULL
DROP TABLE Clean.DirtyCSVFile;

CREATE TABLE Clean.DirtyCSVFile
WITH
(
```

```
    HEAP,
    DISTRIBUTION = HASH([OrderNo])
)
AS
SELECT
    ISNULL(CAST([ID] AS INT),'0'),
    ISNULL(CAST([SkuItemId] AS VARCHAR(18)),''),
    ISNULL(CAST([CustomerId] AS INT),'0'),
    ISNULL(CAST([OrderNo] AS INT),'0'),
    ISNULL(CAST([Quantity] AS INT),'0'),
    ISNULL(CAST([Price] AS DECIMAL(10,2),'0'),
FROM [Ext].DirtyCSVFile
OPTION (LABEL = 'Clean.DirtyCSVFile.CTAS');
```

Note that in the preceding code, the index has been defined as a HEAP; this is because there is an overhead to creating a formal index, and as the whole dataset will be loaded, there is no benefit to be gained. A further detail is the distribution being set to hash on OrderNo. This ensures that all data relating to the same order will be stored on the same storage node of the server and therefore provide better performance for joining downstream. In the SELECT itself, all the columns definitions have an ISNULL and CAST statement which enforces a NOT NULL and the CASTED data type on the destination table (Clean.DirtyCSVFile in our case). Finally a label has been added which allows the engine to identify this query later for gathering aspects such as row counts and error details.

2. The now clean data is to be joined and integrated with other tables. The resulting dataset will no longer resemble the source datasets, and so the CTAS offers maximum capability in terms of table definition but also in optimizing the data for its new purpose; now it has been enriched. A CTAS statement to carry out this step is shown in Listing 4-2.

Listing 4-2. CTAS statement to create a warehouse fact table

```
CREATE TABLE Warehouse.DirtyCSVFile
WITH
(
```

```
    CLUSTERED COLUMN STORE,
    DISTRIBUTION = HASH([OrderNo])
)
AS
    WITH
    cte_Orders    AS
    (
        SELECT
            OrderNo,
            SkuItemId,
            CustomerId,
            Quantity,
            Price
        FROM Clean.DirtyCSVFile
    ),
    cte_DimCustomer AS
    (
        SELECT
            CustomerKey,
            CustomerBusinessKey
        FROM Dim.Customer
    ),
    cte_DimProduct AS
    (
        SELECT
            ProductKey,
            SkuItemId
        FROM Dim.Product
    )

    SELECT
        CAST(o.OrderNo AS INT) AS OrderNo,
        CAST(dc.CustomerKey AS INT) AS CustomerKey,
        CAST(dp.ProductKey    AS INT) AS ProductKey,
        CAST(o.Quantity AS INT) AS Quantity ,
        CAST(o.Price AS DECIMAL(10,2) AS Price
```

```
FROM cte_Orders AS o
INNER JOIN cte_DimCustomer AS dc ON dc.CustomerBusinessKey = o.CustomerId
INNER JOIN cte_DimProduct AS dp ON dp.SkuItemId = o.SkuItemId
OPTION (LABEL = 'Warehouse.DirtyCSVFile.CTAS');
```

In the preceding code, the index definition has changed from HEAP to CLUSTERED COLUMN STORE so that the data is more efficient for analytical queries such as aggregations; however, the distribution configuration has not changed which will ensure that the lowest amount of data movement should occur. The SELECT part of the statement uses more complex logic by employing common table expressions (CTEs); these are common in data integration and demonstrate that all SELECT capabilities exist within the CTAS.

While the CTAS pattern offers a number of efficiencies, there is a functionality gap in that when data is selected from the external table, any filter predicates in the WHERE clause cannot be pushed down to the data lake. In practice, all of the data below the root is read and only then is the filtering done – obviously this is not the most efficient way to extract a small daily batch from what may be a much larger set of data.

One solution to this problem is to use an active partition, where the most recent data is stored, and an inactive partition, where the less recent data is located. As the data is ingested, it can then be copied into the inactive partition so that it is available if needed but will not unnecessarily increase the volumes of data to be loaded to Azure Synapse Analytics. The structure for this might look like that shown in Figure 4-2.

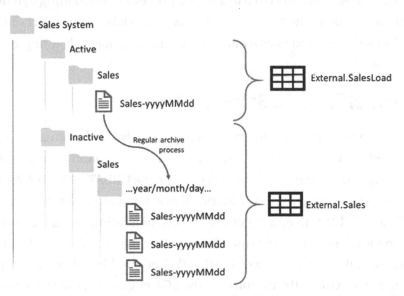

Figure 4-2. *An example of a file structure used to load active data and obstruct loading of inactive data*

In this case, the external table definition would resemble the code in Listing 4-3.

Listing 4-3. Data definition language (DDL) statement to create an external table in Azure Synapse Analytics

```
CREATE EXTERNAL TABLE External.DirtyCSVFile
(
    [ID] NVARCHAR(1000) NULL,
    [SkuItemId] NVARCHAR(1000) NULL,
    [OrderNo] NVARCHAR(1000) NULL,
    [CustomerId] NVARCHAR(1000) NULL,
    [Quantity] NVARCHAR(1000)) NULL,
    [Price] NVARCHAR(1000) NULL,
    [LastUpdateDateTime] DATETIME2 NULL
)
WITH (LOCATION='/Raw/Sales System/Active/Sales',
      DATA_SOURCE  = DataLakeSource,
      FILE_FORMAT  = CSV,
      REJECT_TYPE = VALUE,
      REJECT_VALUE = 0);
```

You can see that by specifying active in the location string, the inactive data will not be read. An alternative solution is to use a stored procedure containing dynamic SQL to create a new external table each time an ETL process is kicked off. This could have the specific location string passed in as a parameter, meaning that only a single file is read at that specific time.

Create External Table As Select (CETAS)

When working with batched data and Azure Synapse Analytics, there may be a need to write transformed data back out into the data lake for consumption by other systems. The way to do this using Azure Synapse Analytics is to use the CREATE EXTERNAL TABLE AS SELECT (CETAS) statement. When considering this statement, remember that a CREATE TABLE AS SELECT (CTAS) statement generates a brand new internal table based on the select that is provided and a CETAS is no different other than the data for the table is stored externally, that is, in the data lake. Provided that the required PolyBase objects are created (the external data source and the file format), the SQL engine can use PolyBase to push data back to the lake. The syntax for this statement is shown in Listing 4-4.

116

Listing 4-4. Creating an external table as SELECT

```
CREATE EXTERNAL TABLE ext_FctOrders
WITH (
        LOCATION='/DWH/Fact/Oders.pqt',
        DATA_SOURCE = DataLake,
        FILE_FORMAT = PqtFormat
) AS SELECT TOP 100 PERCENT FROM Warehouse.FctOrder;
```

One consideration here is that the produced file will be written to the data lake and partitioned according to the storage engine and not how the data was partitioned in Azure Synapse Analytics. There is a method to achieve intelligent partitioning and this is described in more detail in Chapter 7, "Logging, Auditing, and Resilience."

Event Ingestion

Event ingestion is not dissimilar to batch ingestion although instead of multiple files being processed at once, now a single file is considered your batch. Of course, the challenges and opportunities of single file batches are much closer to traditional batch processing than stream processing, which is based on a record by record flow. The primary difference is that files are processed the minute they arrive within the agreed location and not based on an arbitrary schedule. In nearly all cases, this means that files are processed as a single unit, without any dependence on other files that may also arrive throughout the course of the day.

A warehouse will almost always require multiple files to be ingested in order to be refreshed; however, the early cleaning and validation stages for those files can be entirely independent.

Many services within Azure can generate events when things happen, and also many services can listen to these events and take actions when they do. An example is Blob Storage, and therefore Azure Data Lake Gen 2; the storage engine can fire events when new files are added or existing files are deleted. Subsequently, Azure Data Factory can listen for those events and then trigger a pipeline, utilizing the metadata provided with the event, for example, file name and location. Generally speaking, event data is implemented using JavaScript Object Notation (JSON) because many services can process and understand this simple object type while it also is not schema bound, meaning additional attributes can be added to the object without disrupting existing processes. The Azure platform also has a wide number of tools for managing and working with event data, some of which will be discussed later in this section; however, an exhaustive list of event-enabled services is out of scope for this book.

The Risks and Opportunities of Event-Based Ingestion

The primary benefit of event-based ingestion is that files can be processed quicker and the warehouse can be updated sooner. If a file arrives early, then the processing can be completed earlier. Although if a file arrives late, this should not collapse the integration process because the process would not have started until the file arrives. In batch ingestion, files could arrive at any point during the day but still not be processed until the evening, assuming a nightly ETL window is implemented. The only other way to manage file ingestion in such a way is to build intraday ETL loads, but this would require managing multiple schedules and ETL windows; ultimately this can quickly become very complicated. The reason for event-based ingestion being better is that the trigger is the event, perhaps a file arriving in Blob Storage, and the integration engine knows how to respond to the event because of the associated metadata of that event.

This seems like a great way to build upon a batch process; however, it is not without its own pitfalls. In a more simplistic event-based application, you have to realize that you are relinquishing the ability to decide when files are processed. You are no longer telling the engine to get to work when you know the environment is ready; you are granting the data provider that ability. Even if this is done with no intention to negatively affect your system, you must ensure that the platform is always able to process data, day or night. If for some reason it cannot, then you need other options for storing events and returning to them later in the day.

Finally, you will need a mechanism to determine when all the required files have arrived in clean and therefore the warehouse is ready to be refreshed. This can often start out as a simple stored procedure but can quickly become a complex mesh of intertwined dependencies that becomes very difficult to navigate and resolve. The risk here is that the data warehouse will never be processed because the necessary files were never all ready at the right time; it is essential that you manage this process closely and ensure that your warehouse will not be starved.

Implementing Event Ingestion

As discussed, event-based processing can present many benefits, but there are also challenges and technical considerations. This next section aims to focus on the real-world implementation considerations needed when working with events.

Decoupled Processing

The essence of decoupled processing is in the absence of unnecessary dependencies. When datasets are dependent on each other, there is a higher chance of failure, and particularly at early stages of an ETL pipeline, there is little reason to enforce these dependencies. Instead, each dataset can be processed independently, and if there was a failure, this should not disrupt any of the other datasets being processed at the same time.

Often ETL designs originating from a batch-based paradigm tend to favor complete success or complete failure, whereby all datasets are coupled, and a single error means the entire batch must be fixed and reprocessed. The issue is that this is inefficient in terms of compute power, every second counts in a cloud-based environment, but also in the amount of time, it takes to deliver insights to your users. Instead, all successful datasets can be handled according to their individual needs.

In a data warehouse scenario, decoupled ingestion allows the loading process for an individual file to be triggered by an event, usually the file arriving in a storage repository. An event could occur at any time of day and be handled in several different ways, but this concept allows the file to be ingested as soon as it arrives, allowing BI teams to move away from a single, monolithic nightly ETL load. This approach is illustrated in Figure 4-3.

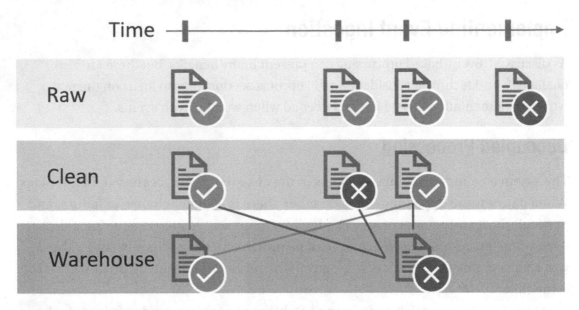

Figure 4-3. *A decoupled process loading data between layers*

In the preceding diagram, files 2 and 4 both have failures between layers; however, files 1 and 3 can be fully processed into the warehouse, if appropriate.

Assuming the cleaning process completes successfully, the next procedure is to transform and integrate datasets to produce warehouse tables. In contrast to the load and clean routines, the transformation procedure needs to interact with multiple datasets in order to add value. With the possibility that some datasets may fail to reach the clean layer, a special type of query is needed that can check the dependencies for each warehouse table and tell the ETL engine which tables can be created and which are not yet ready to run.

Referring to the preceding image, a warehouse table that was dependent on files 1 and 3 could be created; however, a file that required files 1 and 2 could not. In order to resolve this kind of processing logic, a dependency resolution engine is required.

A dependency resolution engine can take many forms depending on the prevalent technologies in your platform though one common method may be to use a stored procedure. This assumes you are storing your dataset processing runs, high watermarks, and dependency mappings in an auditing database, as is the pattern recommended and explained in more detail in Chapter 7, "Logging, Auditing, and Resilience." A dependency resolution query would be triggered each time a dataset is successfully cleaned and would comprise of several steps. These are described as follows using dataset 1 as the dataset just cleaned, with the warehouse tables depending on datasets 1, 2, and 3 in order to be refreshed:

1. Knowing the identifier of the dataset just cleaned, query for all of the subsequent tables that are dependent on that dataset.

2. Using those identifiers, query for all the other datasets that would be required to fulfil each list of dependencies.

3. Using the high watermarks, determine which of those datasets have a watermark that is greater than the warehouse table enforcing the dependency.

4. For those where all high watermarks are greater, run the proc to generate the table. For the others, do not run the proc and check again when the next file arrives into the clean layer.

A more visual example of these steps is shown in Figure 4-4.

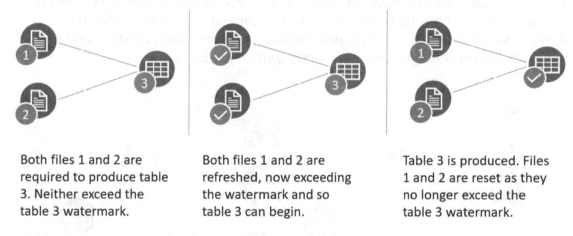

Both files 1 and 2 are required to produce table 3. Neither exceed the table 3 watermark.

Both files 1 and 2 are refreshed, now exceeding the watermark and so table 3 can begin.

Table 3 is produced. Files 1 and 2 are reset as they no longer exceed the table 3 watermark.

Figure 4-4. *An example of a simplistic dependency resolution process*

More complex scenarios can develop of course, and a common requirement is to daisy chain dependencies together, otherwise known as recursion. This can be implemented simply by triggering the dependency engine query from later stages in the process. In Figure 4-5, a warehouse table needs to be produced in order to generate subsequent warehouse tables and so the dependency query would be called as the datasets arrive in clean but also when tables are refreshed in the warehouse layer.

Files 1 and 2 are required to produce table 4, however file 3 AND table 4 are required to produce table 5.

Files 1 and 3 arrive, however no subsequent tables can begin due to the dependency on table 4 and file 2

File 2 arrives, table 4 is produced with table 5 following after.

Figure 4-5. *Using a dependency resolution engine to resolve a meshed dependency structure. In this second scenario, all subsequent processing is blocked until file 2 arrives. If file 2 was a low-priority dataset or did not change often, but its data was still required as in the preceding scenario, it would be reasonable to question whether this is a worthwhile endeavor. To overcome this, we can overlay the dependency engine with a simple policy concept that can override the fact that a required file was not refreshed. This is exemplified in Figure 4-6*

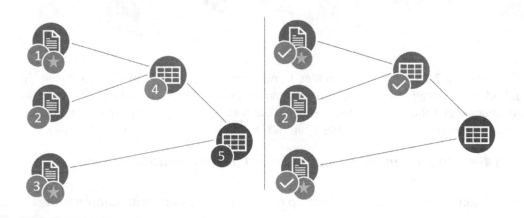

Files 1 and 3 are marked as mandatory and file 2 is set as optional

Files 1 and 3 arrive and so processing of table 4 begins, using the latest available version of file 2

Figure 4-6. *Showing how optional and mandatory files can ensure processing is not held up by late or infrequently arriving files*

In the preceding figure, files 1 and 3 are mandatory; however, file 2 is optional and therefore should not delay processing. A real-world example could be to have file 1 as a product file, file 2 as a product type file, and file 3 as a product sales file. The types change infrequently, so we are happy to take a latest version of that file even if it is not as recent as the other files.

Listening for Events

The ability to listen to events being raised across an Azure subscription is fairly common. While there are many services that can manage and process events, the most relatable to the content of this book is Azure Data Factory, which has the ability to be triggered by either a blob creation or blob deletion event. The event has to come from a Blob Storage account and so Azure Data Lake Gen 1 (ADL Gen1) is out of the question; however, the architecture of Azure Data Lake Gen 2 means that it is compatible with this event trigger. A limitation here however is that the event can only be filtered by the name of the file triggering the event although there is the ability to wildcard this filter to a point. When filtering for events, you can either choose to react to blobs that have a certain prefix or suffix, and this means you can either be entirely specific about a particular blob to look out for or very generic to pick up on any event that occurs within a set directory. See the following Table 4-1 for some examples.

Table 4-1. *A table demonstrating some implementations of event filters*

Filter Type	Filter Expression	Would Find
Blob path begins with (prefix)	Sourcefiles/SalesDetail/	Any file in the SalesDetail folder in any container
Blob path begins with (prefix)	/Sourcefiles/	Any file in the Sourcefiles container
Blob path ends with (suffix)	.csv	Any CSV file in any container
Blob path ends with (suffix)	/Sourcefiles/SalesDetail/ sales.csv	Any files named sales.csv in the specific directory

Queuing Events

In an event-driven architecture, the goal is to listen and process events in real time; however, this is not always possible. Whether it be agreed downtime with the business to maintain analytical consistency throughout the day or a scheduled maintenance window to allow for deployments, there is guaranteed to be a time when your platform cannot respond immediately to events. During these windows, it is essential that the platform has a robust mechanism for queueing the events in the correct order so that they can be processed at a later date or time.

To tackle this, delayed event processing can be employed to listen to all events; however, only process them outside of the agreed downtime, similar to an ETL window. Events that happen within the downtime should be stored in order and processed when the platform resumes. See Figure 4-7 for a diagram of how this would work.

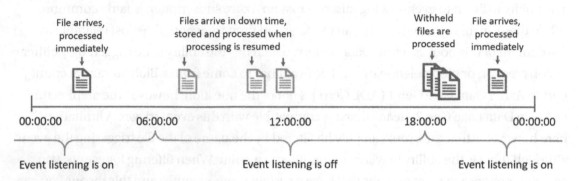

Figure 4-7. *A diagram showing an implementation of delayed event processing*

A similar but alternative pattern is to implement a period of selective event listening whereby some files are allowed to process as they will not disturb the other activities going on in core business hours. However, some may be withheld until the ETL window opens. A diagram for this pattern is shown in Figure 4-8.

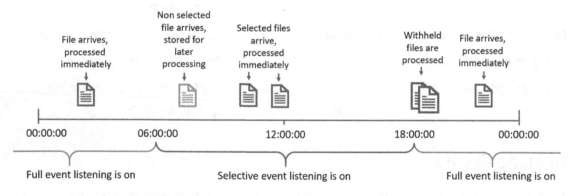

Figure 4-8. *A diagram showing an implementation of selective event processing*

The benefit in both delayed event processing and selective event processing is that your stable period throughout the day is maintained; however, throughout the course of the evening, data is allowed to process freely as and when it arrives, alleviating pressure vs. a single batch load. Further to this, now that file processes are decoupled, a failure for one file has absolutely no bearing on whether any other files will fail to process or not. This can make debugging much simpler because the affected file will be clearly identified and there is less work to do once the issue is resolved. A full explanation and implementation of this pattern is held in Chapter 8, "Using Scripting and Automation."

Event Ingestion for Azure Synapse Analytics

The method for ingesting event-based datasets in Azure Synapse Analytics is broadly the same as for batch-based data. The additional consideration is that you may receive smaller volumes of data more frequently. Because the standard pattern in Azure Synapse Analytics is to use the CREATE TABLE AS SELECT (CTAS) syntax, you essentially have to re-create the entire table for every dataset you want to append, and also you will be more frequently using up limited concurrency slots. In some scenarios, however, you may find there is a disconnect between the rate your data arrives and the frequency that your users need it. Therefore, you should be open to the possibility of batching your data to a frequency that is agreed with your users. Fortunately, because of PolyBase technology, your multiple files can remain separate and Azure Synapse Analytics will be able to read the data in one pass.

Event Ingestion for Azure SQL Database

Azure SQL Database is a good fit for event-based ingestion because it is architected to be more transactional than Azure Synapse Analytics. This means that data arriving in smaller and more regular batches is easily ingested at the same frequency as the originating events, unlike Azure Synapse Analytics where you may group datasets together. Of course, without PolyBase, you still need to use an integration engine such as Azure Data Factory to push the data into the database.

Stream Ingestion

When reading about event-based and batch-based processing, you will see that there are a number of similarities between the two modes. Both use files that can be processed in a decoupled manner although event based perhaps processes smaller files more regularly and is more responsive than a scheduled batch process. Ultimately, however, there is a regular interval in which data is processed and clear beginning and end to the process routine. This third mode, stream ingestion, is completely different from the previous two and relies on a constant flow of data from a source which can then be landed into files or passed directly into a destination system. Many modern systems are now able to offer the ability to tap into data streaming outlets, and with the increasing dependence on Internet of Things (IoT) technology, stream-based ingestion is becoming increasingly popular. Azure has a whole set of technologies dedicated to streaming capabilities, and this is in addition to the open source technology options, such as Databricks that can support a streaming architecture.

The Risks and Opportunities of Stream Ingestion

Data streaming presents a number of benefits against the slower pace of batch- and event-based ingestion, and while the available technologies go a long way to making this approach simple, there are still challenges that need to be overcome. The most obvious benefit is the speed at which data is available to your users. Mere moments after transactions occur in your source system, they will be available to your users via their analytics dashboards and reports. This can lead to incredibly efficient decision making and the ability to react to changes in real time, not hours or days later. This can not only have a commercial benefit to a business but also can allow for critical systems to be monitored continuously. By streaming events from IoT sensors, businesses are able to monitor attributes of hardware such as temperature or pressure to detect the possibility of failure before any real problems occur.

A further benefit of data streaming is the size of data being processed through the system is likely to be very small, usually single records or micro batches of one or two records at a time, and this means that architecture components can be relatively inexpensive as there is no memory pressure.

Though the speed of data streaming is arguably the key benefit it also presents the primary challenge. The rate of the arriving data means that solutions must be always running and available to process records successfully or at least store them securely in a system that can preserve the order in which records arrived. Additionally, the speed of the arriving data means you want to limit the number attributes arriving through your stream to only what is needed to be displayed in real time. This could perhaps mean that some attributes are being removed and therefore a mop-up routine that pulls the remaining data into your data warehouse for later analysis could also be required.

A further challenge is the granularity and isolation of the data. Because each record is isolated from all other records and also not processed in the same scope as any other records, aggregating data to achieve a different grain cannot be done as part of the constant stream but would have to be completed in a subsequent processing phase. This can delay the records arriving in your destination and should encourage you to keep data as granular as possible right through to the destination. The other side of this challenge is the isolation. Unlike in event or batch processing where we, at some point at least, have a chunk of static data for a period of time which can then be used to join and transform, the data is constantly in motion, although streamed records could be joined to reference datasets.

Finally, the layered approach used in both batch-based and event-based processing does not really apply here; the data does not sit still for long enough. Therefore, data cleaning and standardization needs to be written directly into the stream and requires developers to maintain multiple sets of cleaning logic.

Implementing Stream Ingestion

In this section, we will look at a method for stream-based ingestion. The core of this method utilizes event hub and stream analytics; however, there are some differences depending on the location. While one version writes data directly into a destination database, the other writes data into a Blob Storage account and assumes the streamed data will be batched and processed in batch mode. At the time of writing, hierarchical namespace-enabled storage accounts are only supported in preview mode.

Stream Ingestion with Azure Event Hub's and Stream Analytics Jobs

As mentioned, the core of this method uses Azure Event Hubs, which by design makes many sources available as inputs to your streaming job, and likewise, there are many options for destination. This gives ultimate flexibility when working in Azure as streams can be routed to wherever needed through a very simple interface. Another great advantage to this method is that the streaming jobs are written in an approximation of SQL and so are easy to pick up for developers already working in a SQL-based environment. The actual development of these streaming jobs is performed from within the Azure portal and can easily be tested using the UI. This does however pose a problem from a source control perspective, as the streaming jobs themselves cannot be source controlled other than in ARM templates.

A key feature of Azure Stream Analytics Jobs is the ability to integrate with reference datasets. Because records are being loaded very regularly and may only have a minimal amount of data, such as an IoT device, the reference data allows for the streamed records to be enriched while in flight. Azure Stream Analytics supports reference data stored in Blob Storage or in an Azure SQL Database. In the case of Blob Storage, the data is stored under a set path and then split by date and time values as lower levels of the directory; the reference query can then load each set of data as and when it becomes relevant. Alternatively, Azure SQL Database reference data can either be queried fetched once at the start of the job and used throughout or periodically refreshed down to the grain of a minute. For very static data then, a single dataset will likely suffice; however, if you have regularly updated values, then you can make use of this periodic refresh capability. Additionally, if the dataset is very large, then a delta query can be supplied to avoid lengthy operations that would result in timeouts. Reference data is loaded into memory by the streaming runtime, and this allows for very quick joining of data. However, this dataset is limited to a size of 300 MB at a level of six streaming units and above. Less than six and the limit is half of that if not smaller. This means that care needs to be taken when writing the reference data queries to ensure that the snapshot times are correct and that deltas are employed if needed. Further to this, compression is not supported for reference data.

Stream Ingestion for Azure Blob Storage

As previously mentioned, Azure Data Lake Gen 2 is not a generally available destination for a streaming analytics job; it is currently in preview for select regions and therefore not a reliable production option. While this does present an issue from an architectural conformity perspective, it does make the route for inputting data from streaming devices simpler. Data is simply written into a file that is hosted in a specific directory. In order to assist with file management, the stream analytics config UI allows for dynamic placeholders to be used so that file names and directory locations can accurately describe the window of data that is contained. Examples of these are shown as follows. Alongside these placeholders, a minimum batch row count and maximum time window can be set to restrict the size of each batched file. For example, the maximum time parameter can be set so that a batch is written every 5 minutes, even if that does not meet the minimum row count. In this scenario, an event can be raised by the Blob

Storage account when the batch is completed, which is then interrupted and processed by Azure Data Factory. These batch windows can be 1 minute or greater, and while this is not quite record by record immediacy, it certainly is near real time and would comfortably cover off many fast-moving data scenarios.

Stream Ingestion for Azure SQL Database

The preceding streaming approach shows how a stream can be rolled into a batch and then ingested; however, direct integration is also very simple to achieve by using Azure SQL Database as a destination. Records can be inserted near to the rate of generation if required, and while this speed is clearly a benefit, it can pose issues when it needs to be integrated with other datasets. Without the rigorous structure of the ETL processing, you must assume that the data arriving from a stream may have some cleaning problems that are only acceptable given the speed at which the records arrive. To work around these problems and blend the data with the slower moving batch or event-based data feeds, you should employ a lambda architecture.

The Lambda Architecture

The lambda architecture approach is defined as a blend of streaming and batch-based ingestion that allows for historical, well-curated data to be seamlessly integrated with high-velocity data, allowing for a cohesive and contextualized view of real-time information. The technical challenges when implementing a lambda solution are not generally the individual feeds; while streaming and batch-based feeds can present their own challenges, the main issue to overcome is that of integrating the data. Slow-paced, batch, or event data will be well cleaned, prepared, and accurate; however, streamed data will often be very raw and close to its original source format. For this reason, there is the need to have a serving layer that can tightly control the way in which data is presented to querying applications and users. Additionally, a modicum of cleaning can be applied here at the frequency defined by the business requirements without slowing down or interfering with the stream.

Blending Streams and Batches

In all cases, stream data should be loaded into a separate table that is designed specifically for the stream and never into a pre-existing warehouse table. This is so that the accuracy and integrity of your warehouse is not compromised but also so that long running processes for loading dimensions and facts are not continually interrupted by frequently arriving stream data. Given the two tables of information, a view should be built that consistently picks common attributes from both tables and present them in a way that is transparent to the end user or application. Due to the nature of streamed data, the records in this table will be far less enriched than those of a proper warehouse table, and therefore the view should utilize logic that can provide defaults or lookup values in order to make the streamed records meaningful alongside the warehouse datasets.

The Serving Layer

Any tables or views that are exposed to a user or application need to be carefully designed; however, with a lambda solution, this is even more critical. The requirements of the reports need to be well understood so that the real-time data can deliver the metric values to fulfil these requirements but also the absolute minimum set of dimension attributes so that the aggregated values can be sliced and diced. In some cases, the warehouse data may already be aggregated and stored at a higher grain than that of the streamed data. In those cases, the logic behind the view layer will need to aggregate the granular data to the correct grain and then blend the two datasets.

As mentioned earlier, a degree of cleaning could be performed in this layer and in fact this is highly recommended. By allowing the stream processors to focus solely on pushing data to your database or file system, you ensure that records are passed off quickly and reliably. Any increase in complexity midstream only makes the process more likely to fail while also consuming more streaming units without a returnable benefit. Even if the serving layer was queried every 30 seconds, this would allow ample time to apply common data cleansing techniques on the delta of records since the previous 30 seconds.

In most lambda scenarios, the records arriving from the speed layer would be considered fact information in that they are individual transactions or readings from a sensor, for example. Each of these records is then loaded and stored at their lowest grain and aggregated into the serving layer. To enrich the existing fact data, streamed records can be unioned, that is, to join the data vertically like stacking to the existing data. The key here is that both sets of data must have the same schema, and so the stream records must hold a minimum set of attributes to allow this to happen or at least be enriched to that point, within the serving layer. There is however the possibility that the stream data applies to existing dimension records, for example, customer statuses that are regularly changing. In this scenario, dimension data that is already enriched is then further enriched with real-time data. In this case, speed data is joined horizontally and so needs to have at least one joining characteristic, for example, customer id, so that both versions of the record can be aligned.

The following code shows how a core warehouse table and a stream table can be unioned together to present a consistent set of facts to an end user. Additionally, the streamed data is being enriched with product names as part of the view definition, instead of these taking up part of the stream. Listing 4-5 shows how the two tables can be unioned to create a single presentation view.

Listing 4-5. Creating a single presentation view

```
CREATE VIEW Warehouse.Sales
AS
    SELECT
        [SalesPerson]
        ,[SalesAmount]
        ,[ProductName]
        ,[ProductId]
        ,[CustomerId]
    FROM [Clean].[Sales]

UNION ALL

    SELECT
        'Anon Sales'
        ,[SalesAmount]
        ,p.[ProductName]
        ,p.[ProductId]
        ,[CustomerId]
    FROM [Stream].[Sales] AS s
    INNER JOIN Warehouse.DimProduct AS p
        ON p.ProductId = s.ProductId

SELECT * FROM Warehouse.Sales
```

Assessing the Approach

The goal of this chapter was to outline a range or ingestion architectures that can be employed in varying degrees across a data warehouse ETL solution. By having a full understanding of the risks, opportunities, and implementation considerations of each approach, you can determine how each might fit with the data you have to process into your data warehouse. The approaches in this chapter were laid out in order of complexity, and so if ETL in Azure is a new concept to you and the developers you work with, then a batch-based architecture is a great starting point. By implementing this and doing it well, you will have the fundamental building blocks for an event-based architecture. Only once you have a solid grasp of how these two methods hydrate your warehouse should you begin to plan how streamed data could be used to further enrich your data warehouse.

CHAPTER 5

The Role of the Data Lake

As the data needs of a business change, the methods to store, organize, and audit data need to change as well. Big data is the buzz word of the day, and big data needs a scalable storage platform. Multimedia files such as images, videos, and audio files need to be co-located and reported against, and so a platform that can accommodate such diverse data types is required. A modern data platform may also need to ingest data at incredibly high speeds, and having a platform that can cope with streaming and scale accordingly is essential. There is such a variety of requirements for data storage with modern businesses that managing and maintaining storage systems specifically for each would be impossible. What is needed is a simple option that implements a "less is more" approach to offer the scalability and diversity required. What is needed is a data lake.

The term data lake was first used in 2010 by founder and former chief technical officer of Pentaho, James Dixon, who was speaking about the inherent restrictions of a regular data mart. These of course are size, time to deliver value, and research/experimentation capabilities.

> *If you think of a Data Mart as a store of bottled water, cleansed and pack-aged and structured for easy consumption, the* Data Lake *is a large body of water in a more natural state. The contents of the* Data Lake *stream in from a source to fill the lake, and various users of the lake can come to examine, dive in, or take samples.*
>
> —James Dixon 2010
> https://jamesdixon.wordpress.com/2010/10/14/pentaho-hadoop-and-data-lakes/

The way the data lake overcomes these restrictions is by being a much more generic store for raw data, meaning that users can easily deliver data of any type into the lake while rapidly deriving insight from it because the data does not need to be coerced and bound to the schema of a data mart. No longer will analysts have to wait for months to even begin exploring a dataset, only to discover that the essential data they need has been aggregated away into the ether. Now they can dive straight into the data lake,

© Matt How 2020
M. How, *The Modern Data Warehouse in Azure*, https://doi.org/10.1007/978-1-4842-5823-1_5

doing as much cleaning as necessary, and once a proven value has been asserted, a proper process can be built to funnel the data into a warehouse. In practice, the high-value datasets may well go via the data lake and more or less immediately into a data mart; however, with the limitless storage capabilities of a data lake, there is never a reason to throw data away. In fact, these datasets often can hold unprecedented insight that can only be discovered when enough of the data is held in the same place and in its raw, low-level format.

Additionally, users can benefit from unstructured datasets such as images and videos that could never be represented in a traditional data mart. This capability is of particular interest to data science teams looking to extrapolate tags or metadata about images before blending that data with some other dataset such as customer or product. What's more, in a data lake environment, the data can be nicely co-located so that a semi-structured JSON file can easily be joined to a Parquet file which can then be updated to hold the output of some AI algorithm – the possibilities are truly endless when data storage is not a barrier.

The key point here though is that the data in a data lake is in a raw, untranslated state and cannot easily be read or evaluated using traditional SQL-based methods. Depending on the user and their intention this can be beneficial, often data science teams prefer to do all cleaning and loading from raw to model stage themselves; however, to fuel a data warehouse, a degree of structure is required. In order to use a data lake in conjunction with a data warehouse, we must use the lake as a raw storage area that is used as a landing and staging platform. Crucially, we need a structure for the lake that allows us to properly segment business areas for security or logical reasons. Without this kind of structure, we would find ourselves in charge of a data swamp – a place where data comes to die and insights cannot be discovered.

The Modern Enterprise and Its Data Lake

Any organization will likely have a data lake although they may just not call it that. They may call it SharePoint, or "The Intranet," or even just the shared network drive. Branded data lake technologies such as Azure Data Lake Gen 1 and Gen 2 are flagship products that specialize in being data lakes; however, these other systems can also compete in some areas. Just because a data lake is not called a data lake doesn't mean it doesn't do the same job. Often however, a cloud-based data lake holds a special place between these technologies – it is not quite so user friendly as to be used daily by a nontechnical user, yet it is much easier to access and load data to than an SFTP site. What's more, the Azure Data Lake technologies make use of AD integrated security and can be closely tied in with existing security configurations.

So, if your organization does not have an Azure data lake, but you do already use some sort of large-scale file repository, do you still need a data lake? The answer is yes. Whereas systems like an Intranet or SharePoint are built to maximize collaboration, the data lake should be a developer lead initiative so that the structure is conducive to warehouse loading and data science research if required. This may mean breaking apart data silos; where data was previously kept together in isolation, files should be relocated so that they can be loaded more efficiently, and because the lake is easily accessed and defined by users with the right permission, development of the lake in this way can be rapid and agile, lest we forget that the lake is also scalable to almost limitless capacities. It requires very little maintenance or up keep as there are no servers that you need to worry about, Microsoft takes care of all of that for you; the only concern to the business is the structure and quality of the data in the lake. This founding feature of cloud data lakes means that there is never a reason to throw data away without a very good reason (GDPR, etc.). Any data stream that is identified in the enterprise should be directed to output data into the lake in some capacity. Even if there is no actual processing or defined purpose for the data, the fact that it is captured means that it can be profiled, analyzed, and built upon when the time is right.

Azure Data Lake Technology

The Azure platform has three offerings that can be considered candidates for a Data Lake which are

- Azure Data Lake Gen 1

- Azure Data Lake Gen 2

- Azure Storage

From a functional perspective, these products are obviously fairly similar; however, there are aspects about them that are different, and these distinguishing features are important to understand. Additionally, Microsoft are fully bought into the concept of the data lake and therefore continually develop their offerings to ensure they are competitive products that lead the market.

Azure Data Lake Gen 1

The initial data lake offering, Azure Data Lake Gen 1 (ADL Gen1) is a well-matured product at this point and has been the go-to data lake technology in Azure for a good number of years. While this has been moved on in the form of Azure Data Lake Gen 2 (ADL Gen2), it is worth a few sentences to explain why this product was beneficial and how the architecture was structured. ADL Gen1 is built using an Apache Hadoop file system (HDFS) and exposes the WebHDFS REST API Layer to calling applications. This means it is easily integrated into other technologies that understand those APIs such as Spark and Hive. A feature of an HDFS type file system is that it can store files of any type and size; there are no restrictions whatsoever. Files can range from bytes to petabytes in size, and ADL Gen1 will have no problems storing, reading, and writing them. In fact, when files are deposited into the Azure Data Lake Gen 1, they are split across a number of storage servers to offer maximum resiliency but also parallel reading capabilities. This splitting of data means that analytical compute resources that run on top of the lake, such as Spark, Hive, and Azure Synapse Analytics, are able to run as efficiently as possible. Lastly, ADL Gen1 implements Active Directory integrated security, so that access to folders and files can be managed through groups to a high degree of granularity.

Azure Blob Storage

Before Azure Data Lake Gen 2 became generally available in February 2019, the only alternative to Azure Data Lake Gen 1 was Azure Storage or Blob Storage as it is commonly known. Azure Storage also uses the HDFS-based file system client and therefore offers optimizations for parallel reads and analytical queries; however, it exposes its own set of Azure Storage APIs rather than the more generic WebHDFS APIs using its own Windows Azure Storage Blob (WASB) driver. One more major difference between the two technologies is the way that files and folders are implemented. In Azure Data Lake Gen 1, folders are true folders in that they are stand-alone objects in the system, and this is known as a hierarchical file system. In Blob Storage, the files are stored as objects in a container which is a flat namespace. The concept of folders does not really exist; however, virtual directories can be implemented using part of the object name. Despite this, all the tools to work with Blob Storage use the name "folder" to describe levels in the system; however, if you create an empty "folder" and navigate away from it, you will notice that the folder does not appear to exist and this is because there is no object that has that folder as part of its name. Therefore, the "folder" does not exist either. This can be confusing at first although in practice this is rarely an issue. A further benefit that Blob Storage has over the Azure Data Lake Gen 1 is the concept of redundancy. In ADL Gen1, data is locally redundant, meaning copies are stored within the same Azure region. However, Blob Storage can offer locally redundant, zone redundant, and globally redundant levels of geo-redundancy making the recovery options a bit more flexible.

Azure Data Lake Gen 2

Finally, we have Azure Data Lake Gen 2, which is essentially the marriage of ADL Gen1 and Azure Storage. Mostly the technology is based on Azure Blob Storage so that costs are low and features such as geo-redundancy are implemented by default. There are, of course, a couple of differentiating factors that make this a true data lake technology optimized for big data analytics instead of a generic object storage engine. The first is hierarchical namespaces. This feature allows a directory structure to be realized physically rather than being mimicked as is the case in Azure Blob Storage. As mentioned earlier, the folders do not technically exist in Blob Storage, and so any changes to the directory structure incur the need to iterate each object and perform an update. With the implementation of hierarchical namespaces, a directory update becomes a simple metadata change in the storage engine and data access is simplified greatly, thereby improving query performance. Another addition is that of the ABFS driver, which is a driver that is available in all Apache Hadoop environments such as Azure Databricks and Azure Synapse Analytics and is specifically optimized for big data analytics. Previously, the WASB driver was used to complete the complex mappings between the HDFS semantics and the object store interface used in Azure Blob Storage. However, due to the arrival of hierarchical namespaces, the system semantics are now aligned and therefore the mapping exercise is no longer required making reads much more efficient. The security implementation for Azure Data Lake Gen 2 is very similar to that of Gen 1 now that folders are no longer virtualized. Azure Active Directory is fully integrated and permissions can be set for each file and folder. The permissions themselves can be assigned through the Azure Portal and also using Azure Storage Explorer.

Each of these data lake technologies interacts excellently with Azure Synapse Analytics as the PolyBase engine and can make full use of the distributed storage structure to read data into the instance in parallel. However, Azure SQL DB on the other hand is not a distributed system that has support for HDFS type file storage, meaning that data moving from any of the preceding data lake options into Azure SQL DB must be loaded via an integration engine such as Azure Data Factory.

Planning the Enterprise Data Lake

When you first begin using an operating system (OS), such as Windows, the first thing you probably take for granted is that all the files are neatly packaged into folders for you and the OS provider will usually have already created some empty ones that are preconfigured for things that you use regularly such as downloads, music, images, and others. Despite this, there will always be an area where you are encouraged to put in your own organization structure – this is your documents folder for users of Windows. Here, the file system has been well thought out so that when new data arrives in your system, there is a clear place for it to go and files can easily be located when needed. Imagine firing up your PC to find that every file on your machine was stored in a single folder. You would be completely lost! Additionally, some folders are purposefully locked down to avoid you accidentally deleting something that it critical to your system, again, good planning of the file structure.

Moving out of the realm of a user's PC and into that of cloud data lakes, the same principles still very much apply. A data lake without a folder structure is a data swamp and is of very little use to anyone, in much the same way as a machine with all its files stored in one place would be. The first step is to define the purpose of your lake and determine which parts of the data processing pipeline will be hosted in the data lake. Commonly, the data lake is used to store data in its rawest form. However, there are tools that can perform complex cleaning and relational logic to data, all within the data lake. This next section will explore when to use a data lake to fulfil various needs that are common in data warehouse scenarios.

Storing Raw Data

The primary usage of the data lake should be storing files in their raw format and so a specific directory should be defined for that purpose. Once data arrives in this directory, it should be immutable (never overwritten or changed) so that you can always roll back to a previous point in time if needed. Additionally, keeping all files in their raw state means that future solutions developed outside of your data warehouse do not have a dependence on your cleaning and transformation logic, thereby reducing the need for regular changes to the ETL processing. It is also best practice to group data by source system, again to ensure that future solutions can easily be developed without interfering with warehouse processing.

In terms of security, the data in this directory should be tightly locked down so that files cannot be deleted or overwritten, and only new files can be added. Often, the Azure Data Factory responsible for copying the data into this directory would have write-only access, and a separate Data Factory (or at least linked service) with read-only access would be used to move data out of this directory. Generally, only an administrator would have both read and write access, and this configuration ensures that there is isolation of concerns for each Data Factory that is working with the files. This directory could be called "RAW" and an example structure is shown in Figure 5-1.

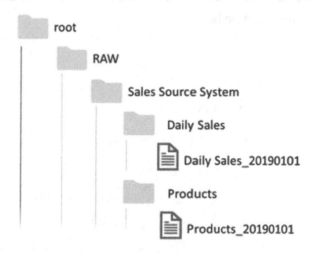

Figure 5-1. *A folder hierarchy showing the RAW directory with one source system and two datasets*

Storing Cleaned Data

Often a SQL engine is used for all processing once RAW data has been ingested because it has all the cleaning capabilities available out of the box. Azure Synapse Analytics and Azure SQL DB could be used to clean and standardize your data from its RAW state into a prepared state, and this is a recommended approach for most integration scenarios; however, there are some exceptions. If, for example, your data is particularly large, it may be much more efficient to leave it in the data lake and use a compute engine, such as Spark or Hive, that can operate on data that is stored in the lake without the need for data movement. Additionally, if your data is a complex semi-structured file or completely unstructured media files, the logic to read and standardize that data may be easier to implement using Spark or Hive. In these scenarios, I recommend cleaning your data within the data lake, and as files are cleaned, sterilized, and perhaps batched or split, they should be stored in a new area that indicates that the aforementioned activity has taken place. It is important to separate this data because it is no longer true to its source and therefore may obscure some detail that is required by another team or process perhaps now or in the future. This could be called "Clean" and is the first step to distilling value. The security here could be more relaxed as there may be analysts wishing to access this cleaned but still relatively untouched data. As with Raw, this space should continue to group data by source system and will very closely resemble the structure of Raw so that the path from Raw to Clean is easily followed. Figure 5-2 shows how both Raw and Clean could be laid out.

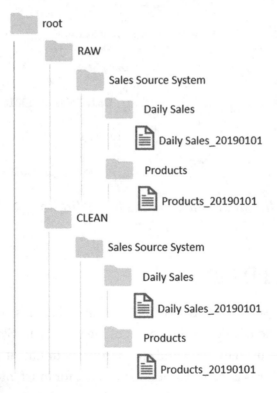

Figure 5-2. *A folder hierarchy showing the RAW and CLEAN directories with one source system and two datasets*

Storing Transformed Data

As with the clean directory, simple tabular data that needs to be transformed in some way should be loaded into a SQL engine. Again, all the capability is built into the engine, and often development teams have pre-agreed patterns or methods for transforming data so that it is ready for ingestion into a data warehouse. However, the same exceptions are still valid because at this point your large or less structured files are cleaned and prepared but not necessarily any smaller or more structured. If they were not tabular to begin with, then they most likely are still not tabular, and therefore it may again be easier to read and transform the data using an HDFS-based engine such as Spark or Hive. The goal of this processing step however is to coerce the data into a tabular format so that it can live in a SQL table as part of your data warehouse. That said, avoid the temptation to transform and load your data into the data warehouse in one step. While this might seem more efficient, having the process split out makes maintenance much simpler and provides a clear checkpoint for data before it arrives in your warehouse. As such, a new directory should be created to store these transformed files separately to your raw and clean files. This new directory will no longer follow the source system-based structure, as nearly all data transformation steps alter the files schema or join rows across datasets, and we should now start to group data by its logical usage. An example would be the processing of customer records from multiple source systems into a single conformed dimension. This file no longer belongs to any single source system and therefore should be grouped under "Customer." As you can see, the data stored here would closely resemble facts and dimensions and so this directory should be called "Warehouse." Here you may have both analysts and applications consuming your data, so security needs to be heavily considered here. Figure 5-3 shows how the data lake may support the Warehouse directory.

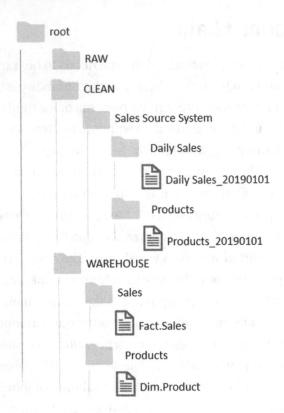

Figure 5-3. *A folder hierarchy showing the RAW, CLEAN, and WAREHOUSE directories*

Facilitating Experimentation

If you have users that want to experiment in the lake, by perhaps transforming data in new, unexplored ways, this may also require a separate "Experiments" area so that the data arriving here will not affect the more defined movement of data through the lake. The security here is very much dependent on the scenario; however, you could have user-specific folders where the security is set up as such. Generally, the usage of this area varies although most organizations that use this concept successfully have analysts or developers pull data from Raw into their own defined spaces and build proof or concept reports to whet the appetite of the business. When a report is considered valuable, then the processing created in the Experiments area of the lake can be replicated easily on top of Raw because the data is in the same state. Figure 5-4 shows how user-specific folders can be used to copy Raw data from RAW that can be used for experimentation.

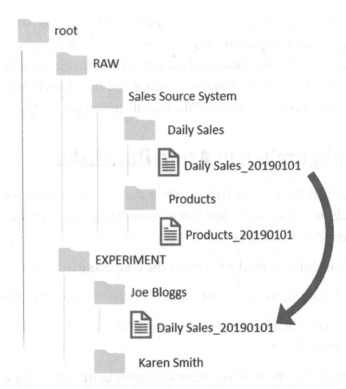

Figure 5-4. *An implementation of an EXPERIMENT area where Joe Bloggs can experiment with Raw data without affecting the warehouse processing*

Implementing the Enterprise Data Lake

When implementing an enterprise data lake on Azure, it is important to remember that the lake should be for the benefit of every single employee – even those users without requirements currently may well have business-critical data in the future, and the goal is to create a solution that is generic and future proof enough to ensure these scenarios can be implemented with the least amount of developer effort. This can easily be achieved with proper planning of directory structure and security, but as the lake develops over time, this principle is important to keep in mind. Despite this point, we are looking at data warehousing and how a warehouse can be feed from a data lake. Therefore, we will begin to discuss the specifics of this approach, but in practice, these steps should only form part of the lake and not dictate the entirety of its purpose.

Another key attribute of the lake is its relative cost compared to its value. A data lake is a way to store immense amounts of data while paying very little to do so, with the added benefit that the implementation of the HDFS APIs means data is very efficiently read from the lake. For any solutions that have a tight budgetary constraint, a data lake means that the expensive compute resource is only spent deriving actual analytical value and not cleaning and transforming data, a task that can be done by a lower-level technology. In this section, we will discuss cleaning opportunities in the lake and how these activities can be completed without the use of an expensive SQL engine.

Security Configuration in Azure Data Lake

Before explaining the details for each directory in the lake, it is important to discuss the nature in which permissions are applied in Azure Data Lake Gen 1 and Gen 2. The permissions that can be set are either

- **Read**: The ability to read a file or list the contents of a folder

- **Write**: The ability to add, delete, and overwrite folders and files

- **Execute**: The ability to iterate through a folder and access the subfolders within it

Each folder and file are treated as a separate object in the hierarchy and therefore have their own set of permissions. A common "gotcha" for people new to administrating a data lake is that of the *EXECUTE* configuration. This permission is essential when a process needs to navigate through the data lake, as the *READ* permission alone does not permit access to any subfolders in a directory structure. Figure 5-5 shows how to correctly configure permissions for file access.

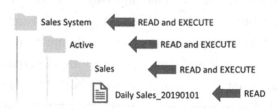

Figure 5-5. *The correct permission setup to allow for file access*

A key aspect to keep in mind is that permissions do not inherit from their parent folders. Where a principal has access to a folder, new files and folders added to that folder will not, by default, be accessible to that principal. This sounds problematic at first because any new file or folder incurs the need to update permissions; however, if we know that a principal will need access to every new addition into the parent folder, we can create a default permission entry that ensures the security configuration of the parent is applied to every new object for that principal. This concept is illustrated in Figure 5-6.

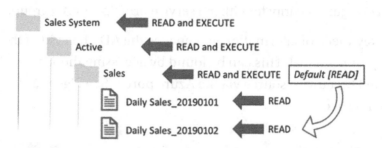

Figure 5-6. *Default permissions are configured on the "Sales" folder to allow for a new file to be accessed by a principal*

If there is a chance that folders will be added to the "Sales" folder, then the "Sales" folder would need *READ* and *EXECUTE* configured as *Default*. Figure 5-7 shows how to configure these permissions correctly.

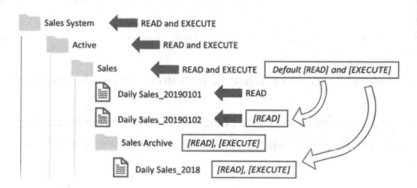

Figure 5-7. *A diagram showing the correct configuration for folders that may become parent folders*

Applying Security in Azure Data Lake Gen 2

In order to apply security configurations to Azure Data Lake Gen 2, you must have the Storage Explorer application downloaded. Assuming you have this application, follow these steps to configure security for either a service principal or AD group:

1. The key piece of information you need is the AD object id of the group or principal. This can be found by accessing the Azure Active Directory resource via the Azure portal. See Figure 5-8 for reference.

Figure 5-8. *Highlighting where Azure Active Directory can be accessed*

2. From here you can locate any of the key principles that you may need to configure security for. Figure 5-9 shows the main areas of interest.

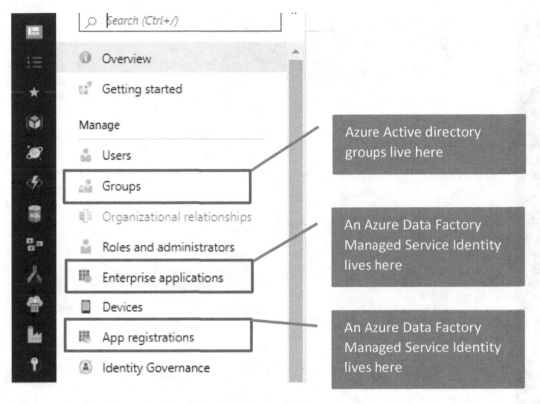

Figure 5-9. *Emphasizing the key areas to configure security in Azure Active Directory*

3.   Within each of these areas is the ability to search for a group or principal by name or application id, and the Object id is then easily located either within the search result itself or by clicking the application and locating the object id item. For reference, an object id is a GUID that could resemble the following: **1abc6475-79cd-4292-8203-c6c926b3b679**.

4.   Once you have your Object id for the object you want to configure permissions for, open the Azure Storage Explorer application and locate your Data Lake Gen2 instance from the tree menu on the left-hand side. Click it to open the folder view in the main window and right-click the first folder to see the dialog box shown in Figure 5-10.

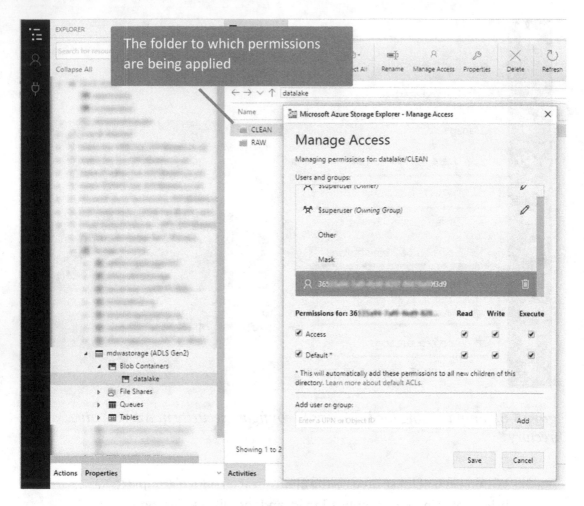

Figure 5-10. *An image showing the "Manage Access" dialog in Azure Storage Explorer*

5. In the bottom text box, copy the object id in and click Add. Once the object id is validated, you will see the new object id highlighted and the boxes below unchecked. From here you can check the "Access" boxes to determine what permissions are applied directly to the folder and the "Default" boxes to determine what permissions are applied to new files and folders that are created underneath the selected object.

Implementing a Raw Directory

As mentioned previously, the first area for inbound data should be the Raw directory of the data lake. The route into this area should be simplistic and low maintenance so that there is little to no barrier to entry and data can quickly be consumed and stored securely away in a place where it will not be lost. Immediately within the Raw folder should be top-level source system folders that group related data together. By operating in this way, security can be configured to meet any requirement. If you have a source system that is capable of writing data directly into the lake, then this system can be granted access to write into this single folder without the ability to affect any other source systems. Conversely, if you need to obtain data yourself using Azure Data Factory, then you could allow this Data Factory the ability to write into each of the folders as required. Further to this, with the advent of GDPR, there is the need to understand and process sensitive data separately to nonsensitive data. For reference, sensitive data includes attributes such as race, ethnic origin, politics, religion, genetics, and others that can be linked to specific individuals by either a unique identifier or more natural aspects such as name, email address, and phone number. As such it may be prudent to subcategorize Raw into Sensitive and Non-Sensitive, also ensuring that any processes that are writing into the lake are only able to do so into the correct folders. This could therefore mandate the need for two Data Factories, one that operates with Sensitive and one that operates with Non-Sensitive.

A further key benefit of the Raw directory is the resilience that it offers to the overall solution. By storing data redundantly in the lake, you can ensure that you always have the ability to rehydrate your data warehouse should the need arise. Of course, the larger the data volumes, the more difficult a full hydration may be, but at least with the data stored in Raw, you always have the option.

Partitioning

A common pattern in any file system that is updated daily is to partition the data by a batch id or arrival date. This is so that deltas can be easily derived and lineage accurately tracked. A data lake is no exception to this, and it is encouraged that any writing processes can create a daily folder or batch folder for each of the loads. Were the frequency to be even higher, for example, hourly or minutely, then you could weigh up the pros and cons for partitioning the structure to that level or grouping data by date. If you are receiving data from a source provider, then it should be mandated that they create date folders within the lake, underneath their source system folder. Alternatively if you have to obtain data yourself with Data Factory, then these folders can easily be created using an expression. Listing 5-1 shows some code that could be inserted into the sink dataset directory to create folders for the year, month, and day.

Listing 5-1. Data Factory expression to concatenate current datetime values with directory paths

```
@concat(
    'raw/Source System 1/',
    formatDateTime(utcnow(),'yyyy/MM/dd'),
    '/'
)
```

Once this pattern is in place, most tools that operate over a data lake (including Azure Synapse Analytics) can begin reading data at the table root level which in this case would be /raw/Source System 1/. All of the date partitioning and subfolders underneath are completely transparent to the engine, and the data can therefore be treated as a single dataset, regardless of which year, month, or day partition the file is stored under. It does not matter how many files are included within the hierarchy; Azure Synapse Analytics will have access to them all. A key point to understand here is that over-partitioning of data can be a bad thing. This is known as the small file problem and generally arises when files are split up to a point that the overhead to read multiple files exceeds the benefit that is generated through parallelism. Essentially the engine has too many files to read, and because the files are so small, the engine reads them too quickly and then has to go through the overhead of reading the next file. Depending on the scale of your data warehouse, you can achieve different amounts of parallelism when reading data from your data lake. For example, an Azure Synapse Analytics running at 500 cDWU can have a maximum of 40 external readers, meaning that 40, 512 MB chunks of data can be read at once. Be aware that compressed files can bottleneck performance because although there may be less data to retrieve from disk, PolyBase cannot open multiple threads on a compressed file.

An additional consideration when implementing an enterprise data lake that needs to feed Azure Synapse Analytics is that the PolyBase engine cannot push filtering predicates down onto the data lake layer. This means that an external table that is pointed at the table root will have to read the full dataset every single time, and this will gradually degrade performance over time. In order to mitigate this issue, files could be loaded into an *Active* table location so that only relevant files are exposed to the external table and any nonrelevant files are moved out of this location so that a full history can be accessed when needed, but daily loads are optimized.

Choosing a File Format

A major consideration with any data platform implementation is that of the file formats used throughout the system. In principle, the data lake can house files of any type; however, best practice dictates that a standard file type convention is used so that standards can be maintained. The formats available to PolyBase are

- Delimited text files: CSV files and alike.

- RC files: Record columnar format that generates groups of rows and then processes these into key value pairs.

- ORC files: Optimized row columnar format that uses encoding and lightweight indexes.

- Parquet: Similar to ORC files, however also lend support for nested attributes and hard data typing. PolyBase, however, cannot read nested Parquet files but can utilize the internal metadata that defines data type information.

With delimited text files, the data types are not enforced, and so the external table should define each column as a NVARCHAR(1000) type so that any value can be read in. However, this also then mandates that an additional processing step is implemented to coerce the untyped values into strongly typed values. To mitigate this, Parquet files could be your default because the files themselves contain metadata describing each column, meaning data does not have to be loaded into an untyped table and then transformed into a table that is strongly typed.

Implementing a Clean Directory

Up until now we have discussed mostly the Raw area of the data lake, and while this is arguably the most critical area to get right, there are other areas to focus on. Depending on how you choose to clean your data, there are some major considerations to evaluate and the route into this area can vary greatly depending on the technology choices of the platform.

Cleaning Within a Database

Both Azure SQL Database and Azure Synapse Analytics are highly capable of applying complex and repeatable cleaning rules to datasets, and therefore if your data is all tabular, then this should be your primary method. The T-SQL language that is native to both Azure Synapse Analytics and Azure SQL DB contains reams of functions designed to help developers achieve these goals. Common functions that are used heavily are TRIM, SUBSTRING, LEFT, RIGHT, UPPER, LOWER, COALESCE, REPLACE, CAST, CONVERT, and CONCATENATE, and often they are used in conjunction with each other. Further benefits of this approach include easier deployment and source control using Visual Studio. While the code to clean the data can be common across both Azure SQL engines, the method to hydrate your database with Raw data to be cleaned would be different. Of course, Azure Synapse Analytics would use PolyBase to obtain the data directly from the data lake, while Azure SQL DB would have to use Azure Data Factory to bulk copy the data. When using Data Factory, you may be tempted to call a cleaning stored procedure from the copy activity itself as per Figure 5-11; however, this is poor practice as this changes the insert from a minimally logged bulk operation into a highly transacted one, and this hits performance. Figure 5-11 shows the configuration to use a stored procedure as part of the Data Factory copy activity.

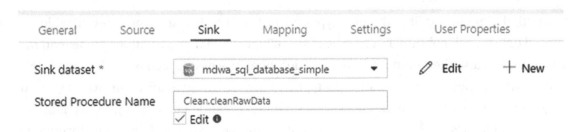

Figure 5-11. *Image of Data Factory using stored procedure called from Copy activity*

There is of course a redundancy benefit to writing the cleaned data out into the lake which could also enable subsequent solutions that require clean data to piggyback on this output. Were this to be of interest, then Azure Synapse Analytics can again use PolyBase to do the opposite of the import. By creating an external table from an internal table, you create a new file in the data lake that could be picked up by a subsequent process. An example of this is shown in Listing 5-2.

Listing 5-2. An example of a Create External Table As Select (CETAS) statement

```
CREATE EXTERNAL TABLE dbo.CleanCustomer
WITH
(
    LOCATION = '/Clean/Sales System/Customer/',
    DATA_SOURCE = AzureStorage,
    FILE_FORMAT = TextFile
)
AS
SELECT TOP [N]
*
FROM
clean.Customer;
```

The preceding code shows how to create the external table from the internal clean.Customer table specifying the location and file type. Additionally, note the use of TOP here. This is used to force all the data into the control node of the Azure Synapse Analytics engine and thereby producing one file instead of 60, one per storage distribution.

While processing data in Azure SQL engines should be your primary choice, there are also issues with this approach. The first is that Azure Synapse Analytics is expensive. The massively parallel processing (MPP) engine that is the core of Azure Synapse Analytics is designed for blazing fast analytics and should not be thought of as a regular SQL engine in terms of cost or capability. To maximize on your investment in Azure Synapse Analytics, you want to ensure that you are using it to serve users queries across giant datasets rather than consuming concurrency slots to perform menial ELT tasks. To avoid placing these activities on your Azure Synapse Analytics, you could of course utilize the cheaper SQL engine, Azure SQL Database. The drawback here is that data movement pipelines need to be defined and orchestrated to move data into and out of your SQL engine. Figure 5-12 shows how data can be moved between different components of a solution.

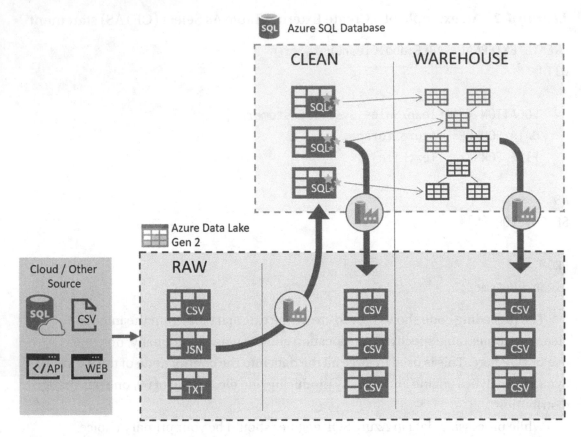

Figure 5-12. *A diagram showing a polyglot approach to ingest, process, and egress data to and from the data lake*

Cleaning Within a Data Lake

A different approach is to leave the data in the lake and not move it into a SQL engine at all. This relies on specialist data lake processing tools which are becoming increasingly popular due to their flexible nature and their ability to really capitalize on the underlying storage engine. Databricks is one such processing tool and is built upon the Apache Spark engine, therefore using clusters to scale out compute jobs and in-memory storage to enhance performance. Working with Databricks to clean data is beyond the scope of this book; however, all required cleaning activities can be easily undertaken using either

- Spark SQL: A SQL language that abstracts a set of dataframe APIs

- Python: The world's most popular programming language with a whole heap of external libraries to solve every possible scenario

- R: Traditionally a statistical language that can perform complex data transformations

- Scala: The native language of Spark and the language that Spark SQL, Python, and R compile into

The benefits of this approach are that the data does not have to move as far; Databricks connects to the data lake by impersonating a service principal and then exploits its deep integrations with the HDFS ecosystem. Additionally, a truly immense file that would be difficult or too time consuming to load into SQL can easily be processed by Databricks as its partitions will be exploited and the workload parallelized. Databricks can also rack up a cost; however, be cautious with features such as auto scaling and default sizing as often you can begin to consume compute resources long before you realize how much it is costing and be sure to terminate a cluster when not needed.

Cleaning Within Azure Data Factory

A final option that coincides nicely with the topic of Databricks is that of Azure Data Factory Mapping Data Flows. These are graphical data flows that are created using Azure Data Factory but executed as Scala jobs on a Databricks cluster. They allow developers to drag and drop well-defined activities into a left to right flow and configure properties at each step. Similar to SSIS Data Flows, they can perform row- and column-based transformation operations while also handling aggregations lookups and filtering. At the time of writing, Mapping Data Flows were recently released (May 2019) and are therefore a fairly immature offering at this stage; however, they do provide a low/no code option to working with data not within a SQL environment.

Implementing a Transformed Directory

Once again, certain characteristics of your data may dictate that the role of your data lake extends all the way to implementing business logic using Spark or Hive instead of using a traditional relational engine. In this case you would want to carve out a further area of the data lake likely to be named "Warehouse." "Warehouse" is the area where clean data is *joined* and transformed into a shape that resembles facts and dimensions, although the data has not been surrogate and dimension keyed or undergone slowly changing dimension logic. The operative word here is "joined" and joining requires a relational engine because often we are combining two or more source entities to create a single conformed warehouse entity that encompasses the constituent parts. Databricks has a relational capability through the implementation of Spark SQL and PySpark, which allows a developer to write traditional looking SQL that can perform joins without the need to actually move data into a SQL engine. This approach can drastically decrease the overhead to process data as the relational engine is brought directly to the data, rather than the data being brought to it. Additionally, Spark's performance is founded upon processing data in memory and can perform such tasks at a very large scale due to its distributed architecture.

Regardless of SQL or data lake being chosen for each step, all of the cleaning and warehouse operations can be orchestrated using Azure Data Factory. ADF can call stored procedures in either SQL engines and also invoke Databricks "notebooks," like repeatable scripts, and this means that wherever the processing of the data is done, the orchestration and control of the processing is handled by ADF. This approach is now known as ELT.

- **Extract** data from source files or source database.

- **Load** data into a SQL engine or data lake.

- **Transform** data using SQL stored procs or notebooks that are executed by Azure Data Factory.

This approach is most effective when datasets begin to cross the boundary into that of "big data" as the data is now transformed, aggregated, processed, and so on in a proper engine that can have the scale to cope with such a task, rather than inflight between a source and destination, as is the pattern with SQL Server Integration Services. Essentially the compute resource is brought to the data and is transformed in place.

In summary, the role of the enterprise data lake is to support a SQL engine when the data becomes too large or too loosely structured. And in either of these cases, there is very little trade-off between using the data lake against using SQL because of the quality of tools that are available, such as Databricks. Further, the integrations between the lake and Azure Synapse Analytics mean that the two can work cohesively to provide a "best of both" solution. Of course the data lake holds another benefit in that no matter what the data, the lake can handle it. Whether it be multimedia files, frequently arriving log files, or ginormous data files, the lake cannot only store this data but provide a base for rich analytics against these datasets. Of course, multimedia files cannot be read into a relational SQL data warehouse, but by being in an accessible location, their metadata can be used for reporting and analytics if needed.

Another key point is that when a new stream of data is uncovered, it can simply be pointed at the data lake to be stored away safely until a team of developers is ready to do something with it. With no limits on storage, there is never a reason not to store everything. Even if no value is derived specifically from that data immediately, by storing the data in a platform such as a data lake, it is ripe for analytics as soon as the need arrives. While I mention that technologies such as SharePoint and Shared drives can be treated as data lakes in many organizations, the offerings within the Azure platform implement features that ensure the storage platform is not only limitless and accessible but also easily integrated into database engines and existing security structures. This ensures the data lake is flexible to the needs of the business but robust enough to underpin mission critical systems such as a data warehouse.

Example Polyglot Architectures

The following figures and explanations discuss a number of different ways the technology offerings could be blended to produce a solution that covers all bases.

Example One

Figure 5-13 contains a diagram displaying a solution with the following characteristics:

- Small/medium data warehouse that ingests moderate amounts of data per day

- Has little need for processing data back to lake after RAW

- May have a need for regular micro inserts or updates

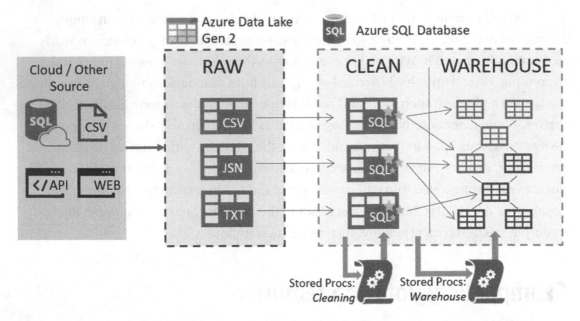

Figure 5-13. *A diagram showing a polyglot architecture with a SQL preference*

Example Two

The diagram in Figure 5-14 displays a solution with the following characteristics:

- Large warehouse that ingests massive amounts of data per day

- Has need for processing data back to lake after RAW

- Ingests data only in large batches – no micro batches

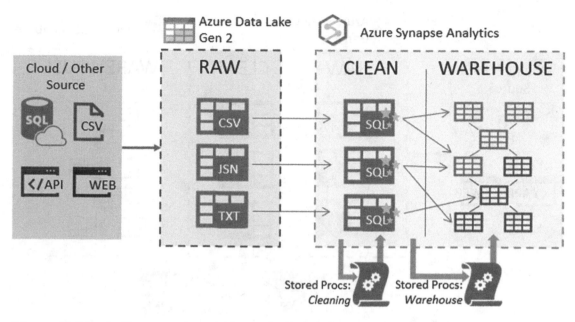

Figure 5-14. *A diagram showing a polyglot architecture with a blend on Azure Synapse Analytics and Azure Data Lake Gen 2*

Example Three

Figure 5-15 displays a solution with the following characteristics:

- Small/medium warehouse that needs Spark or Hive to clean complex or ginormous datasets

- Has ability to accept smaller batches or micro inserts

- Needs to serve a broader analytical community of analysts

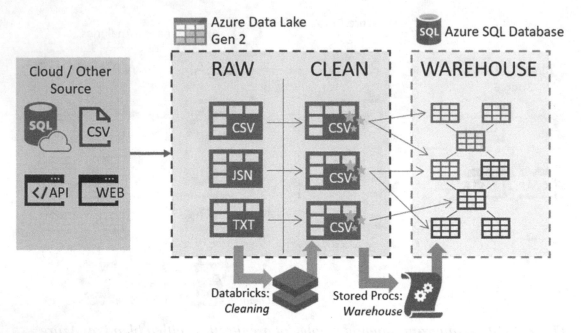

Figure 5-15. *A polyglot architecture that utilizes Databricks to assist with data cleaning and preparation*

Example Four

Figure 5-16 displays a solution with the following characteristics:

- Large warehouse capable of processing highly complex and ginormous datasets

- Has ability to ingest giant datasets from the lake in parallel

- Seamless lake integration via PolyBase

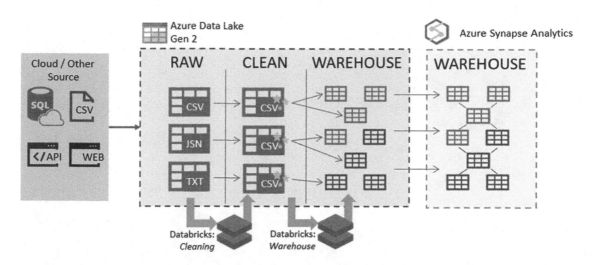

Figure 5-16. *A polyglot architecture that utilizes mostly lake processing, with a SQL engine layer for presentation*

CHAPTER 6

The Role of the Data Contract

In all data integration projects, there is always a concern about datasets changing their properties. This could be changing columns, changing data types, or even changing the degree of quality instilled in the data. The technical name for this is "Schema Evolution," sometimes known as Schema Drift, and whether that be new columns arriving or known columns dropping off, how these situations are handled can have a huge effect on the success of the project. At a basic level, you need to be able to detect and react to occasions when a datasets schema has evolved, and with the vast amount of file and database types available, this task is getting more complex. Not only do you need to detect changes in tabular data (CSV files, database extracts) but also in semi-structured datasets such as JSON and XML. Expanding on this basic concept, you need to be able to handle the schema drift so that you can continue to integrate the data without having to manage multiple extraction methods for the same type of data. This may be manual to begin with, but there are tools out there now that can automatically handle schema evolution. As you begin to write ingestion procedures, remember that maintaining these schemas through schema evolution needs to be simple. If you get to a point where you are ingesting over 20 different files or datasets, then you do not want to have to visit each script to update the schema. Instead we need a centralized schema store so that we can easily make updates in a controlled way.

Another major component in data integration is the rules that are applied to data to transform and clean it, ready for ingestion to the data warehouse. Often these rules are used all over the integration solution, and there may even be a subset of these rules that are applied to all values, such as a trim to remove excess whitespace. Of course, the bane of a developer's life is duplication of code as this causes consistency and maintenance issues, and so to avoid having versions of these rules in every script, the rule definition itself should be stored centrally and distributed as needed. This means that as the

© Matt How 2020
M. How, *The Modern Data Warehouse in Azure*, https://doi.org/10.1007/978-1-4842-5823-1_6

understanding of the incoming data matures, and therefore the rules implemented change and develop, all rules across the solution are updated together but from a single source. An additional benefit here is that anybody looking to understand the transformation and cleaning logic applied in the ETL phase can simply look in one place to review the entire set of rules.

Any integration system that ingests data from more than one source likely needs to manage scheduling and dependencies to some degree. Often these schedules and dependencies can become intertwined in complex ways, and if they are spread out across scripts, then locating an out-of-date schedule or invalid dependency can become very difficult. Ultimately this makes debugging and maintenance very difficult, and given that you may need to change scheduling and dependencies frequently, it makes sense to store this information centrally so that changes are made once and in a single place.

All these problems are common and have been solved many times and in several different ways. However, the solution that I always opt for is that of an overarching set of metadata known as a *data contract*. In much the same way as a legal contract enforces obligations to partaking parties and specifies details of how they can operate together, the data contract does the same for how the data should look when it arrives and how it should be treated in the solution. Because the data contract is stored centrally, it ensures all the key elements as mentioned previously are managed from a single access point. Importantly, however, a data contract should not have to be long winded and difficult to read like a legal contract. In fact, they should only hold exactly what is needed to be useful and nothing more.

What Is a Data Contract?

In reality, a data contract could take several forms; however, the nature of this book suggests that a set of related SQL tables is the best option for a reader who is a data warehouse specialist. Of course, the concepts can be applied to many other data storage platforms such as document databases and key value pair stores, but it is important to remember that the data contract will be called upon frequently and so should be in a format that is comfortable with your development team and will fit easily into your intended architecture. To satisfy basic requirements, your data contracts should store the incoming and intended schemas of datasets; however, these could then be extended to include transformation rules and scheduling logic. Arguably the easiest way to understand a data contract is to see one and there is an example of a SQL table implementation in Figure 6-1.

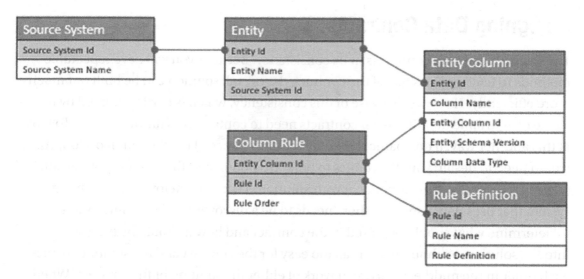

Figure 6-1. *An entity diagram showing how the primary elements of a data contract can be implemented in SQL tables. A detailed SQL script to create the tables shown in Figure 6-1 is included in the appendices*

As you will see, the diagram is relatively simple to understand and is normalized so that rule definitions are only stored once. And clearly data contracts do not need to be complex to be useful as their benefit comes from their consistency. Being able to connect to the database and know exactly how to retrieve the schema, or the cleaning rules, or both, in every single ingestion scenario can make ETL development much more efficient. Common patterns for implementing the schema or rules can be built and then used across the platform wherever needed.

Working with Data Contracts

Data contracts can be useful for any organization or integration solution, and there are two main elements to consider for the implementation to work well. First is how you will design your data contracts so that they cover all requirements consistently. Second is how you will integrate the contracts into a solution so that the contract can become useful. This next section will focus on both design considerations and integration considerations respectively.

Designing Data Contracts

The strength of a data contract is in its consistency. Because you will have repeatable methods to fetch each aspect of the contract, the overall solution can be built out much more efficiently. However, because of this consistency, which is partly enforced by the virtue of SQL table definitions, all contracts need to contain the same attributes. To look at this another way, if one particular entity requires a special configuration option, you would need to design your SQL tables to hold this option and therefore supply a value (e.g., NULL) for every other entity in your solution. Therefore, before implementing a system that uses data contracts, there needs to be a discovery and planning exercise to determine what should be stored in the contract and how it should be translated into the solution. Without this, it is all too easy for the contract and the solution to miss each other in the middle, incurring rework of either the solution or the contract. When planning your data contracts, there are several points to consider. These are

- **Generating data contracts**: How you will create and populate data contracts in a consistent way?

- **Storing data contracts**: Determining a location that is easily accessed by your integration components.

- **Modifying data contracts**: Detailing the process for ongoing work with data contracts including how to handle schema drift.

Generating Data Contracts

The way in which data contracts are built can greatly affect their uptake in an organization. Having to manually write INSERT statements for schemas that have many columns is not going to be a fun exercise, and because these contracts will be largely repeatable, there should be a thought given to the possibility of automation. However, you may decide that due to the importance of these contracts, you want to ensure a human has validated the contract before it is deployed to the metadata store. Of course, you may also find that the sheer number of contracts needed renders the task of manually creating them impossible to achieve in the given time frames. Bear in mind that the contract structure may go through several iterations as they are first being introduced.

An easily adopted option for automating the creation of data contracts is PowerShell, which provides an easily scripted approach to the generation process. There needs to be a balance here of course as automation requires metadata, and we are now at a point of creating metadata to then create more metadata. An ideal solution would be to read a file and inherit its data types and column names. This would mean that you could point your script at a repository of source files – ideally with one source file of each type – and have the script iteratively generate metadata for each file in a consistent and repeatable way.

The output of this script could of course be SQL insert or merge statements that can write data directly into the metadata store or be added to post deployment scripts that are executed each time the database is deployed from Visual Studio. This ensures that the metadata is regularly up-to-date and also offers developers a consistent way to work with metadata. Chapter 8, "Using Scripting and Automation," will go into more detail about how a script such as the one described could be written; for now, consider that data contract generation should be automated as much as possible. An example of a post deployment script that uses a MERGE statement to insert data into the Entity table is shown in Listing 6-1.

Listing 6-1. A post deployment script for merging entity metadata

```
SET IDENTITY_INSERT Metadata.Entity ON;

MERGE INTO Metadata.Entity AS tgt
USING (
    VALUES
        ('1','Daily Sales', '1'),
        ('2','Product', '2'),
        ('3','Product Category', '2')
) AS src ([Entity Id], [Entity Name], [Source System Id])
ON src.[Entity Id] = tgt.[Entity Id]

-- UPDATE MATCHED ROWS
WHEN MATCHED THEN
UPDATE
    SET
        [Entity Name]     = src.[Entity Name],
        [Source System Id] = src.[Source System Id]
```

```
-- INSERT NON MATCHED ROWS
WHEN NOT MATCHED BY TARGET THEN
INSERT
    (
        [Entity Id],
        [Entity Name],
        [Source System Id]
    )
VALUES
    (
        src.[Entity Id],
        src.[Entity Name],
        src.[Source System Id]
    );

SET IDENTITY_INSERT Metadata.Entity OFF;
```

The preceding script uses a SQL MERGE statement to allow for entities to be inserted into the metadata store if the entity does not exist. If, however, the entity does exist, then it can be automatically updated to reflect any changes. This approach allows metadata to be created automatically using scripting but can also be tweaked easily by developers as and when needed.

Validating Data Contacts

Regardless of how the contracts are generated, it is essential that there is a degree of validation before they are deployed into the metadata store. These contracts will define how the system operates and so a faulty contract could cause a wide swathe of issues across your solution. Of course, with SQL tables, there is the reliability of a schema that enforces correct data types and that essential values are not left NULL; needless to say, these best practices should be followed. In addition however, there may also need to be a business sense check to ensure that a dataset is handled properly and this is why contract authoring should be limited to a small group of super users and each contract supplied should be approved by a data steward before being committed to the system.

Any contracts that are found to be invalid or non-(business) sensical should be rejected and sent back to the author. This could be done with some kind of alerting mechanism depending on how sophisticated the validation mechanism is.

Storing Data Contracts

When storing data contracts, there are some critical considerations to bear in mind. In order to protect your SQL engine that would host your data warehouse, it is important to store data contracts on a separate SQL database. For this job, Azure Synapse Analytics would not be suitable as the volumes are small and transactions and concurrency are potentially quite high. A further benefit is that changes to metadata can be deployed without affecting any of the business-critical processes that run the data warehouse. Figure 6-2 shows how such an architecture would be deployed.

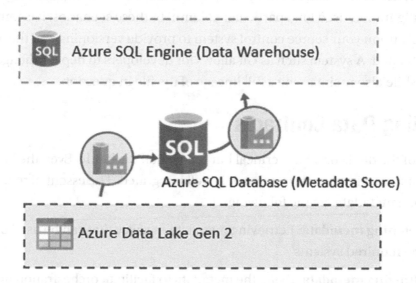

Figure 6-2. *A diagram showing the data contract host database as a pivotal element in the processing of data between data lake and the SQL engine*

Once the data contracts are located on an independent SQL database, the next consideration is that of versioning. It is key that as a schema of a file evolves, the contract is evolved with it. However, it is also key that the previous schema is preserved so that comparisons can be made and that older files can be reconciled to newer versions if required. As you can see from the data model shown in Figure 6-1, the Entity Column table contains a version attribute that allows each set of columns attached to an entity to be associated to a particular version of that entity.

The second consideration of the metadata store is that it is central to your solution and widely available. It is likely that this metadata will be called upon very frequently and by a variety of services, so ensuring that the store can interface with every required service is crucial. One solution may be to surface all data using SQL stored procedures and ensure that all services that require metadata can execute those stored procedures.

Modifying Data Contracts

In some scenarios, you may want to modify data contracts. This may be the case when the schema itself has not evolved but you want to change something less critical such as the rule configuration used for a particular column. In these scenarios, it is important to be able to rely upon your source control system to provide versioning and the ability to roll back if needed. A system such as Git allows for developers to deploy changes to the repository while also maintaining a full lineage of the file in question.

Integrating Data Contracts

The design of the data contract is critical but is only half the battle. Even the best designed contract will be useless unless it is well integrated. The essential requirements for integrating metadata are the following:

- **Fetching metadata**: Retrieving metadata in a way that can be used by the required systems

- **Utilizing metadata**: Using the metadata to facilitate orchestration or provide entity information

- **Harmonizing schema evolution**: Writing scripts that can move files with an older schema to a newer schema

- **Utilizing orchestration metadata**: Using scheduling metadata to ensure processes run at the correct time and in the correct sequence

Fetching Metadata

The method by which your system fetches its metadata should be well thought out. It is important to consider if other solutions outside of your data warehouse processing will need to read your metadata and if so, how you will facilitate that. Additionally, given the size and scale of your ETL processing, how available and powerful the mechanism is that powers the metadata fetch.

Fetching Orchestration Metadata

Orchestration metadata is generally needed at runtime to determine the way in which the processing should proceed. This could be scheduling information or details on how to fetch the relevant data. Given that Azure Data Factory is the primary Azure native integration engine, a simple starting point is to use Data Factory's native connectivity to query your metadata store and fetch the elements you need.

As mentioned in previous chapters of this book, Azure Data Factory has the ability to connect to a great number of data stores. These can be databases, semi-structured stores, and even file storage engines, both on premises and in the cloud. This means that however you decide to store your data contracts, there is a very strong chance that Data Factory can connect and read the metadata from them. While Data Factory will not limit which data store you can connect to, you want to ensure that Data Factory can actually query the data store, so that you can fetch specific metadata as and when you need it.

The key activity to facilitate the metadata fetching in Data Factory is the *Lookup activity*. This activity provides the ability to either execute a query or stored procedure and then expose the result to Data Factory in a way that can be utilized later in the processing pipeline. A simple and common request might be to fetch a SQL query string that is used to obtain the correct data from a table. A query performed using the lookup activity against a SQL metadata store, using the database structure shown previously, might resemble the code in Listing 6-2 and the result set shown in Figure 6-3.

Listing 6-2. SQL code used select an entity record using the Lookup activity

```
SELECT
    [EntityName] AS EntityName
    ,[EntityObtainString] AS EntityObtainString
FROM [Metadata].[Entity]
WHERE [EntityId] = 1
```

The preceding code would fetch the entity name and obtain SQL string for entity 1.

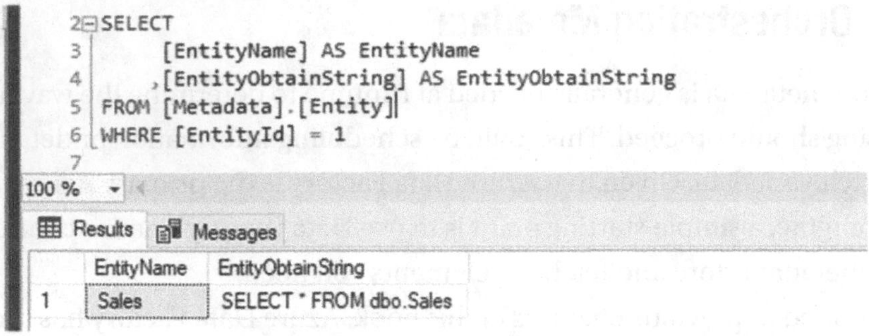

```
2  SELECT
3        [EntityName] AS EntityName
4       ,[EntityObtainString] AS EntityObtainString
5  FROM [Metadata].[Entity]
6  WHERE [EntityId] = 1
7
```

100 % ▾

▦ Results ▨ Messages

	EntityName	EntityObtainString
1	Sales	SELECT * FROM dbo.Sales

Figure 6-3. *An image showing the query results that will be returned to Data Factory*

However, when the result of this query is returned to Data Factory, it must be in JSON format, as that is the object notation used by Data Factory. Therefore, the following query would return a result set resembling the JSON code shown in Listing 6-3.

Listing 6-3. JSON code that represents the query results shown in Figure 6-3

```
{
    "count": 1,
    "value": [
        {
            "EntityName": "Sales",
            "EntityObtainString": "SELECT * FROM dbo.Sales"
        }
    ],
    "effectiveIntegrationRuntime": "DefaultIntegrationRuntime (West Europe)"
}
```

As you will notice, the tabular result of the query is now transformed into a JSON array of objects where each column of the table is represented as a JSON attribute within the object. When creating this type of activity in Data Factory, be sure to untick "First row only." It is on by default but will restrict your query to returning only one row and will also change the attributes that are included in the response. To walk through a guide on using the Lookup activity, refer to section "Getting Started with the Lookup Activity," in Chapter 3, "The Integration Engine." Now that we can access the data, we need to start using it in Azure Data Factory.

Utilizing Orchestration Metadata

In the preceding example, we use a lookup activity to fetch a simple SQL select query that we could use to fetch a relevant set of records. In order to utilize this metadata in a way that ensures reusability, we need to be able to reference the object and attributes that are returned. This is the reason why it is so crucial to use a Lookup activity in Data Factory and not a standard stored procedure activity, only the Lookup makes the result available for later use.

To use the obtained SQL string, we need to pass it to the "Query" attribute for the dataset that is linked to the source of a Copy activity. This is easily done using the Data Factory UI, and provided the Lookup and Copy activities are connected, the syntax shown in Listing 6-4 can be used to reference an attribute from a previous activity output.

Listing 6-4. Data Factory expression to fetch value from previous activity

```
@activity('Metadata Lookup').output.value.EntityObtainString
```

This same approach can be used for any number of attributes that need to be passed around your processing pipelines and can also be used to provide parameter values for child pipelines executed using an Execute Pipeline activity.

You may notice however that the preceding method of identifying an attribute assumes there is only a single entity object returned. If multiple entity objects were returned, such as the JSON snippet shown in Listing 6-5 you would need to handle each individual record iteratively.

Listing 6-5. Multiple entities returned from the metadata lookup

```
{
    "count": 2,
    "value": [
        {
            "EntityName": "Sales",
            "EntityObtainString": "SELECT * FROM dbo.Sales"
        },
        {
            "EntityName": "Product",
            "EntityObtainString": "SELECT * FROM dbo.Product WHERE
             ProductName IS NOT NULL"
```

```
        }
    ],
    "effectiveIntegrationRuntime": "DefaultIntegrationRuntime (West Europe)"
}
```

The preceding expression would not be able to determine which entity obtain string to fetch. In these scenarios, we would want to iterate the result objects using a *ForEach activity*. This is simple to do; however, the key difference is that we now have to obtain the required values from *inside* the scope of the For Each loop so that we can reference a single object, even though multiple were returned. Because each iteration of the loop is anonymous (we don't know which item we are on while iterating the objects), we can use the @item() syntax to reference the necessary attributes:

```
@item().EntityObtainString
```

Now, depending on whether you are working with a single entity or multiple, you can use these approaches to utilize the obtained metadata in your downstream data processing.

Fetching Entity Metadata

The primary purpose of entity metadata is to grant your solution the ability to understand the datasets that you will be processing. By telling your system what columns are needed and how they should be treated, you can automate much of the repetitive processing. However, complex, business-driven transformations cannot be automated without a great deal of complex metadata, more than I could possibly describe in this book. While full automation could be achieved, the developer would need to consider the following as a start:

- Complex transformations such as pivoting and mapping

- Columns that use layered conditional logic such as CASE statements and IIFs

- Joins that use several different predicates and span multiple tables

To refer to the layered structure mentioned previously, entity metadata should allow you to process data from raw to stage to clean very efficiently. Subsequent processing would need to be written by hand and tailored to each specific target dataset.

With this in mind, it is clear that entity metadata needs to be implemented at the point where data is cleaned and standardized. In a traditional on-premises ETL solution, cleaning was regularly done in SSIS packages, meaning the data was altered "in-flight" as opposed to at rest. Due to the potential scales of modern data warehouses, an "in-flight" approach is not always appropriate due to the increased overhead of picking the data up, cleaning it, and then putting it back down again. Not to mention, the current Data Factory solution, Mapping Data Flows, cannot be parameterized to a point where data cleansing pipelines can be generically applied to any given dataset. Therefore, it is clear that SQL stored procedures are the most appropriate way to approach this task, albeit with Data Factory invoking those procedures at the appropriate time. In short, we need to provide entity metadata to the appropriate SQL engine, although without using cross database queries (cross database queries are not supported in Azure SQL Database unless using a managed instance).

Utilizing Entity Metadata

As you now know, you need to pass metadata into your SQL engine so that it can dynamically check column names, enforce data types, apply rules, and transform values so that they are ready to be ingested into your data warehouse. The most reliable method I have found for this is *code generation*.

Code Generation

Code generation describes the process of generating all of the SQL artifacts (stored procs, table definitions, etc.) ahead of time and then deploying them onto the database ready for execution at runtime. The role of the data contract here is to supply entity metadata to the code generation tool in order to produce all the required scripts. This approach is so reliable as it ensures the orchestration is kept simple but still allows developers to update stored procs relatively quickly when a schema evolves. Additionally, the objects that are deployed to the server are readable and easily maintained. This is opposed to be a dynamic SQL approach whereby values are supplied at runtime. While this approach may be more agile, it makes debugging a troublesome stored procedure very tricky.

To implement code generation, I often use a PowerShell script that queries for the metadata, does some text replacement against a preformatted template, and then saves the new .sql files back into a source-controlled folder structure. The program flow for such a script would resemble the diagram shown in Figure 6-4.

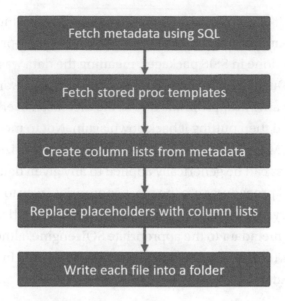

Figure 6-4. *An example program flow diagram for a code generation application*

Getting Started with Code Generation

The following guide walks through how to use a PowerShell script to create completed SQL objects from pre-existing templates and metadata fetched from a SQL database:

1. Check that the correct proc exists on your Azure SQL Database. The name of the proc is Metadata.ObtainEntityMetadata and the result of the proc when run should be three tables resembling that in Figure 6-5.

```
SQLQuery3.sql - m...DB (MattHow (121))*  ↔  ×  SQLQuery2.sql - os...se (MattHow (100))*        SQLQuery1.sql - os...se (MattHow
    1   EXEC Metadata.ObtainEntityMetadata 'Sales'
```

	EntityName	EntityType
1	Sales	Source

	EntityName	EntityType	EntityColumnName	EntitySchemaVersion	ColumnDataType	ColumnOrder	IsPrimaryKey
1	Sales	Source	SalesSystemId	0	INTEGER	0	1
2	Sales	Source	SalesPerson	0	NVARCHAR(100)	1	1
3	Sales	Source	SalesAmount	0	DECIMAL(10,2)	2	0
4	Sales	Source	ProductName	0	NVARCHAR(100)	3	0
5	Sales	Source	ProductId	0	INTEGER	4	0
6	Sales	Source	CustomerId	0	INTEGER	5	0

	EntityColumnName	RuleDefinition	RuleOrder
1	SalesPerson	LTRIM(RTRIM(REPLACE(REPLACE(REPLACE([%%COLUMN_NA...	0
2	SalesAmount	COALESCE([%%COLUMN_NAME%%],0)	0
3	ProductName	REPLACE(REPLACE([%%COLUMN_NAME%%],'Unknown',NULL),'...	0
4	ProductName	LTRIM(RTRIM(REPLACE(REPLACE(REPLACE([%%COLUMN_NA...	1
5	ProductId	REPLACE(REPLACE([%%COLUMN_NAME%%],'Unknown',NULL),'...	0
6	CustomerId	REPLACE(REPLACE([%%COLUMN_NAME%%],'Unknown',NULL),'...	0

Figure 6-5. *An image showing the correct result of the ObtainEntityMetadata stored procedure*

2. Locate the GenerateScripts.ps1 file from the GitHub repo. It can be found in the following directory: PowerShell/Code Generation/ GenerateScripts.ps1. Be sure to open this script in the 64-bit version of PowerShell ISE, not x86.

3. Update the critical parameters. As you can see from the screenshot in Figure 6-6, there are some key parameter values that are used to create a connection to your SQL database and template repo.

```
# Define variable values
$TemplateRepo = "C:\@Source\Modern Data Warehouse in Azure\Modern-Data-Warehouse-In-Azure\SQL\Control Database\Templates"
$AzureSQLDatabaseServer = "mdwa-sqlserver.database.windows.net"
$AzureSQLDatabaseName = "Demo Control DB"
$AzureSQLDatabaseAdminUserName = "MattHow"
$AzureSQLDatabaseAdminPassword = "*********"
$Query = "EXEC Metadata.ObtainEntityMetadata 'Sales'"
```

Figure 6-6. *An image showing the critical parameters in PowerShell*

TemplateRepo: The folder that contains the templates. This can again be downloaded from the GitHub repo (`https://github.com/MattTheHow/Modern-Data-Warehouse-In-Azure/tree/master/SQL/Control%20Database/Templates`); however, you may need to change the location here slightly to match the location of your repo.

AzureDatabaseServer: The name of the SQL database server. This can be found via the portal. Use Figure 6-7 as a guide to help locate the correct property.

sqlserver/Demo Control DB)

Resource group (change)	: moderndw
Status	: Online
Location	: North Europe
Subscription (change)	: Visual Studio Enterprise – MPN
Subscription ID	: d6c9085f-1bef-4f0b-85e8-a30400cbbd0c
Tags (change)	: Click here to add tags

Server name	: mdwa-sqlserver.database.windows.net
Connection strings	: Show database connection strings
Pricing tier	: General Purpose: Serverless, Gen5, 1 vCore
Auto-pause delay	: 1 hour
Oldest restore point	: 2019-09-03 00:00 UTC

Figure 6-7. *An image highlighting where you can obtain the server name property for your Azure SQL Database in the Azure portal*

AzureSQLDatabaseName: The name of the SQL database

AzureSQLDatabaseAdminUserName: The admin username supplied when creating the Azure SQL Database

AzureSQLDatabaseAdminPassword: The admin password supplied when creating the Azure SQL Database

Query: The query to be run against the SQL database. In this case, it is just executing the proc shown previously.

4. Once these parameters are completed, you should be able to execute the script using F5. By default, the script will create a new "Complete" folder within your **TemplateRepo** and drop the completed files in there. Check this folder once the script has completed. You should see the templates as per Figure 6-8.

« Local Disk (C:) › @Source › Modern Data Warehouse in Azure › Modern-Data-Warehouse-In-Azure › SQL › Control Database › Templates › Complete

Name	Type	Size
CleanSourceData.sql	SQL Source File	3 KB
CleanTable.sql	SQL Source File	1 KB
StageTable.sql	SQL Source File	1 KB

nthem - General
scovery - General
n Cancer Support - General
JK - NGAHR
e Survey - General

Figure 6-8. *An image showing the three completed templates*

5. Now that the files have been generated, they can be deployed to the SQL engine that will host your data warehouse. The output of the script is a stored proc that copies and cleans data between stage and clean schemas and two table definitions, one de-typed for the "Stage" schema and another typed definition for the "Clean" schema.

By using the preceding approach, you can see how the metadata provided from the data contract can drastically improve your ability to onboard new datasets. As these new datasets arrive, all that is needed is some data profiling to understand the columns and required cleaning. Once these elements are known, they can be implemented as a data contract and the code generation can build all the SQL required to process those new datasets. Couple this with orchestration metadata and the process becomes even more efficient.

For a more detailed walk-through and explanation of this process, refer to Chapter 8, "Using Scripting and Automation."

Harmonizing Schema Evolution

As datasets change over time, a key task of a data warehouse developer is to update the processing routines so that they keep step with the dataset provider. To assist with this process, data contracts can store schema versions, meaning every change to the dataset can be tracked over time. When the time comes to harmonize files with differing schemas, the delta between the two structures can very easily be determined. The term harmonize here refers to the process of updating older versions of a dataset so that they match a newer version. By instilling this consistency, it ensures tools such as PolyBase and Data Factory can easily read all the data when needed, without having to hold multiple definitions of that dataset.

In some simple cases, datasets can be harmonized automatically. If you imagine a scenario where a dataset simply has one additional column and all the other columns remain identical, a script could easily be written that would match columns by name, identify the new column, and simply provide NULLs for new column in the older datasets. See Figure 6-9 for an example diagram.

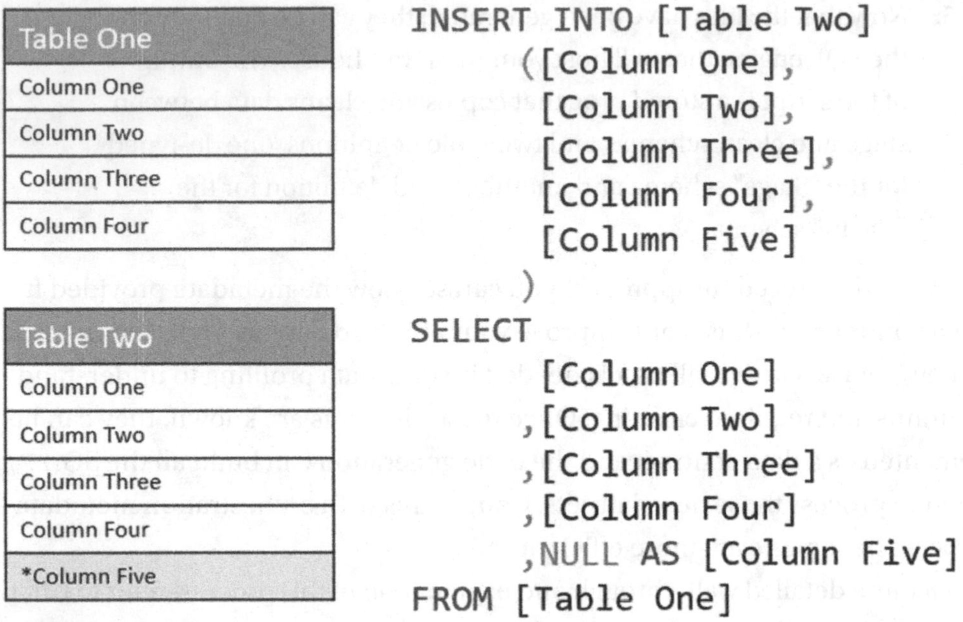

Table One
Column One
Column Two
Column Three
Column Four

Table Two
Column One
Column Two
Column Three
Column Four
*Column Five

```
INSERT INTO [Table Two]
    ([Column One],
     [Column Two],
     [Column Three],
     [Column Four],
     [Column Five]
    )
SELECT
     [Column One]
    ,[Column Two]
    ,[Column Three]
    ,[Column Four]
    ,NULL AS [Column Five]
FROM [Table One]
```

Figure 6-9. *A diagram showing how two tables with a simple difference could be harmonized using SQL*

While the preceding change is very simple, it is very common for schema drift to be much more complex. In fact, it is likely that a developer would need to write a bespoke script in order to harmonize data, as often you may want to provide more than NULL to a new column. In these cases, it is highly recommended that data harmonization occurs as soon as possible and that the scripts are stored and source controlled so that should the harmonization need to happen again, it can be done so consistently.

CHAPTER 7

Logging, Auditing, and Resilience

Things will go wrong in your data processing pipeline. I wish there was a less blunt way to say it, but it is true. In the majority of cases, it may not even be the fault of the platform or the developers. It could be the source provider updating their software, or an intermittent loss of connectivity to an Azure service, or even a harmless comma manually entered into just the wrong place. Whatever the fault is or how trivial it may be, they all have the ability to disrupt your warehouse and ultimately cause loss of service to your users.

Something to bear in mind is that your platform is about data integration, and rarely do source system designers consider downstream data warehouse processes when they build systems, and you can never expect them to put off updates that may well contain breaking changes to your platform. For that reason, you and your development team are obliged to not just know how your platform behaves when running smoothly but also to have a deep understanding of how it behaves when things go wrong. In these moments, when processing grinds to a halt and all the little green ticks turn to red crosses, what your platform tells you about what is happening and why will make all the difference to how efficiently that issue is resolved.

Logging the Data Movement Process

Imagine a scenario where no logging is in place, a large yet critical file that is essential to one of your most used reports fails to load. Manually checking the file indicates that the data is not corrupted and the correct number of columns are present; however, eyeballing each row is not an option due to sheer volume. Checking the SQL database is online proves successfully and all credential checks come back positive. As you begin to take calls from impatient users expecting the report, you begin to suspect the issue is

181

© Matt How 2020
M. How, *The Modern Data Warehouse in Azure*, https://doi.org/10.1007/978-1-4842-5823-1_7

with the SQL Db layer, although without any evidence to suggest whether the problem is with the table, column, or a single value, you realize you need to look at the data row by row. Perhaps a PowerShell script would work? Maybe a profiler session while the data is run through a second time? Either way, you are hours away from implementing and testing a fix for this issue. Logging is a must.

Now, fast forward a few weeks and logging is fully enabled. A similar issue occurs, so you check your audit database. Against the problem file is an error message captured using data factory that states there is an extra field on line 356,789. Depending on the contents, you reject the file back to the user or fix the issue yourself and reprocess. The logging here enables the fix to be done confidently and in minutes.

While logging is always a good idea, excessive logging can be painful to work with, and applications that are too chatty in the logs will frustrate developers and support teams more than they help them. Finding the right balance of logging, and layering different sets of logs, is therefore important to ensure your solution does not log itself into disuse.

Basic Logging Requirements

To avoid over-logging, there should be some basic log requirements that are met. These ensure that a base level of information is held consistently without it disrupting the day-to-day running of your platform.

Where to Store Your Logs

The first question to ask when planning a logging approach is "where should we store our logs?" The answer is simply somewhere that is easy to access for all users, being you, your team, and Data Factory, and also somewhere that provides the ability to be queried efficiently. Logs can often get large and generally have a fair amount of repetition, and so the ability to write detailed filtering logic is very useful. For these reasons, Azure SQL Database is always my recommendation and I generally embed a logging schema in the same database that would serve as a metadata store. These databases could be separated if that was required by the teams managing the different parts of the solution, although bear in mind that it can be occasionally useful to join logged data to entity metadata. An example Audit schema is shown in Figure 7-1.

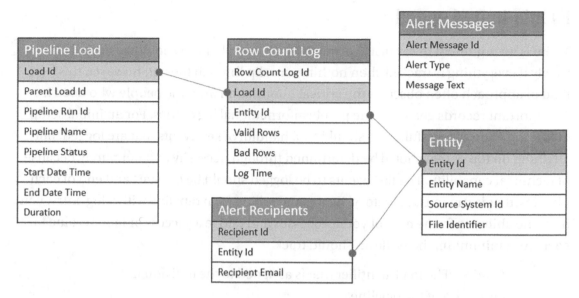

Figure 7-1. *An example schema that logs pipeline execution and provides storage for alerting metadata*

Some users may be tempted to use a completely Azure native logging strategy, employing Azure Monitor and the Operations Management Suite; however, I personally find this cumbersome and liken it to a square peg in a round hole. I feel strongly that there is no substitute for well thought-out, customized logging routines.

Azure SQL Database is one of many options that could be employed here; however, the only other option that I feel is really worth mentioning is Azure Cosmos DB. Cosmos DB is a document database that stores semi-structured JSON documents and can be very efficient for logging due to its less structured nature. Essentially log records can take any shape and do not have to conform to a set schema the way SQL records do. If, for example, a log from an ingestion routine holds vastly different attributes to that of a transformation routine, then Azure Cosmos DB would allow you to store these two differing records side by side in the same database. Of course, a SQL log platform requires that every log entry holds the same attributes or has to be loaded into a different table. Additionally, Cosmos DB uses extensive indexing that can be queried using a SQL-like language, so it can offer up log insights very quickly and easily.

Events to Be Logged

There is an argument to say that every activity in your platform should be logged. Surely if everything is tracked, then nothing can slip through the net; however, this kind of approach often obscures the critical information from the people who need it as important records get lost in the purely informational log entries. For an initial setup of logging to be successful, there should be a handful of key events that are logged, but anything on top of that should be determined through necessity and not purely because of technical capability. The first events to be logged should be the start and end of each pipeline that is run in Data Factory. By top and tailing each pipeline with a log entry, you have the ability to frame each of your processes and derive a success or failure value for each. As a minimum, the platform should track

- Load id: The load identifier that is assigned to the individual execution of the pipeline

- Date and time: The date and time the log event occurred

- Pipeline name: The Data Factory pipeline name pulled from a system variable

By logging these basic attributes, additional insights can be established such as duration of process and even duration of process based on time of day, a very important metric when working with a system that has fluctuations in usage. By trapping these two events, you have the ability to know which pipelines have failed and when, but you can also begin to plan when those pipelines are run in order to achieve the shortest durations.

Importantly, any pipelines that are executed as a child of a parent pipeline should log not just their own unique load id but also that of the parent, so that a hierarchy can be established. This allows developers and support staff to understand the context in which a child pipeline was run, providing critical detail when trying to debug a failure. Figure 7-2 shows how top and tail logging should be implemented for all pipelines in a hierarchy.

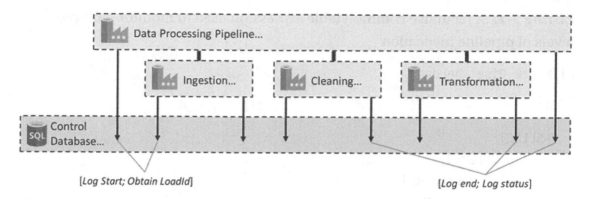

Figure 7-2. *Diagram showing the structure of top and tail logging*

Logging in such a way can easily be captured and Figure 7-3 is an example of such a logging structure.

Load Id is parent for the following child pipelines.

Load Id	Parent Load Id	Pipeline Name	Pipeline Status	Start Time	End Time	Duration
101037	101036	Ingest Source Parent	Success	18:11:34	18:12:38	65
101038	101037	Ingest DB Full Table Child	Success	18:11:43	18:12:28	45
101039	101037	Ingest DB Incremental Table Child	Success	18:11:43	18:11:58	14
101040	101037	Ingest DB Incremental Table Child	Success	18:11:43	18:12:09	26
101041	101037	Ingest File Child	Success	18:11:45	18:12:08	22
101043	101042	Ingest Source Parent	Success	19:11:24	19:12:27	62
101044	101043	Ingest DB Full Table Child	Success	19:11:34	19:12:17	43
101045	101042	Process Platform	Success	19:12:38	19:19:50	432
101046	101045	Process Notebook Parent	Success	19:12:42	19:19:45	422
101047	101046	Process Notebook Child	Success	19:12:50	19:19:38	408

Figure 7-3. *An example table showing the how parent-child processes can be tracked in a SQL table*

This logging structure means that infinite descendant pipelines of the parent can be captured; however, in order to tie each back to the original, you need to use a query like the one shown in Listing 7-1 which employs a recursive common table expression (CTE) to recreate the hierarchy.

Listing 7-1. A recursive common table expression used to monitor multiple levels of pipeline invocation

```
WITH cte_PipelineLoad
AS
(
    SELECT
        pl.LoadId,
        pl.ParentLoadId,
        pl.PipelineName
    FROM
        Audit.PipelineLoad AS pl
    WHERE
        LoadId = 101042
    UNION ALL
    SELECT
        pl.LoadId,
        pl.ParentLoadId,
        pl.PipelineName
    FROM
        Audit.PipelineLoad AS pl
    INNER JOIN cte_PipelineLoad AS cte
        ON cte.LoadId = pl.ParentLoadId
)
SELECT * FROM cte_PipelineLoad
ORDER BY LoadId
```

The preceding code locates every descendant pipeline of load id 101042 and produces the result set shown in Figure 7-4. Related pipelines have been highlighted in darkening shades of blue, showing how the hierarchy is constructed.

LoadId	ParentLoadId	PipelineName
101042	NULL	Processing Master
101043	101042	Ingestion Parent
101044	101043	Ingest Table Child
101045	101042	Process Platform
101046	101045	Process Warehouse Parent
101047	101046	Process Enriched Child
101048	101046	Process Curated Child

Figure 7-4. A result set highlighting how a processing hierarchy can be reported or queried

The next set of events to be logged are anything that involves an external process. If the pipeline calls a SQL activity, log the output. If the pipeline calls a web service, log the output. Particularly if the pipeline relies upon an external compute resource, log the output. These integration points are common areas for failure, as the execution has to be passed outside of Data Factory, and so logging a success or failure with an accompanying message can shortcut a great deal of investigative work that would have to be otherwise carried out. Often these external services return varying amounts of information. Some may provide standard error messages, and some may pass back a detailed stack trace. However, others may just provide a link to their own suite of logging reports. In these cases, it can be useful to use the Cosmos DB logging approach mentioned before as the schema-less nature of a document database is conducive to data that regularly has different attributes. The alternative is to store the JSON data returned to Data Factory in a text column within your SQL database. With this approach, you can easily store the data consistently and also neatly package the additional detail into a single structure. You can then use the JSON_QUERY functionality to read that data when needed.

The table in Figure 7-5 shows that schema-less JSON data can be stored in a SQL column. Note that the rowsSkipped value does not exist for the first row within the *Pipeline Info* column.

Load Id	Parent Load Id	Pipeline Name	Pipeline Info	Pipeline Status

1	NULL	Copy Raw to Stage	{
			
			   "rowsRead": 9,
			   "rowsCopied": 9,
			   "throughput": 0.121
			
			}
				2

2	1	Copy Raw to Stage	{
			
			   "rowsRead": 9,
			   "rowsCopied": 0,
			   "rowsSkipped": 9,
			   "throughput": 0.121
			
			}
				2

Figure 7-5. *A table showing JSON data stored alongside regular tabular data, allowing for schema-less information to be logged*

Listing 7-2 shows the code to read the table shown in Figure 7-5.

Listing 7-2. Code used to extract JSON data from the Audit.PipelineLoad table

```
SELECT
    LoadId,
    JSON_VALUE(PipelineInfo, '$.rowsRead') AS RowsRead,
    JSON_VALUE(PipelineInfo, '$.rowsCopied') AS RowsCopied,
    JSON_VALUE(PipelineInfo, '$.rowsSkipped') AS RowsSkipped,
    JSON_VALUE(PipelineInfo, '$.throughput') AS KbThroughput
FROM
    Audit.PipelineLoad
```

The code in Listing 7-2 uses the JSON_VALUE function to extract several scaler values from the JSON stored within the table. This query will produce the result set shown in Figure 7-6; note the NULL value returned for the missing rowsSkipped value.

Load Id	Rows Read	Rows Copied	Rows Skipped	Kb
1	9	9	NULL	0.121
2	9	0	9	0.121

Figure 7-6. *The result set of a query that blends tabular data with schema-less JSON data fed from the Data Factory pipeline*

Extended Logging Capabilities

The events mentioned previously should be considered mandatory when creating a reliable platform; however, there are additional events that may also be considered useful of even mandatory depending on the type of workload your platform undertakes. One such example is when you need to schedule the startup of an external compute resource. Often in Platform as a Service (PaaS) environments, services can be paused to save cost and therefore need waking up again before they can do any processing. When working with these services, you may find you need to schedule the "waking up" of a resource and regularly check to see if that resource is ready or not. In these cases, you are likely to want to log the fact that a check happened and the result of that check. Additionally, if the resource is paused, then you should log that you had to start it and couple that with a final start time or "duration to start" type calculation. By storing these events, you can begin to see if your processing speeds are being extended purely through wait times for services to become available. If this were the case, then you could review their busy times and bring the schedule forward by 10 minutes to avoid those waits in future.

A further "nice to have" logging opportunity is when you refresh any semantic layers that sit on top of but outside of your data warehouse, for example, Azure/SQL Server Analysis Services (SSAS). The Analysis Service database itself will track when it was last refreshed, but it can be very useful to you as a developer to know how long the process took to complete and then also at what point in time the data that is presented to a user was last refreshed. Often teams measure success by delivering on service level agreements (SLAs), and the time that it takes to refresh the presentation layer is often a critical key performance indicator (KPI). By logging the semantic layer process complete time, this KPI can easily be calculated.

Aggregating Your Logs

In some cases, a single log record does not warrant much attention although several hundred of a similar nature may well indicate a significant problem. When relying regularly on external compute services, you may occasionally get transient failures where the service is offline for short periods of time. These may log a single failure and would be rectified with a simple retry; however, were you to see many of these type of failures in a given time window, you would be fairly certain that there was a problem with that service that needs to be investigated or worked around.

The preceding example is common but not very close to the actual data. There could also be scenarios where a particular type of file occasionally has specific errors on a column. Again, single instances of failures might be expected and can be resolved with some specific data cleansing; however, if every file of that type begins failing, you could make the assumption that the file has changed significantly and therefore some work needs to be done on the data contract. Similarly, when loading very large files, it is often preferential to accept an amount of failures or data quality issues in the interest of loading the majority of rows into the warehouse. Despite this, a threshold should still be maintained to ensure that the quality of data in the warehouse is not lowered too drastically.

In both of these cases, your logging system would need to be smart enough to know that some types of log records are only a problem when they are aggregated together and that simply tracking individual failures does not go deep enough. This is where the logging tables can actually take on a dual role and act akin to a fact table in an analytical system. By regularly running jobs to aggregated failures of a certain type or that are attached to a certain entity, you can easily start to flag alerts that are only relevant at that aggregated level. In order to support these scenarios however, you should design the table with this in mind and ensure all the attributes that you may need to group by are first-class attributes of the logging table. This means that queries over many rows can perform sufficiently. To further support this type of log analysis, you should store threshold values at the appropriate grain which can then be joined to the fact table as per the diagram in Figure 7-7 and Listing 7-3.

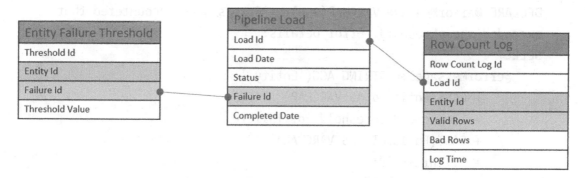

Figure 7-7. *A diagram showing how a threshold table can be related to an audit table to generate threshold-based aggregated log analysis*

Listing 7-3. Code to count the number of each failure type and flag any types that exceed the threshold

```
SELECT
     rtp.EntityId
    ,pa.FailureId
    ,COUNT(pa.FailureId) AS FailureCount
    ,eft.ThresholdValue
INTO #tmpError
FROM
    audit.PipelineLoad AS pa
INNER JOIN audit.RowCountLog AS rtp
    ON rtp.LoadId = pa.LoadId
INNER JOIN audit.EntityFailureThreshold AS eft
    ON    eft.EntityId    = rtp.EntityId
    AND    eft.FailureId    = pa.FailureId
GROUP BY
    rtp.EntityId,
    pa.FailureId,
    eft.ThresholdValue
HAVING
    COUNT(pa.FailureId) >= eft.ThresholdValue

IF @@ROWCOUNT > 0
BEGIN
```

```
    DECLARE @errorMessage VARCHAR(250) = 'Errors were encountered that
    exceeded the threshold. Error Details: '
    SELECT
        @errorMessage += STRING_AGG('Entity '
            + CAST(EntityId AS VARCHAR)
            + ' exceeded threshold for failure '
            + CAST(FailureId AS VARCHAR)
            + '. Threshold: '
            + CAST(ThresholdValue AS VARCHAR)
            + ' Failure count: '
            + CAST(FailureCount AS VARCHAR)
            ,', ')
    FROM #tmpError
    RAISERROR(@errorMessage, 16,1)
END
```

The code in Listing 7-3 counts the number of specific failure types according to the threshold table and entity values and will return any combinations that exceed the threshold. It will then raise a detailed error message back to Data Factory detailing the entities that failed and what the failures were. By using the *RAISERROR* function, an "On Failure" path can be used in Data Factory which could fire off an alert email as detailed later in this chapter.

Auditing the Data Movement Process

Logging that data movement occurred is perhaps the most important part of your platform, given its use when things go wrong. However, there will always come a time when you need to know what normal looks like for your platform so that you estimate what a strenuous load might look like. This is particularly important in sectors such as retail where seasonal milestones can cause huge peaks in traffic. While a data warehouse is unlikely to be too heavily involved in an operational process that utilizes many transactions, if your users are expecting downstream reports to be refreshed frequently, then being able to estimate peak data processing needs is important.

Basic Auditing Requirements

There are two main basic auditing requirements that will allow you to measure what normal looks like for your solution. These are

- Data volumes: The amounts of data flowing through your platform

- Processing times: The frequency of ingestion jobs and the time it takes to complete them

- Watermarks: The max values for each dataset after each ingestion run, helping to detect change

Auditing Data Volumes

By tracking volumetric information about the data that flows through your platform, you can begin to assess the need to scale services, increase storage sizes, and spot potential issues before they become problematic. The most common metric when talking about data volumes is row counts. This metric succinctly indicates the amount of data a file may hold in a single integer and is also generally easy to get hold of. Certainly Microsoft SQL engines provide useful functions to get this number, as does Data Factory and Databricks if you were to be working more in a data lake.

When working within Data Factory, a successfully completed copy activity can, depending on the source and sink settings, produce 22 data points that detail the specifics of that action. The most useful of these regarding row count audit information are

- **rowsRead**: The number of rows read from a data. source

- **rowsCopied**: The number of rows copied into the sink.

- **rowsSkipped**: The number of rows that were skipped. For rows to be skipped, a setting needs to be configured on the copy activity.

- **redirectRowPath**: The path to the "skipped rows" file that sits within the Blob Storage location of the Azure Storage account, supplied when configuring the "rowsSkipped" setting.

In order to obtain these values from within Data Factory, you can use the following snippets in any activity that comes after the copy activity, assuming it is connected:

rowsRead: @activity('Copy Data').output.rowsRead

rowsCopied: @activity('Copy Data').output.rowsCopied

rowsSkipped: @activity('Copy Data').output.rowsSkipped

redirectRowPath: @activity('Copy Data').output.redirectRowPath

These snippets could be used to assign values to stored procedure parameters as per Figure 7-8, which passes the *rowsCopied* and *rowsSkipped* values into a logging stored procedure.

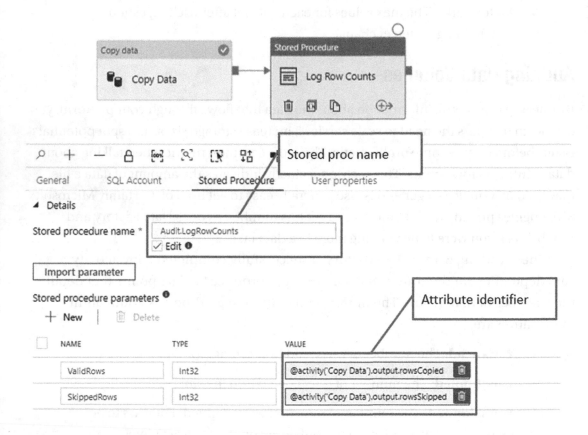

Figure 7-8. *An example showing how copy activity outputs can be passed into a SQL stored procedure for logging in the control database*

Once datasets have been copied into a warehousing database, the movement will be done using stored procedures and not through the Data Factory copy activity, meaning the copy activity outputs will not be available. In order to audit this information and log row counts, they will need to be obtained using the stored procedure and passed back to data factory so that the numbers can be pushed into the logging database. Critically, any stored procedures that are called from Data Factory, where an output is expected, must use the *Lookup* activity, not the stored procedure activity. A stored procedure activity *will not* produce an output to Data Factory, even if one is generated from the stored procedure.

Listing 7-4 shows how an insert statement can be written in SQL that will produce the associated row count of that statement.

Listing 7-4. SQL code to execute an operation and store the row count into a variable

```
DECLARE @InsertCount INT = 0

INSERT INTO dim.Product
SELECT
    ProductName
    ,ProductCategory
FROM clean.Product

SET @InsertCount = @@ROWCOUNT
```

In Listing 7-4 the @@ROWCOUNT system function is used immediately following the insert statement and assigns the value to a variable, storing its value for later use. These exact same methods can be used against *UPDATE* and *DELETE* statements also. In order to surface these values back to Data Factory, a simple select of the variable values at the end of the procedure will suffice:

```
SELECT
    @InsertCount AS InsertCount
```

Full implementation of the methods used in Listing 7-4 can be seen as part of the Code Generation pattern in Chapter 8, "Scripting & Automation". Once the Lookup activity has completed, the InsertCount output can be retrieved from the output using the following snippet:

```
@activity('Exec SQL Stored Proc').output.firstRow.InsertCount
```

The "firstRow" element is used to avoid the use of an array in the activity output.

While knowing row counts are useful, it doesn't cover all bases, as rows themselves can massively vary in size, and so 1000 small rows could in fact store less data than 5 massive rows. This is why it is also useful to audit data sizes, as these give a truer impression of the load on your platform. Similar to row counts, Data Factory has some useful copy activity outputs that can be fetched and logged very simply. The following snippets should be considered when logging data size:

dataRead: `@activity('Copy Data').output.dataRead`

dataWritten: `@activity('Copy Data').output.dataWritten`

throughput: `@activity('Copy Data').output.throughput`

The "dataRead" and "dataWritten" values will provide either the data read from source or written into the sink as an integer in bytes. The throughput value details the kilobytes per second for the data transfer operation.

By logging row count information and file sizes against each incoming dataset, you can begin to analyze the load on your system by file type. Once you have a base level of data, you could compare the new, incoming values to a rolling average to quickly catch any datasets that arrive outside of the normal boundaries. This could help you avoid processing bloated files that contain additional data that is not required or empty files that could fail validation steps.

Auditing Processing Times

Row counts and data sizes are useful when plotting the storage used within your system; however, they only offer half of the story. When coupled with processing times, you can build a fuller picture of the capability of your platform.

Again, Data Factory offers some valuable data as part of the standard output from the copy activity, and so when using Data Factory to physically move the data, this audit information is easily gathered. The key values that are returned from the copy activity are listed here:

- **copyDuration:** The total number of seconds the copy activity executed for.

- **throughput**: The number of kilobytes per second at which Data Factory copied the data.

- **queueingDuration**: The number of seconds before the integration runtime (IR) began running the copy. Large value here on a self-hosted IR can indicate the need to scale according to your workload.

- **preCopyScriptDuration**: The number of elapsed seconds between the start of processing by the IR and the completion of the pre-copy script.

- **timeToFirstByte**: The number of seconds between the completion of the pre-copy script and the retrieval of the first byte of data. Long durations here indicate poor-performing SQL or under-powered servers. This value is for non-file-based sources only.

- **transferDuration**: The number of elapsed between the first byte and the last byte.

The **copyDuration** and **throughput** can be gathered in the same way as the preceding row counts; however, the later four values are actually contained within a **detailedDurations** object which itself is contained within an **executionDetails** array. Therefore, some additions to the preceding snippets are required so that the values can be recovered. An example for **queueingDuration** is as follows:

```
queueingDuration: @activity(
'Copy Data').output
.executionDetails[0]
.detailedDuratons
.queueingDuration
```

Note that while these values are available, the schema may change and null checks should be used when fetching these values from Data Factory.

Once data is stowed inside the database, you can use logging stored procedures to mark the start and end of group of tasks. If needed, this could be very granular such that you log the start and end time either side of each activity. Alternatively, you could simply log the start and end of the entire pipeline, giving a total figure for the process including any overhead processes. Finally, you could use SQL inside of the stored procedure to derive the required duration information and report it back to Data Factory so that it can be used in a log entry. Listing 7-5 shows how that could be achieved.

Listing 7-5. Code to report on the start time and end time of processes with SQL

```
DECLARE @StartTime DATETIME = GETUTCDATE()
DECLARE @EndTime DATETIME
DECLARE @Duration INT
```

```
INSERT INTO dim.Product
SELECT
    ProductName
    ,ProductCategory
FROM clean.Product

SET @EndTime = GETUTCDATE()
SET @Duration = DATEDIFF(Second, @EndTime, @StartTime)

SELECT
    @StartTime AS StartTime,
    @EndTime AS EndTime
    @Duration AS Duration
```

These outputted values, which must be called using a Lookup activity, can be retrieved as per the following snippet:

```
@activity('Exec SQL Stored Proc').output.firstRow.Duration
```

Storing High Watermarks

Storing high watermarks allows developers and support staff to track incoming data using a simple mechanism. Additionally, a high watermark can be used to resolve dependency constraints that may be placed on the system. A watermark can be implemented using either a sequential ID column, something that is very common in transactional systems, or a date column such as record creation date. In some cases, a source system may use a globally unique identifier (GUID) which is great for ensuring uniqueness but is not sequential, and therefore it is not possible to identify the latest of records using it.

A high watermark should be maintained at the entity level so that is can be used as a point of comparison between source entities that may form part of a target entity. In order to obtain the watermark value on each load, a simple MAX function should be applied to the selected column, or columns, as the data is loaded using a SQL stored procedure. This MAX value can then be passed out of the stored procedure using a mechanism similar to the one described in Listing 7-3 and logged in the auditing database using Data Factory.

A key value of this watermark is its ability to indicate change. For example, if there are two source datasets that produce a single target dataset, a simple comparison can be made between the two source watermarks and the target high watermark to work out if the data has changed in source and therefore needs refreshing in the target table.

By engaging one or more of these logging mechanisms, you should be able to build up a repository of telemetry and volumetric data which can be helpful when planning for new datasets or monitoring the current scale and state of the services that make up the platform. Be sure to consider what metrics are important to you and whoever supports to solution however, as excessive logging can be problematic and can even obscure the data that is giving you the real insight.

Incorporating Resilience into the Data Movement Process

Logging information about steps that have happened within a data processing pipeline is useful when looking retrospectively; however, to become resilient, there needs to be a native ability to handle problems that might occur. Additionally, being able to alert certain members of a team when something has gone wrong also drives toward a more resilient platform.

Basic Resiliency

As with audit information, there is a base level of data that should be captured and then there are numerous ways in which that can be extended to offer specific insight into an area that may be of particular interest. The first step toward resiliency is to incorporate some basic defensive checks, allowing the platform to detect problems before they become problematic. The second is then being able to act on those problems autonomously, whether that be by alerting a person or redirect the logical flow so that downstream issues do not occur.

Using Metadata for Troubleshooting

Throughout several previous chapters I have mentioned metadata and how it can be used for a number of different purposes, well here is another. By using metadata to tell the platform about what inbound data *should* look like, you can check to ensure that that image aligns with reality, and if not, steps are taken to ensure the data does no harm downstream.

The sooner these defensive checks can be performed, the better, and so Data Factory is an ideal place to conduct such activities. Given its ability to read and copy files at scale, it can also be used to profile such files and detect if there any differences to what is expected.

Primarily these checks are conducted using the **Get Metadata** activity which, when pointed to a particular dataset, can return a variety of attributes about the data. For a basic level of checking, the primary attributes to obtain are listed as follows:

- **itemName:** This can be used to fetch name of a file or folder. You could then compare this value to some metadata to ensure the file name has the correct date or other attributes within it.

- **Size**: By retrieving the size of a file before copy, you could pre-emptively scale a set of resources or delay loading until a less busy period of the day.

- **childItems**: This attribute can confirm that a folder contains files or other folders, thereby indicating some processing needs to occur. Where this check to come back empty, you can pause processing or alert a user of an upload failure.

- **columnCount**: By fetching the number of columns to be copied, you can easily detect if additional columns have arrived; be aware that this does not check column order.

See Figure 7-9 for an example of how the Get Metadata activity can be configured to retrieve these values and feed them into a downstream stored proc. By using a stored procedure, you can easily develop logical checks in SQL, using metadata, which can then pass instructions back to Azure Data Factory (ADF).

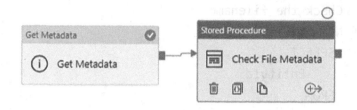

General   SQL Account   **Stored Procedure**   User properties

▲ Details

Stored procedure name *   Audit.CheckFileMetadata

☑ Edit ❶

Import parameter

Stored procedure parameters ❶

+ New | 🗑 Delete

NAME	TYPE	VALUE
ColumnCount	Int32	@activity('Get Metadata').output.columnCount 🗑
Filename	String	@activity('Get Metadata').output.itemName 🗑

Figure 7-9. *Configuration of Data Factory to pass metadata values into subsequent activities from the Get Metadata activity*

Listing 7-6 shows the code for such a checking stored procedure.

Listing 7-6. Code to check the metadata of the given file

```
CREATE PROC Audit.CheckFileMetadata
(
    @EntityId INT,
    @ColumnCount INT,
    @Filename VARCHAR(100)
)
AS
BEGIN
```

```sql
    -- Check the filename
    IF NOT EXISTS (
        SELECT
            EntityId
        FROM
            Metadata.Entity
        WHERE
            @Filename LIKE '%' + FileIdentifier + '%'
        AND EntityId = @EntityId
    )
    BEGIN
        RAISERROR('The filename did not match the specified identifier' ,16,1)
    END
    -- Check the column count
    IF NOT EXISTS (
        SELECT
            EntityId
        FROM
            Metadata.EntityColumn
        WHERE
            COUNT(EntityColumnId) = @ColumnCount
        AND EntityId = @EntityId
    )
    BEGIN
        DECLARE @ErrorMessage VARCHAR(100) = 'The column count ' +
        @ColumnCount + ' does not match the specified column count'
        RAISERROR(@ErrorMessage ,16,1)
    END

    Further procedure logic...

END
```

Creating Alerts Using Azure Data Factory Alert Rules

There will be occasions when you need a specific event, such as the result of a metadata check or a connection failure, to trigger an alert immediately. Initially, you may decide that the majority of platform issues should raise alerts as this will help uncover issues and bugs more efficiently. At present, Data Factory does not have a "Send Mail" task, as was available when using SSIS, and so any custom email alerts will be delivered using an alternative method. However, what Azure Data Factory does support is the use of the Azure native alerting service which uses Azure Monitor to detect instances where certain metrics, such as number of failed activities, exceed a threshold. At these times, alerts are fired to members of an action group, detailing which metric was exceeded and when.

To configure a Data Factory alert rule, you can follow these steps:

1. Open Data Factory and navigate to the monitor UI using the red icon on the left-hand menu. Choose "Alerts & metrics."

2. Click New alert rule as shown in Figure 7-10.

Figure 7-10. *Creating a new alert rule in ADF*

3. Name the alert appropriately and choose an appropriate severity. Click "Add criteria" to begin nominating the events that will raise an alert event. There are many options to choose from here; however, the most useful to begin with is likely "Failed activity runs metrics." See the example in Figure 7-11.

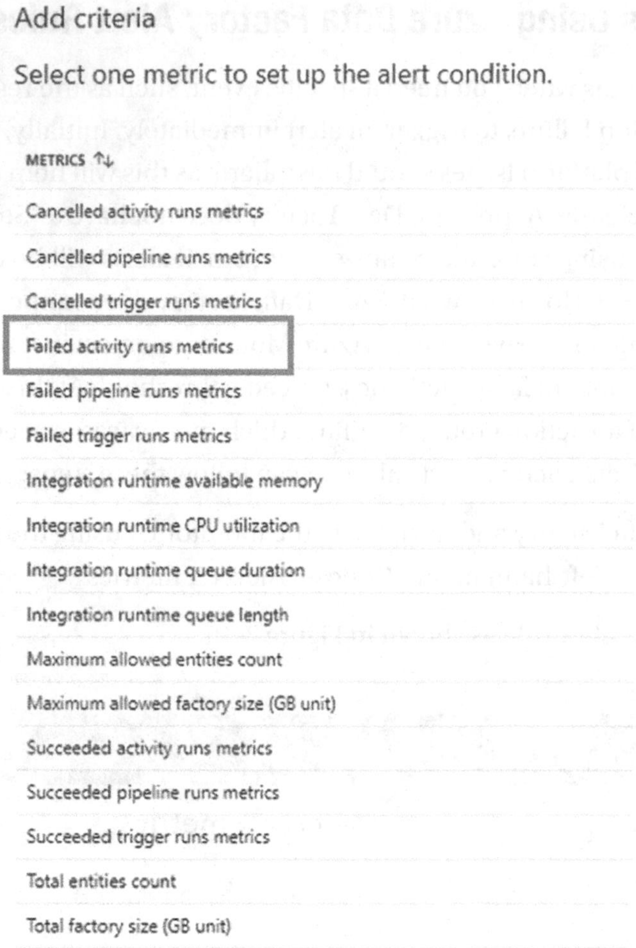

Add criteria

Select one metric to set up the alert condition.

METRICS ↑↓

Cancelled activity runs metrics

Cancelled pipeline runs metrics

Cancelled trigger runs metrics

Failed activity runs metrics

Failed pipeline runs metrics

Failed trigger runs metrics

Integration runtime available memory

Integration runtime CPU utilization

Integration runtime queue duration

Integration runtime queue length

Maximum allowed entities count

Maximum allowed factory size (GB unit)

Succeeded activity runs metrics

Succeeded pipeline runs metrics

Succeeded trigger runs metrics

Total entities count

Total factory size (GB unit)

Figure 7-11. *Image showing the metrics available for flagging alerts*

4. Choose "Continue." Here you can select certain dimensions that will filter failure events, meaning that you can set specific thresholds for each activity, activity type, failure type, or pipeline name. This allows the logging to be highly flexible and granular.

5. Set conditional logic to determine what constitutes an alert event by specifying the condition, the time aggregation, and the threshold count.

6. Specify the period over which to evaluate failures by setting the period and the frequency. Refer to Figure 7-12 for an example.

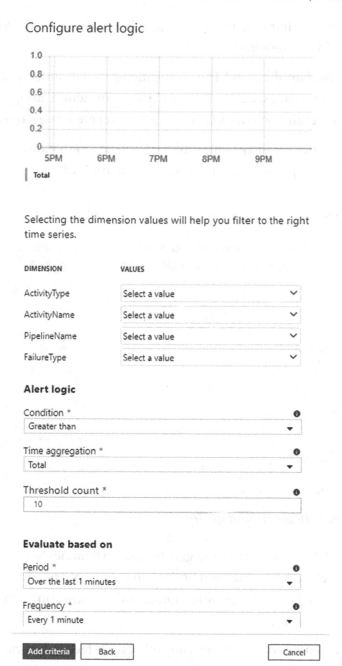

Figure 7-12. *An image showing the configuration of the alert*

Tip   Use the chart at the top of the configuration pane to see the history of the selected metric over a range of time values.

7. Choose "Add criteria" to create the alert event. Further criteria can also be added if required.

8. Choose "Add notification." The notifications are submitted using Azure action groups, and so if you have existing action groups, these can be supplied here. Otherwise you can create new ones.

9. To create a new action group, supply an action group name and short name as per the example shown in Figure 7-13.

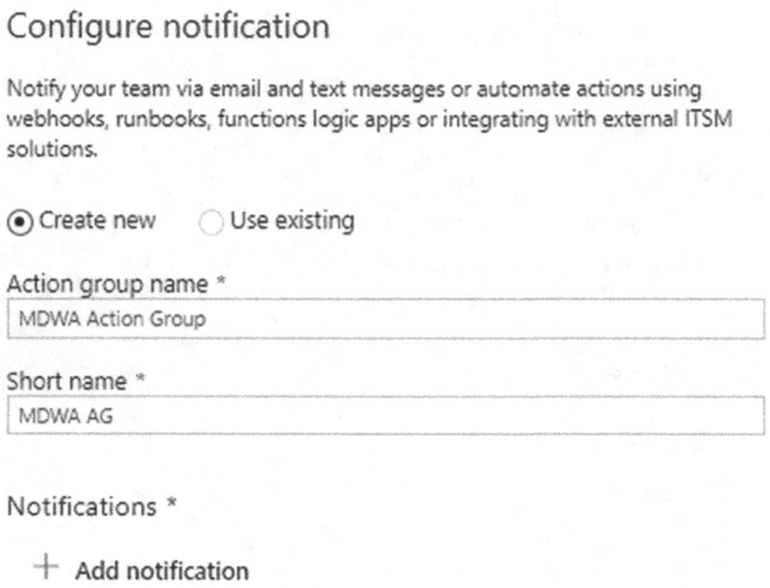

Configure notification

Notify your team via email and text messages or automate actions using webhooks, runbooks, functions logic apps or integrating with external ITSM solutions.

◉ Create new   ◯ Use existing

Action group name *

| MDWA Action Group |

Short name *

| MDWA AG |

Notifications *

    + Add notification

Figure 7-13. Creating the action group

10. Choose "Add notification" and give the action a name. Now you can select the notification options that you want to add to the group. These can be either Email, SMS, Azure app push notification, or Voice.

11. Supply at least one "Email" and any others you feel appropriate as per the example shown in Figure 7-14.

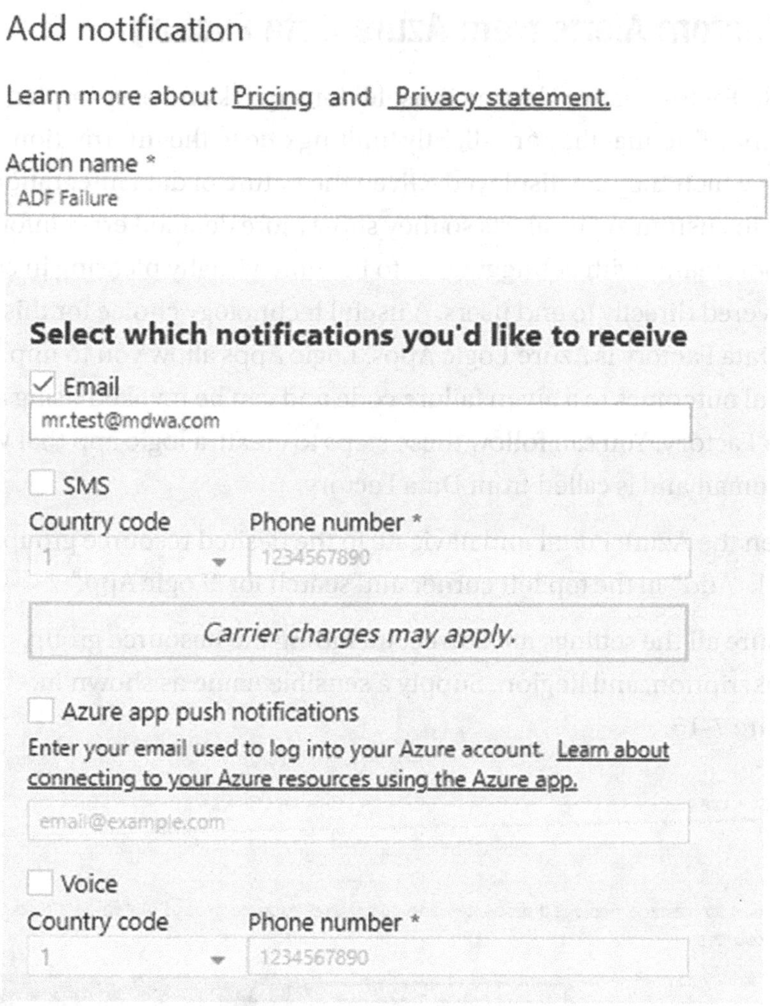

Add notification

Learn more about Pricing and Privacy statement.

Action name *

ADF Failure

Select which notifications you'd like to receive

☑ Email

mr.test@mdwa.com

☐ SMS

Country code   Phone number *

1   ▾   1234567890

Carrier charges may apply.

☐ Azure app push notifications

Enter your email used to log into your Azure account. Learn about connecting to your Azure resources using the Azure app.

email@example.com

☐ Voice

Country code   Phone number *

1   ▾   1234567890

Figure 7-14. *Creating a notification for the action group*

12.   Choose "Add notification" and then "Add action group." Finally, ensure "Enable rule upon creation" is set to on and choose "Create alert rule."

13.   You can now test the rule in your Data Factory pipeline and view the alert messages produced.

Creating Custom Alerts from Azure Data Factory

The Azure Data Factory native alerting is useful for a quick and easy implementation; however, you may find that they are slightly limiting due to the information they provide and the way in which they are displayed. Given the nature of data integration platforms, you may want to customize the alerts so they show more detailed error information, assisting support teams with debugging, or to be more visually pleasing in case they are being delivered directly to end users. A useful technology choice for this kind of extension to Data Factory is Azure Logic Apps. Logic Apps allow you to implement many different logical outcomes to a given failure code and can be invoked using a REST API call from Data Factory. You can follow these steps to create a logic app that will alert users with an email and is called from Data Factory:

1. Open the Azure Portal and navigate to the desired resource group. Click "Add" in the top left corner and search for "Logic App."

2. Ensure all the settings are correct including the Resource group, Subscription, and Region. Supply a sensible name as shown in Figure 7-15.

Basics *   Review + create

Project details

Select the subscription to manage deployed resources and costs. Use resource groups like folders to organize and manage all your resources.

Subscription *	Visual Studio Enterprise – ▓▓▓▓▓▓▓▓▓▓▓▓▓▓▓ ⌄
└─ Resource group *	moderndw ⌄
	Create new

Instance details

Logic App name *	mdwa-alertLogicApp ✓
Select the location	⦿ Region ◯ Integration Service Environment
Location *	(Europe) North Europe ⌄
Log Analytics ⓘ	On (Off)

Figure 7-15. *Creating a logic app in the North Europe region*

3. Click "Review + create" and click "Create" to complete the step.
    Once the deployment is finished, choose "Go to resource."

4. From the designer page that opens up, choose the "When a HTTP
    request is received" option shown in Figure 7-16.

Logic Apps Designer

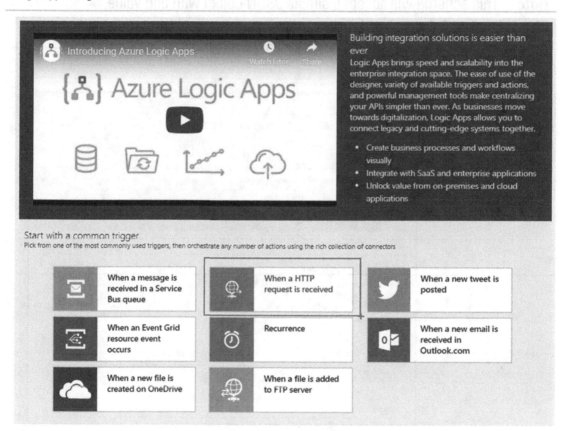

Figure 7-16. *Highlighting the correct template to begin your Logic App*

5. Now in the Logic Apps Designer, add the following JSON schema
    into the "Request Body JSON Schema" input box:

```
{
    "type": "object",
    "properties": {
        "AlertMessage": {
            "type": "string"
```

```
            }
          }
        }
```

This is also shown in Figure 7-17.

Note   This schema will accept a simple JSON object with one value, "AlertMessage." You can add more values in here to provide more flexibility.

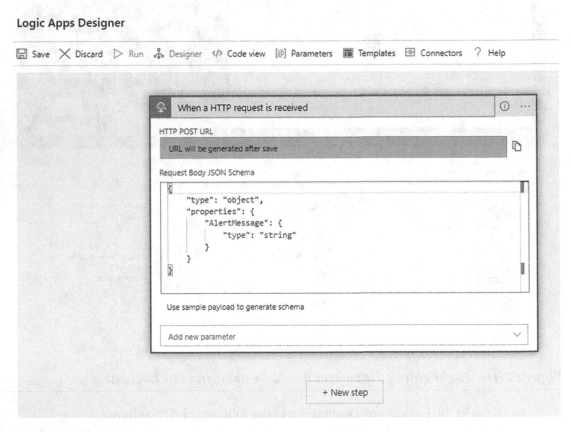

Figure 7-17.   *Configuring the "When a HTTP request is received" trigger*

6. Click "New step" and search "Send email." Scroll through the list until you see the Office 365 Outlook option and choose "Send an email (V2)" as shown in Figure 7-18. You will notice many other providers are on offer here if you already subscribe to a mailing service.

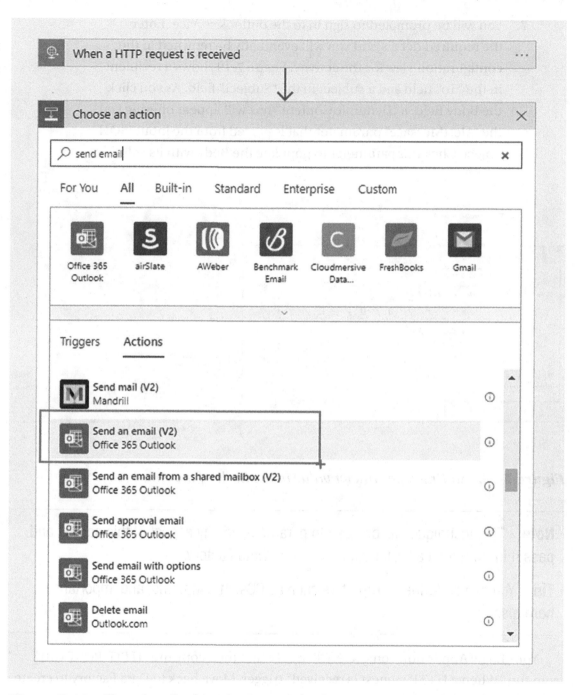

Figure 7-18. *Choosing the "Send an email (V2)" activity*

7. You will be prompted to sign in to the outlook service. Enter the required details and you will eventually be returned to the configuration view for the activity. Figure 7-19 shows a recipient in the "To" field and a subject in the "Subject" field. As you click the Body field, a "Dynamic Content" box will appear offering you the "AlertMessage" parameter that is parsed from the input JSON object. Click this parameter to populate the Body with its value.

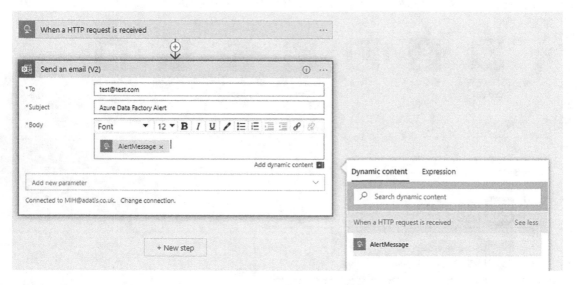

Figure 7-19. *Adding a parameter value in the Body of the email*

Note   This technique can be used to parameterize any aspect of this activity and pass it in from the caller, for example, Azure Data Factory.

Tip   You can add other parameters such as CCs, Attachments, and importance here also.

Your Logic App is now complete. Click Save and then copy the "HTTP POST URL" from the "When a HTTP request is received" trigger. Move back to Data Factory to create the activity that will call the Logic App.

1. Navigate to Azure Data Factory and create a pipeline. Add a single Web activity that can be selected from the General folder.

2. Figure 7-20 shows how to configure the Web activity. Firstly paste the
    URL copied from the Logic App into the "URL" field of the activity. Set
    the method to POST and set the Body to the following JSON object:

```
{
    "AlertMessage": "Data Factory Failed!"
}
```

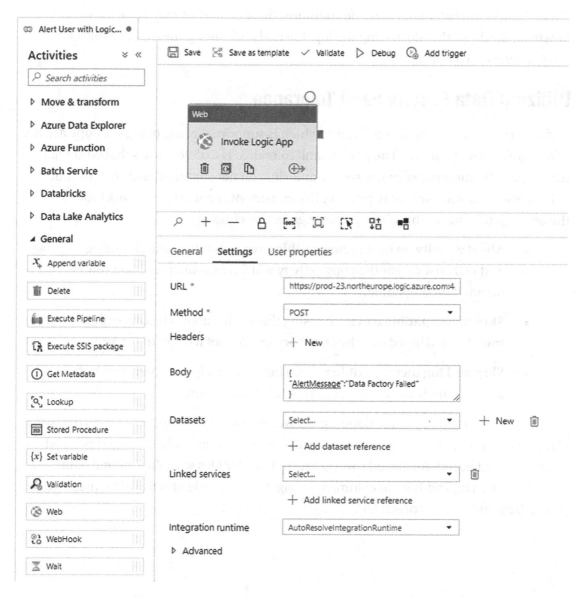

Figure 7-20. *Configure a Data Factory Web activity to call an alerting Logic App*

This pattern can then be used anywhere in your Data Factory pipelines and hooked onto the "On Failure" constraint.

Extending Resiliency

Implementing a basic level of resiliency will give you the confidence to run and manage your platform day to day. However, there will be scenarios that this basic level of checking will not cater for. For some solutions, these scenarios may not even occur; however, for those that do, having the logging and resiliency patterns available can resolve numerous issues.

Utilizing Data Factory Fault Tolerance

Data Factory has built in fault tolerance which is supported when using the copy activity in a nonbinary copy mode. The goal of fault tolerance is to detect rows that either fail data type validation between the source and sink, do not contain the correct number of columns for the sink, or violate primary key constraints applied to the sink table. From the settings tab, one of the following settings can be chosen:

- **Abort activity on first incompatible row**: This is the default setting and will ensure that the copy activity will fail as soon as a single row is deemed incompatible.

- **Skip incompatible rows**: Choosing this setting allows incompatible rows to be skipped over by Data Factory and not written to the sink.

- **Skip and log incompatible rows**: This setting skips the bad rows but also logs their values into an Azure Storage account.

Copy activities that permit skipping of rows will detail the number of rows that were skipped in their activity output and also provide the redirect path for logged skipped rows if so configured. All logged rows get stored as CSV files with the original data enhanced with two additional columns, listing the error code and the error message so that debugging can be conducted.

Checking File Structure Using Data Factory

As part of a basic resiliency setup, you may count incoming columns and compare that number to the number of columns stored in metadata; however, this will not tell you if columns change position or are swapped for different columns. In order to get this level of detail, you should call upon the *structure* attribute from the Get Metadata activity. By specifying the structure attribute as per the basic attribute listed previously, Data Factory will return a more complex array of column objects that contain column names and data types. An example of this structure is shown here:

```
{
    "structure": [
        {
            "name": "Column One",
            "type": "Int64"
        },
        {
            "name": "Column Two",
            "type": "String"
        }
    ]
}
```

Given this object from Data Factory, you could easily generate what should be a matching object from your control database using SQL and then compare the two strings to determine a match. In order to generate the preceding object from your SQL tables that store your data contract, you can use the query shown in Listing 7-7.

Listing 7-7. SQL code used to generate JSON objects for use in Azure Data Factory

```
SELECT
    ColumnName AS 'name',
    DataType AS 'type'
FROM
    Metadata.EntityColumn
FOR JSON PATH, ROOT('structure')
```

If this check were to fail, then you could send off an alert and halt the file loading process without causing any downstream issues.

Creating Alerts from Skipped Rows

When working with large files, often the approach leans toward skipping and/or logging bad data rows than failing the entire file out of principle. This is because consistency can be achieved eventually, and it is often more important to get the majority of the data into the system than depriving the warehouse of data. However, there may be a point at which it is no longer acceptable to load rows as the failures are too numerous. For example, if a file with 1,000,000 rows has 10 rows that are incompatible, it is clearly better to process the 900,990 rows into the warehouse and worry about the 10 later. However, if 100,000 rows were incompatible, perhaps you want to fail the file as there is clearly a more significant issue.

Data Factory's copy activity can produce a skipped row count and a copied row count which can be used to determine if the ratio between these two numbers exceeds a given threshold. For this to be available, skipping rows must be turned on using the fault tolerance settings in Data Factory copy activity. The following snippet can be placed in the expression for an IF activity to calculate the ratio between the two numbers:

```
@greaterOrEquals(div(activity('Copy File').output.rowsSkipped,
activity('Copy File').output.rowsCopied), 0.5)
```

This expression will derive a true or false depending on whether 50% or more of the file is skipped during the copy. This approach means that the loading process can have a degree of intelligence about it when processing large files. However, it does not understand the types of failure, just that the row was incompatible.

Monitoring the Data Movement Process

The auditing and alerting methods mentioned already are useful tools, enabling instant notification in case of failures or anomalies. Being able to react quickly to these scenarios can drastically reduce the time it takes to resolve any damage caused to your data warehouse. These systems can be greatly complemented however with a less instant, steadier paced monitoring method that allows developers to peek at the platforms health and performance through easy-to-understand dashboards and reports. Often these then form the basis of regular canned reports that go out to management to give detail of data volumes, failure percentages, and average durations. As time goes on and the maturity of your platform increases, these reports can begin to highlight numerous other data points such as platform running costs, data quality scores, and even report usage.

Ultimately the richness of these reports comes down to what is logged into your Audit schema, and clearly a base level of logging will only enable a base level of reporting. Think carefully about the platform elements that need to be reported on when designing the Audit schema.

The most basic method of platform monitoring is a set of views that sit on top of your Audit schema tables. Views such as this provide an easily customizable approach to monitoring that can be flexible to your developing requirements. See Listing 7-8 for an example view definition.

Listing 7-8. A definition of the SQL view to report on the data movement process

```
CREATE VIEW [Audit].[ExecutionReport] AS
SELECT
     child.ParentLoadId AS [Parent Load Id]
    ,child.LoadId AS [Load Id]
    ,child.PipelineName AS [Pipeline Name]
    ,CASE child.PipelineStatusTypeId
        WHEN 1 THEN 'In Progress'
        WHEN 2 THEN 'Successful'
        WHEN 3 THEN 'Failed'
      END AS [Pipeline Status]
    ,SourceSystemName AS [Source System]
    ,EntityName AS [Entity]
    ,parent.PipelineName AS [Parent Pipeline]
    ,child.PipelineName AS [Pipeline]
    ,child.StartTime AS [Start Time]
    ,child.EndTime AS [End Time]
    ,child.Duration AS [Duration]
    ,rt.ValidRows AS [Valid Rows]
    ,rt.BadRows AS [Bad Rows]
FROM
    Audit.PipelineLoad AS child
    LEFT OUTER JOIN Audit.PipelineLoad AS parent
        ON child.ParentLoadId = parent.LoadId
    INNER JOIN Audit.RowCountLog AS rt
        ON rt.LoadId = child.LoadId
```

```
    INNER JOIN Metadata.Entity AS e
        ON e.EntityId = rt.EntityId
    INNER JOIN Metadata.SourceSystem AS s
        ON s.SourceSystemId = e.SourceSystemId
```

Eventually views such as this will become relied upon, and so in order to make consumption easier, some form of data visualization is usually required. The tool itself is nonspecific; so long as it can connect to your control database and be developed and accessed by the relevant people, then the tool is the correct choice, although I generally choose either Power BI or excel.

CHAPTER 8

Using Scripting and Automation

A common attribute of many developers is the desire to do things quickly, consistently, and once only. To address this desire, scripting and automation are often used as they provide a hyper consistent method to complete regularly occurring tasks. This chapter aims to walk through three of my most used scripts in the hope that they can also be useful to readers of this book. All the scripts featured in this chapter are written in PowerShell and operate or automate key pieces of a modern data warehouse, the SQL engine, Data Factory, and data lake.

The Power of PowerShell

PowerShell is the go-to scripting language for system administrators and power users looking to rapidly automate common tasks across their enterprise. As an open source language built on .Net, the command-based shell and integrated scripting environment provide an intuitive way to write scripts that can easily be extended as per the needs of the developer. Developers looking to craft their own PowerShell scripts will find the language rich with useful functionality complimented by lots of documentation online and the ability to integrate their scripts with many Azure services. In honesty, this chapter does very little to expose the true power of PowerShell; however, entire books are written for that purpose and I strongly recommend Don Jones and Jeffrey Hicks' *Learn Windows PowerShell in a Month of Lunches* if the reader wants to enhance their PowerShell skills.

© Matt How 2020

M. How, *The Modern Data Warehouse in Azure*, https://doi.org/10.1007/978-1-4842-5823-1_8

Commonly Used Scripts

The following sections of this chapter describe in detail the scripts and patterns that I use very often when developing data warehouse solutions in Azure. All of these can and should be further developed to meet any specific needs, but my hope is that these scripts guide the way for what can be achieved with a low level of effort when using PowerShell.

Code Generation

Code generation is an accelerator that allows warehouse projects to get off the ground quickly. Often one of the most time-consuming tasks when starting a data warehouse project is fetching the data in order to begin development against it, and so the goal of code generation is to use a pattern that works for all scenarios and replicate this quickly as many times as needed. There are three elements that are required to facilitate a code generation approach. These are

- **Data contracts**: SQL tables and procedures that hold the entity-specific metadata

- **SQL templates**: Predefined SQL procedures and tables that will have placeholders for text replacement

- **The PowerShell script**: A PowerShell script that unions the other two elements to create numerous implementations of a pattern within seconds

Data contracts play a major role here as it is the contracts that supply the specific configurations that make each implementation of the generic pattern work for each data source.

To begin working with this script, the metadata database needs to contain the following objects:

- **Metadata.Entity**: The main table that stores a row for each dataset, otherwise known as an *Entity*.

- **Metadata.EntityColumn**: This table is logically aligned to Metadata. Entity; however, it stores a row for each column of the related entities.

- **Metadata.RuleDefinition**: This table stores a row for each rule definition. A rule can be any valid SQL code.

- **Metadata.ColumnRule**: This table is a bridge between *RuleDefinition* and *EntityColumn* as columns can have many rules and rules can be applied to many columns.

- **Metadata.ObtainEntityMetadata**: This stored procedure pulls information from each of the preceding tables and presents it to the PowerShell script in a uniform way.

These tables and procs are discussed in more detail in Chapter 6, "The Role of the Data Contract," and Figure 6-1 shows how the tables relate to each other. The full set of DDLs for the metadata scheme can be obtained from this link: `https://github.com/MattTheHow/Modern-Data-Warehouse-In-Azure/blob/master/SQL/Control%20Database/Scripts/CreateDatabase.sql`

The next objects that are required are the templates. The code generation templates are pre-written SQL scripts or table definitions that have placeholders for various items produced by the PowerShell code. For example, a template may have a generic statement such as

```
SELECT
    <ENTITY-COLUMNS>
FROM
    <ENTITY-TABLE>
```

In this case, the `<ENTITY_NAME>` and `<ENTITY-TABLE>` values would be generated by the PowerShell script and replaced in the template to produce valid and properly configured SQL script. When adopting a code generation approach, it is important to review these templates to ensure the required patterns and processes are implemented properly but that any specific components are supplied by the PowerShell code. Generally, this will mean that the earlier stages of the data processing are code generated, whereas the more volatile and business-oriented transformations are written manually until such time as they can be scripted. The templates supplied using the following link illustrate how ingestion and cleaning processes can be scripted for code generation: `https://github.com/MattTheHow/Modern-Data-Warehouse-In-Azure/tree/master/SQL/Control%20Database/Templates`

The final piece of the code generation setup is the PowerShell script that unions the other two elements. The script itself is nearly 200 lines of PowerShell and so too long to paste directly in this chapter; however, the script is well commented to aid understanding and I will now describe the code as blocks, instead of individual lines.

From lines 0 to 41, the script is configured so that it connects to the correct SQL database and executes the *Metadata.ObtainEntityMetadata* stored procedure. The script then assigns the output of that stored proc to PowerShell variables for use later in the script.

Lines 44–159 do the bulk of the code generation work. Initially there is a check to see if the entity requires SCD type 2 logic and if so sets up a variable that contains a string that can be used to create HASH values. SCD changes are detected using HASH values as this avoids the need to check each and every column.

From line 78, the script enters a series of ForEach loops which perform various actions at different levels. First is the iteration over each entity; this ensures that the code is specific for each entity and generates and replaces each placeholder before moving onto the next entity. Within this outer loop is a ForEach loop over each column that belongs to the given entity. This allows specific column lists to be created, some with full-type and nullability definitions for tables and others with just column names for simple SELECT statements. Additionally, an *isMapped* attribute is used to allow a simple method to trim columns from source datasets that are not required for further transformations. A further ForEach loop is then used to process each rule that is applied to each column. This level of operation allows each rule to be nested so that a single SQL statement is created from potentially numerous separate rules. In particular, this means that rules can be written to be granular and not duplicated to cover off specific column needs. If a rule definition needs to change, then it only needs to change in a single place in order to be updated in all instances of that particular rule.

From lines 162 to 182, the PowerShell script performs replace operations for each placeholder in the template. Each placeholder has a corresponding variable value generated by the PowerShell script for that specific entity.

Finally, the lines 185 to the end simply name each output file and save it into the output folder specified in the variables at the start or the script.

Invoke Data Factory Pipeline

The ability to invoke and monitor a data factory pipeline from PowerShell can come in handy when performing specific tasks. Remember that Data Factory has its own scheduler and event handling capabilities and so rarely is this method used in production. However, the following scenarios do highlight why this script can be useful:

1. Scripting a process that copies data from one data lake into another.

2. Fetching data for an environment that is created using PowerShell.

3. Sequentially invoking long running processes that require
   different configurations each time. I have often used this approach
   when needing to populate large tables overnight and, instead of
   configuring many versions of the same ADF pipeline, would rather
   script this using PowerShell.

The code for invoking a Data Factory pipeline is very simple. This is because ADF is native to Azure and therefore the PowerShell support is very strong. The code shown in Listing 8-1 shows the most basic way of invoking a Data Factory pipeline.

Note   In order to access any Azure service, you must log in interactively via the PowerShell terminal with `Connect-AzAccount`.

Listing 8-1. PowerShell code used to invoke an Azure Data Factory pipeline

```
$resourceGroupName = "moderndw"
$dataFactoryName = "mdwa-datafactory"
$pipelineName = "Copy Sales Data - Lookup"

$invokeParams = @{
    resourceGroup = $resourceGroupName
    dataFactoryName = $dataFactoryName
    PipelineName = $pipelineName
}

$runId = Invoke-AzDataFactoryV2Pipeline @invokeParams
Write-Host "Run ID: $runId"
```

The preceding scripts can be broken down into three parts. The first three lines assign resource-specific values to variables that will be used throughout the script. The next five lines create an object that contains all the variables we want to pass into our invoke function. This technique is known as PowerShell splatting and can be investigated further here: https://docs.microsoft.com/en-us/powershell/module/microsoft.powershell.core/about/about_splatting?view=powershell-7

The final two lines invoke the Data Factory pipeline as specified in the parameters and assign the returned Run Id to the variable, "$runId," so that it could be used later in the script if needed. Of course, this script could be extended in numerous ways as alluded to in the list contained in the section title "Invoke Data Factory Pipeline", however the next obvious requirement is the ability to then monitor the pipeline also using PowerShell (required when creating scenarios similar to number 3 in the list).

Tip   Pipelines invoked by PowerShell are still shown in the monitor view of ADF alongside every other executed pipeline.

By adding the code from Listing 8-2, the script will then continually check in on the pipeline every 30 seconds until a completion status is reached.

Listing 8-2. PowerShell code used to monitor an Azure Data Factory Pipeline run using a specific Run Id

```
while($True) {
    $pipelineRun = Get-AzDataFactoryV2PipelineRun -DataFactoryName
$dataFactoryName -PipelineRunId $runId -ResourceGroupName
$resourceGroupName
    if($pipelineRun) {
        if($pipelineRun.Status -ne 'InProgress') {
            Write-Host "Pipeline run finished. Status: $($pipelineRun.Status)"
            break
        }
        Write-Host "Pipeline is running"
    }
    Start-Sleep -Seconds 30
}
```

While these scripts show some of the Az-DataFactory cmdlets (the name of PowerShell functions), there are a great deal more that can display things such as

- Activity-specific outputs and status/error messages

- Static objects such as datasets and pipelines

- Integration runtime metrics and credentials.

Recurse Data Lake Structures

This script is very useful when reviewing an existing data lake that you need to become more familiar with or as a way of scripting functionality that can check if certain folders have been created by an ETL process. Essentially the script is made up of a PowerShell function that can be called recursively, thereby by continually working through a folder hierarchy flushing out all folder names as it goes. The function definition is shown in Listing 8-3.

Listing 8-3. PowerShell code that allows developers to recurse data lake strucutures to determine entire folder hierarchies

```
Function Recurse-DataLakePath
{
    param
    (
        [Parameter(Mandatory=$true)]
        [ValidateNotNullOrEmpty()]
        [string] $startPath,

        [Parameter(Mandatory=$false)]
        [ValidateNotNullOrEmpty()]
        [int] $level = 0
    )

    if($level -eq 0)
    {
        Write-Host $startPath
    }

    $level++

    $adlParams = @{
        FileSystem = "datalake"
        Path = $startPath
        Context = $ctx
    }
```

```
    Get-AzDataLakeGen2ChildItem -FileSystem "datalake" -Path $startPath
    -Context $ctx |
    ForEach-Object {
        if($_.IsDirectory)
        {
            Write-Host "$(" " * $level * 2)|- $($_.Path -replace $startPath,
            '' -replace '/', '')"
            Recurse-DataLakePath -startPath $_.Path -level $level
        }
    }
}

$ctx = New-AzStorageContext -ConnectionString <your connection string goes here>

Recurse-DataLakePath -startPath "RAW/"
```

The first eight lines define the parameters for the function. These are the input path from where we want to start our search and the level at which the function has recursed to. This parameter should not be configured by the user and is used for internal purposes. The next important part of the function begins at "Get-AzDataLakeGen2ChildItem" and this is where the actual query is run against the data lake. This cmdlet will return each child item of the directory specified in the input path and write its name out into the output window. Note the filter on the "IsDirectory" attribute which ensures the function only records folders and not files; however, the function could easily be adapted to list out files within each directory.

Once the function has logged the children of the current path, it passes each child path into itself, creating a recursive process that continually navigates the hierarchy until every folder has been explored.

The final part of the script, outside of the function, simply defines a storage context which is required in order to connect to a storage account and then call the function for the first time supplying the starting path. If this function is called with a start path of "/", then the function will traverse the entire lake; however, any path could be supplied, and the function will only look in folders below that path in the hierarchy.

The output of this script over a simple data lake is shown here:

```
RAW/
 |- MarketingSystem
   |- Campaign
     |- Recipients
     |- Responses
   |- Customer
   |- Opportunity
 |- SalesSystem
```

CHAPTER 9

Beyond the Modern Data Warehouse

In days gone by, a data warehouse stood as a slow-moving, often large, unwieldly part of a wider decision support system. While tools and technologies that feed to or read from the data warehouse may develop, the complexity of such an artifact and the investment in its development mean that the warehouse would rarely benefit from such upgrades. Throughout this book, I have explained and demonstrated the highlights of building a modern data warehouse in Azure – one which can be developed rapidly and be highly flexible to source system requirements, one which can move and develop with the times and not cause sleepless nights worrying over the SQL version going out of support, one which can ingest in batch-, stream-, or event-based modes offering ultimate speed and time to insight. The focus of this final chapter is now to look at what sits beyond the modern data warehouse. There is a wealth of BI products in the market that provide a range of capabilities and visualizations to the end user, and it can be very difficult to choose between them without a thorough review. This chapter is not a thorough review of BI products but instead give examples of downstream options for warehouse data. Initially this chapter will look at Power BI, as that is the de facto visualization tool for any data but will also examine some other Microsoft products for data as it leaves the data warehouse such as Azure Analysis Services and Azure Cosmos DB.

For each technology, we will examine a use case and flesh this out into a walk-through example.

© Matt How 2020
M. How, *The Modern Data Warehouse in Azure*, https://doi.org/10.1007/978-1-4842-5823-1_9

Microsoft Power BI

Microsoft Power BI (Power BI) is the flagship data visualization and BI product from Microsoft that burst onto the market in 2014. In its early days, it boasted some excellent visualization capabilities but has now extended that to include ETL tooling, interactive functionality, and a host of built-in connectors, making Power BI a leading product in the marketplace. At its heart, Power BI uses the same analytical engine that is used for Analysis Services, optimizing analytical queries over tabular data using in-memory processing, although this is coupled with a rich set of visualization capabilities that allows developers to easily experiment with chart types.

Working with Power BI

Power BI provides a first-class visualization platform for data and offers enterprise grade capabilities for slicing and dicing all kinds of information. Wherever users require regular, pre-built reports, Power BI should be the delivery platform for those reports. With the tools available through Power BI, both IT-led reports can be built and self-service capabilities can be realized, meaning users can be in charge of their own reporting. This can be dangerous if done wrong but liberating if implemented correctly.

Power BI is made up of several key components:

- **Power BI desktop**: The primary development tool for Power BI files that is free to use for all report developers.

- **Power BI report builder**: The report builder used for creating paginated reports as opposed to dashboards.

- **Power BI service**: The web-based portal where dashboards and reports are published to. This is accessible to users with Power BI Pro licenses and extends to mobile devices such as phones and tablets.

All reports should be developed using Power BI desktop or report builder and then published up to the service for wider consumption. The service supports the concept of workspaces allowing users to collaborate on reports and dashboards.

The data for Power BI can be derived from a widespread of sources and *mashed* together to form consolidated datasets. This could mean blending public data with internal data from a data warehouse or analyzing multiple Excel sheets alongside files in a data lake. Additionally, Power BI can be connected to Azure Analysis Services in a method known as *live connection*, which allows the Power BI front end to push queries back to the Analysis Service engine, meaning that data does not have to undergo a lengthy import operation.

Building a Power BI Report

Building a Power BI report is simple and intuitive and getting started is simple. This walk-through will explain how to connect Power BI desktop to your data warehouse, whether that be in Azure SQL Database or Azure Synapse Analytics.

1. Download and open Power BI; this link is regularly updated with the latest version of Power BI desktop: `https://powerbi.microsoft.com/en-us/blog/category/uncategorized/`

2. From the splash screen shown in Figure 9-1, choose "Get data."

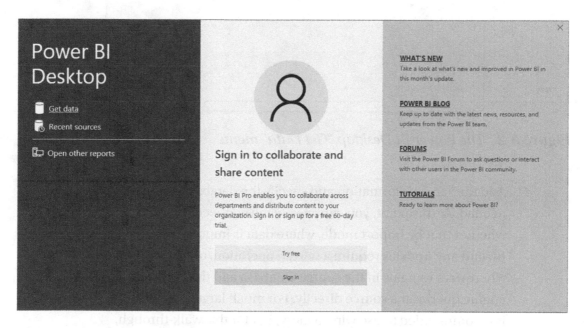

Figure 9-1. *The Power BI Desktop splash screen*

3. From the "Get data" menu, choose "Azure" and then the appropriate SQL engine from the list. For this walk-through, I have chosen Azure SQL Database. Click "Connect" as shown in Figure 9-2.

Figure 9-2. *The Power BI Desktop "Get Data" menu*

4. Add the server information and specify the database name if needed. At this point, you can specify the connection mode, whether that be Import mode, where data is imported into Power BI, and any updates require a refresh operation, or DirectQuery, where data remains in the source database and the Power BI engine queries the source directly. For much larger datasets, it is recommended to use DirectQuery, but for this walk-through, Import mode will be best. Configure each option and click "OK." See Figure 9-3 for an example.

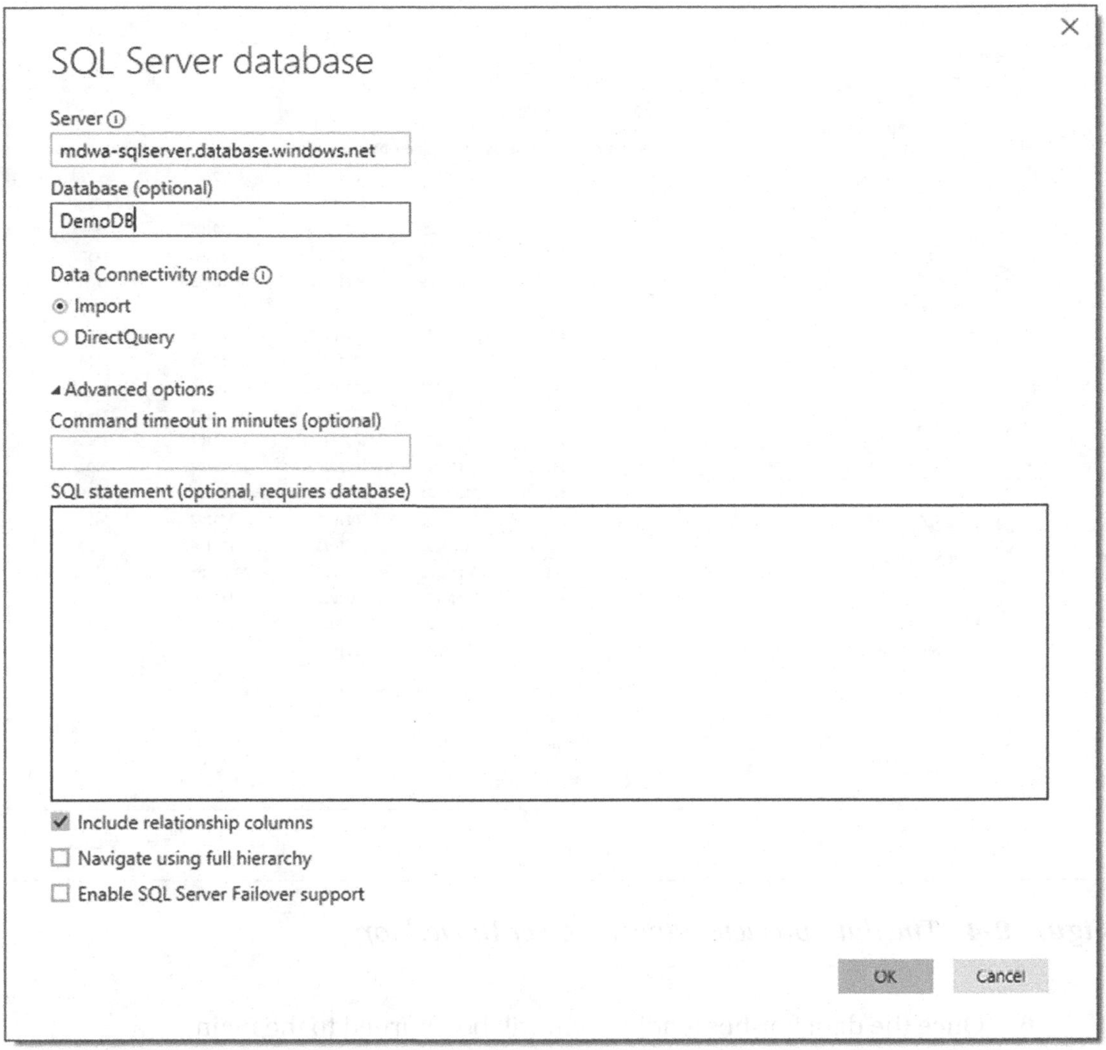

Figure 9-3. *Supplying the Azure SQL Server and database details to Power BI Desktop*

5. Enter your SQL login details and click "Connect." This will prompt the data preview dialog as per Figure 9-4. Choose the tables you want to load and click "Load."

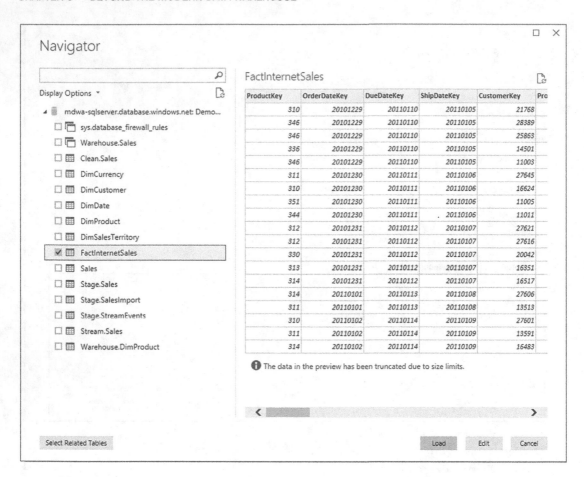

Figure 9-4. *The data preview pane in Power BI Desktop*

6. Once the data finishes loading, you will be returned to the main report designer. Click the Model view and preview the data model that has been imported into Power BI. As per Figure 9-5, you should notice that Power BI has included relationships automatically.

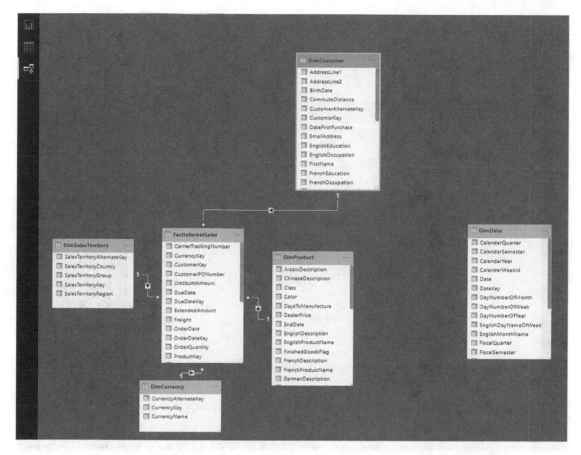

Figure 9-5. *The Power BI model view, showing automatic relationships*

If required, you can build new relationships between tables here, and in some cases, such as when in live connection mode to Analysis Services, it is necessary to build them in Power BI as they are not imported.

7. Open the Data view shown in Figure 9-6 so you can preview the actual columns and rows contained in the model. Here you can create new columns, measures, and hierarchies as per the requirements of your reports.

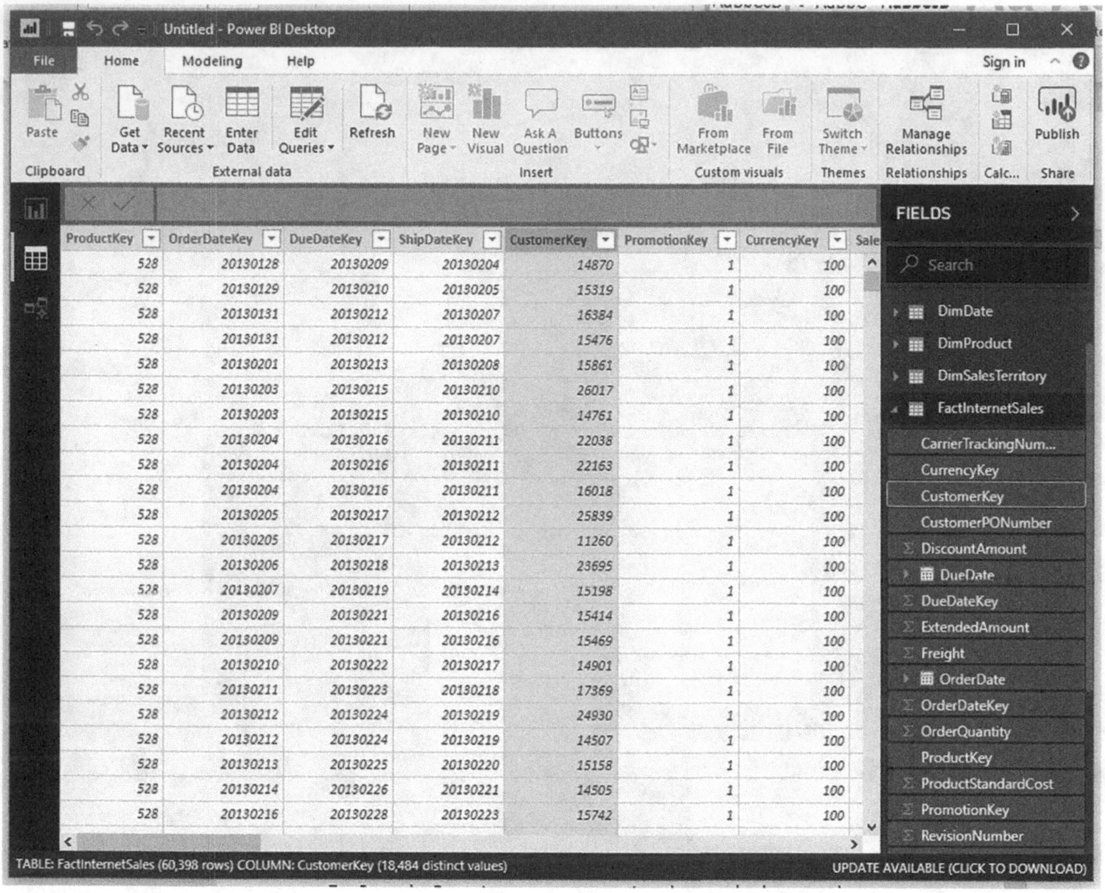

Figure 9-6. *The Power BI Desktop data view showing rows and columns in the dataset*

8. Navigating back to the main designer, you can begin building charts, graphs, cards, tables, and other visualisations until you are satisfied with the result. To create a basic bar graph, select the "Clustered column chart" visual from the "visualizations" pane and drag it onto the design surface. Prior to adding data, the report should resemble the image shown in Figure 9-7.

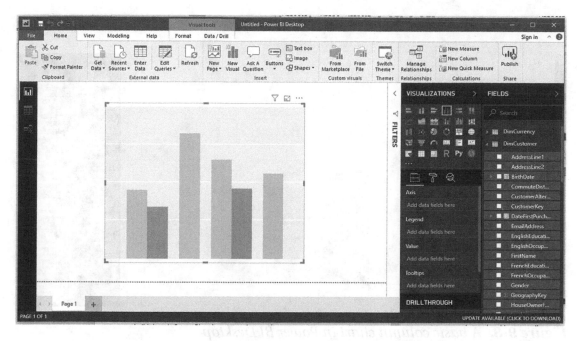

Figure 9-7. *The basic design pane in Power BI Desktop*

9. Now drag the "Sales Amount" column from the
    "FactInternetSales" table onto the chart to see the total sales
    amount as a bar. Then, drag the "EnglishOccupation" column
    from the DimCustomer table onto the graph to act as a slicer.
    Figure 9-8 shows the result.

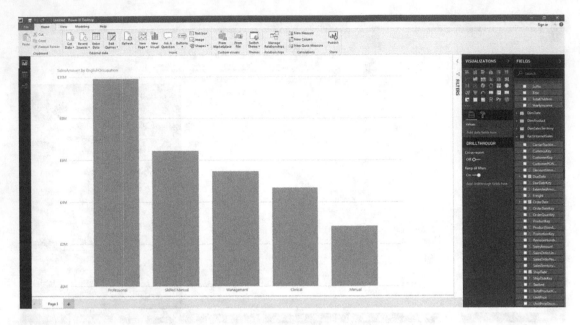

Figure 9-8. *A basic column chart in Power BI Desktop*

Publish Report to Power BI Service

In order to publish a report to the service, you will need a work or school account. Assuming this is the case, then you can proceed.

1. Click "Publish" in the ribbon bar. Figure 9-9 highlights the location of the button.

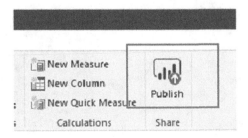

Figure 9-9. *Close-up of the "Publish" button in Power BI Desktop*

2. As shown in Figure 9-10, you will be prompted to sign in with your
    work or school account and then choose a workspace to publish
    the report to.

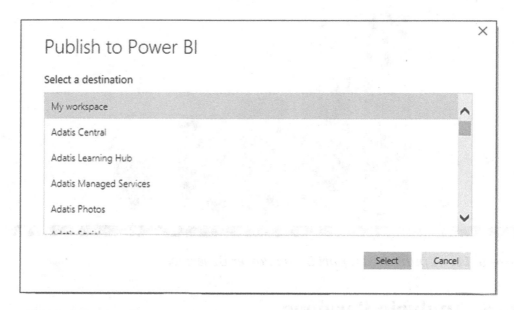

Figure 9-10. *The workspace selection pane in Power BI Desktop*

3. Once the Publish has completed successfully, you will be offered
    a link to the report as it is in the service. Click this to check out
    the report. Figure 9-11 shows the report displayed in the Power
    BI service.

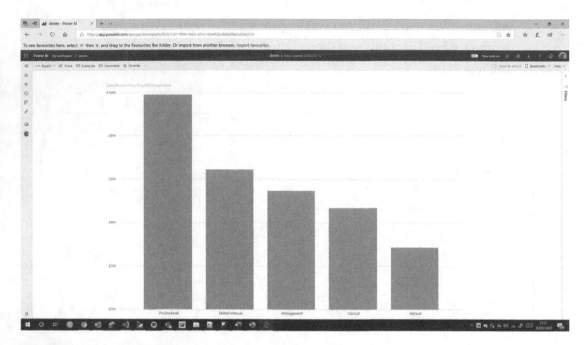

Figure 9-11. *A published report in the Power BI service*

Azure Analysis Services

Azure Analysis Services (AAS) is simply a PaaS implementation of the on-premises product that came as part of the SQL Server Data Tools pack. The nice part of this implementation is that the development experience is exactly the same as before. All models, measures, calculated columns, and security are created in Visual Studio, and the vertiPaq (`www.sqlbi.com/tools/vertipaq-analyzer/`) engine that makes Analysis Services so powerful is unchanged in the Azure implementation. The difference is that you deploy the model to an Azure server instead of an on-premises server. Of course, using a PaaS-based platform means that additional benefits can be derived as well. First and foremost, AAS can support scale-out replicas, meaning that client queries can be distributed across these replicas at times of peak usage. Additionally, processing activities can be separated from the query pool so that the act of processing an AAS model does not disrupt the execution of incoming queries. It's important to note here that only the initial synchronization is automatic, allowing for new replicas to be hydrated from the primary node at the point of creation. From this point on, the synchronizations are invoked manually (or by an orchestration tool – read Data Factory) using the REST API, a PowerShell cmdlet, or the Analysis Services management aspect of SQL Server Management Studio (SSMS). A further PaaS benefit is that the instance can be paused when not in use, providing better cost optimization. Bear in mind that queries will not be answered while the instance is paused.

The Basics of Azure Analysis Services

For those not familiar with Analysis Services, there are two types of calculation engine that can be used in an on-premises deployment; however, if you are to deploy the Analysis Service to Azure, you would need to build a tabular model and not a multidimensional cube. The differences between the two types are minimal to an end user but can have important differences for developers. While multidimensional cubes will still be around for a while, my view is that tabular models are the way forward and should be used as a matter of default.

Azure Analysis Services provides an ability to scale the model to meet demands of processing and querying. To begin with, you must determine service tier which can be either Developer, Basic or Standard. Developer is a cheap tier that provides all the functionality of the Standard tier only with some limitations. This allows developers to evaluate the service before investing in a standard tier service. The Basic tier is best for smaller tabular models that have limited data processing needs and can get by with lower concurrency allowances. The Standard tier is for full production workloads that have scalable concurrency needs and complex data refresh requirements. This tier ranges from an S0, which has a 10 GB model storage limit, all the way to an S9, which has a 400 GB model storage limit. As a general rule, data stored in Analysis Services models benefit from roughly 10x compression meaning the largest dataset available could be around 4 TB. The details of this compression are covered later in this chapter.

Analysis Services as a Semantic Layer

Often it is asked why Analysis Services is required at all, when the data warehouse is designed specifically for the job of performing analytic queries. The answer is that the data warehouse is a storage layer, whereas Analysis Services is a semantic layer. This layer of semantic abstraction allows for much more flexibility when joining the worlds of a BI developer and an end user. It means that column names can be made friendly with spaces and capitalization, unwanted values can be hidden but not removed, hierarchies can be shaped based on custom logic, and role-based access control (RBAC) can be implemented at a very granular level. Without this semantic layer, it would be very difficult to meet the needs of the end user without a huge amount of complexity on the part of the developer.

Analysis Services Security Model

The security for Analysis Services is based around roles which can be associated with individual users or entire Active Directory groups, meaning access to models can be controlled by a centralized IT function and not solely by the BI team.

The primary security mechanism in AAS is a role, which can have model level assigned permissions, row filters, and object level controls to give a very fine-grained level of access to users. The permissions that can be assigned to a role are

- **None**: Members of this role have no access to the model.

- **Read**: The model can be read by the users of this role but not processed.

- **Read and process**: This permission allows users to both read the model and also process new data into the model from SSMS or the Azure Portal.

- **Process**: Members of this role cannot read the model but can process it.

- **Administrator**: The level of permission allows users full access to do anything with the model. The model owner is an administrator by default.

Row filters provide the ability to filter the entire model when users of the role view data. A good example is filtering by region, assuming a region code is applied to the fact table, this could be used to ensure European analysts were confined to see data that corresponds only to their region. Also, within roles developers can specify object level permissions which control whether a user can see a specific table or column. The following figures show how these two aspects of roles are configured.

Often there is a temptation to use perspectives to implement security; however, these are not designed for this purpose. Perspectives are built to allow role-based users the ability to see a subset of a larger model (a perspective), purely to avoid excessive numbers of objects being displayed in the model viewer.

Even more fine-grained security can be implemented using dynamic, row-based security. This method involves creating filters in DAX, the functional language used in Analysis Services Tabular projects, that uses the USERNAME() function to look up the user against a table which stores the access permissions of the user. In the following example, the user ACL/MIH has access to region 3 in the "User Security." When this user signs into the model, this filter is then passed through the territory dimension onto the fact table, thereby only revealing data from the fact table that is associated to that region. This traversal is demonstrated in Figure 9-12.

Figure 9-12. *An example relationship to implement dynamic security within the Analysis Services model*

The Vertipaq Engine

The vertiPaq engine is the proprietary calculation engine that underpins all versions of tabular Analysis Services and also Power BI. The power of this engine is that it stores all data in memory and therefore makes running large calculations very efficient. The trade-off is that large amounts of data require large amounts of memory, and so a key aspect of the vertiPaq engine is its ability to compress data. There are a number of algorithms that are used; they are listed as follows:

1. **Value encoding:** This algorithm applies a mathematical operation to numeric data with the goal of reducing the number if bits required to store each value. The reverse operation is then carried out when the data is read by a query. Figure 9-13 shows this more clearly.

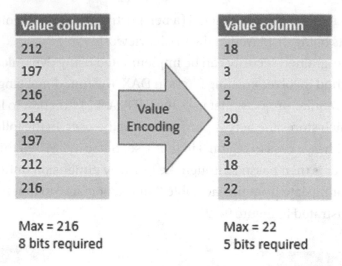

Figure 9-13. *An image explaining the implementation of Value encoding*

2. **Dictionary encoding**: Because mathematical functions won't work on text values, dictionary encoding is used to transpose a set of words into an indexed dictionary. By storing the dictionary in the model and replacing the text value with its dictionary id, a great deal of compression is achieved. This effect is highlighted in Figure 9-14.

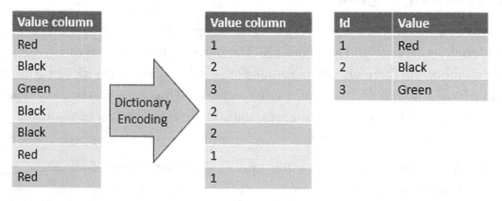

Figure 9-14. *An image explaining the implementation of Dictionary encoding*

3. **Run length encoding (RLE)**: The goal of this algorithm is to remove the amount of redundant data in the model. Often in tables of data, the same value is repeated row after row and RLE reduces this by storing the value and the number of rows it *runs* for in a separate

dictionary which can then be interrupted at query time. The original column and its corresponding dictionary are shown in Figure 9-15.

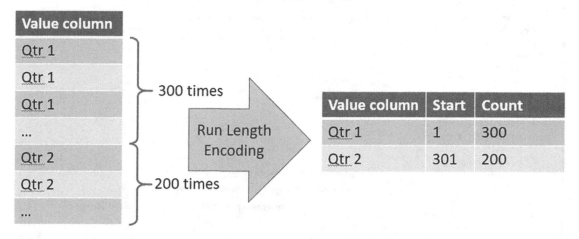

Figure 9-15. *An image explaining the implementation of Run Length encoding*

RLE can also be used in conjunction with Value and Dictionary encoding, compounding the amount of compression available for each individual column.

The next few walk-throughs will help you get started using Analysis Services by creating the project in Visual Studio, deploying the model to Azure and processing new data into the deployed model.

Creating an Analysis Services Project

This walk-through requires you have Visual Studio 2019 with Azure Analysis Services Projects installed. The Analysis Services Project add-in can be downloaded from here: `https://marketplace.visualstudio.com/items?itemName=ProBITools.MicrosoftAnalysisServicesModelingProjects`

1. Open Visual Studio and click "Tools" and then "Options." Scroll through the options to find "Analysis Services Tabular" and expand that node.

2. In the "New project settings" submenu, set the compatibility level to "SQL Server 2019/Azure Analysis Services (1500)" and tick "Ask default project settings…." Older version can be used; however, they will not have the richest set of features.

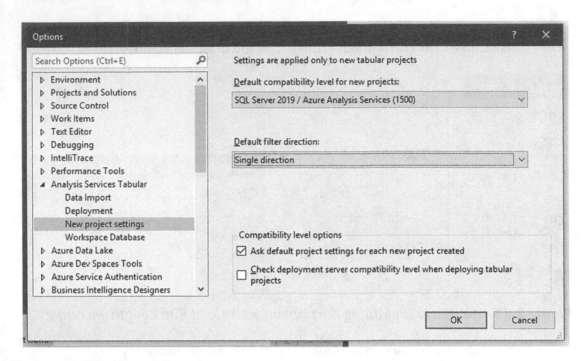

3. Select "Workspace Database" and check "Integrated workspace."
   Also tick "Ask new project settings..."

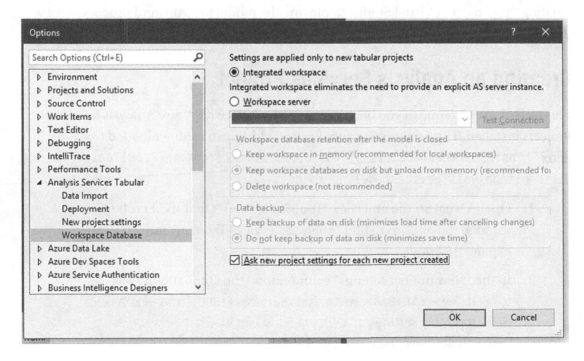

4. Click "File," "New," and then "Project," and type "Analysis Services Tabular" into the search box. Give the project a name and click "OK." All settings should then be correct because of the previous steps, but now you can change them if needed.

Note   Azure Analysis Services only supports tabular projects, not multidimensional.

---

5. From the solution explorer, open the Model.bim file; you should enter the "Tabular Model Explorer" view.

6. Open the "Extensions" menu and choose "Model" and then choose "Import from Data Source." Select "Azure" and then "Azure SQL database" and choose "Connect."

7. Provide the required details – Server and Database name (use the adventure works one that was deployed using the script). Click "OK."

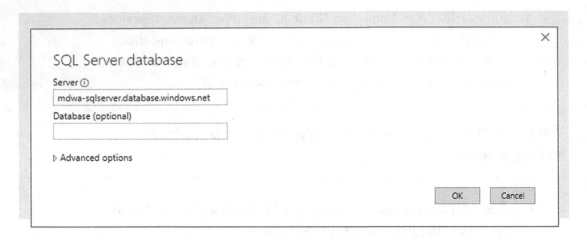

8. On the following screen, provide your SQL username and
   password, then select all the listed tables except for those
   regarding firewall rules.

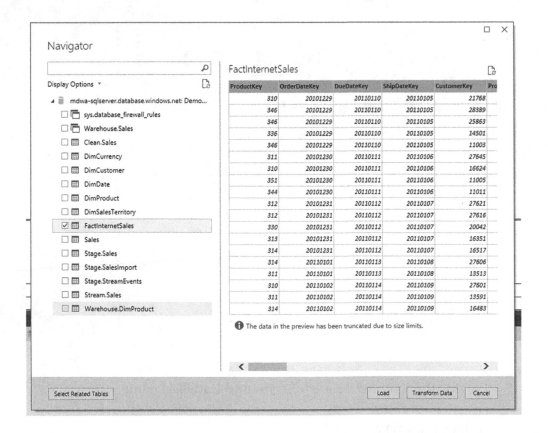

At this point, you should note the similarities here between the Analysis Service "Get Data" wizard and the Power BI "Get Data" wizard. The reason for this similarity is that they are fundamentally built on the same Power Query engine, meaning the experience is largely the same.

9. Choose "Load," and once the import is complete, you should see data in the main Visual Studio window with the tables listed as tabs across the bottom.

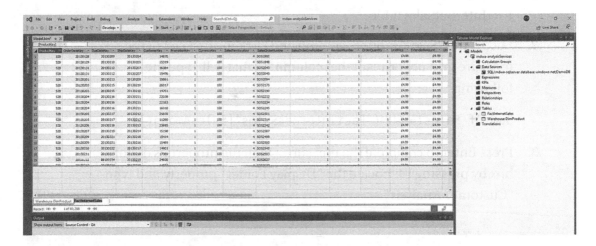

Create Analysis Objects

You now have an Analysis Services project where you can build measures, calculated columns, hierarchies, roles, perspectives, and others. The next walk-through shows how to build some of these analytical objects.

Create a Calculated Column

1. Open Visual Studio and access the Model.bim file in data view mode.

2. From the tabs across the bottom of the data table, choose DimCustomer. Between "LastName" and "NameStyle," right-click and choose "Insert Column."

3. When the new column appears, double-click its header to rename it to "FullName." Now in the formula bar, add the following:

    ```
    =DimCustomer[FirstName] & " " & DimCustomer[LastName]
    ```

4. Complete the calculated column by pressing Enter.

Create a Measure

1. With the Model in data mode, navigate to the FactInternetSales table.

2. Locate the "SalesAmount" column and click the first cell of the measure grid underneath that column. In that cell, type the following:

    ```
    Sum Of Sales:= SUM('FactInternetSales'[SalesAmount])
    ```

3. Press Enter to complete the measure. Open the properties dialog box by pressing F4. Locate the "Display Folder" property and type "Customer Analysis."

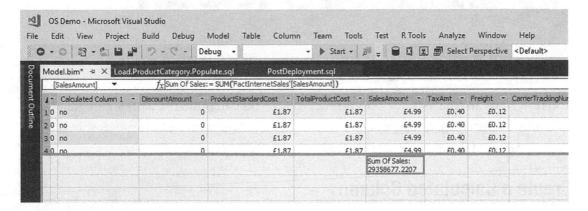

4. In the next column across, "TaxAmt," click the first cell of the measure grid beneath that column and open the "Auto sum" menu Σ▾. From the drop-down, choose "Average" to create an automatic average for the "TaxAmt" column. Open the properties dialog box by pressing F4. Locate the "Display Folder" property and type "Customer Analysis."

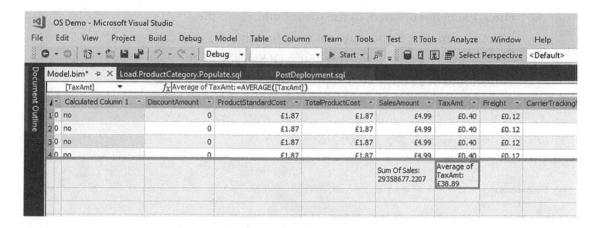

5. To test the preceding objects, click the "Analyze in Excel" button to
    open the model as a pivot table in Excel.

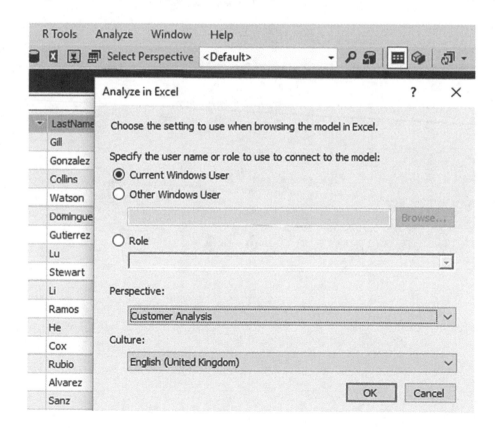

6. Once Excel has opened, in the pivot table, open the
"FactInternetSales" measure set and then the "Customer Analysis"
display folder. From here, drag "Sum Of Sales" into the values box.
You should see a large value appear in the pivot table view.

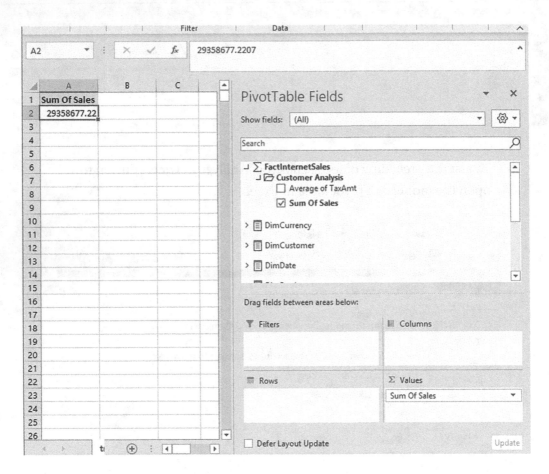

7. Expand the "DimCustomer" table and locate the "FullName" calculated column created earlier. Drag this into the "Rows" box to validate your measure and your column can interact.

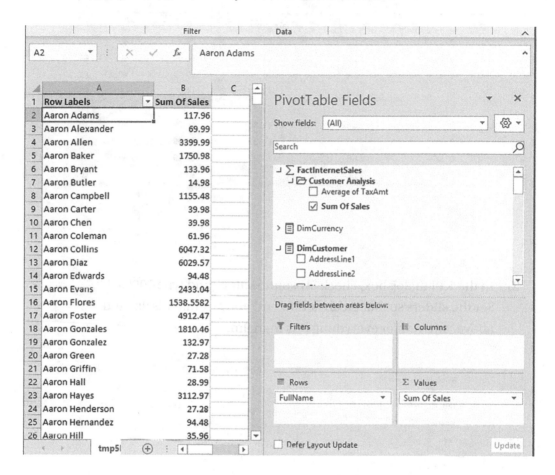

Create a KPI

1. Back in Visual Studio, select the "Sum Of Sales" measure created previously and then click the "KPI" button.

nount ▾	ProductStandardCost ▾	TotalProductCost ▾	SalesAmount ▾	TaxAmt ▾	Freight
0	£1.87	£1.87	£4.99	£0.40	£0.:
0	£1.87	£1.87	£4.99	£0.40	£0.:
0	£1.87	£1.87	£4.99	£0.40	£0.:
0	£1.87	£1.87	£4.99	£0.40	£0.:
0	£1.87	£1.87	£4.99	£0.40	£0.:
0	£1.87	£1.87	£4.99	£0.40	£0.:
0	£1.87	£1.87	£4.99	£0.40	£0.:
0	£1.87	£1.87	£4.99	£0.40	£0.:
0	£1.87	£1.87	£4.99	£0.40	£0.:
			Sum Of Sales: 29358677.2207	Average of TaxAmt: £38.89	

2. In the KPI dialog box, check "Absolute value" and type 10000000. Set the sliders so that green is 10m and above, amber is 9m and above, and red for everything less than 9m.

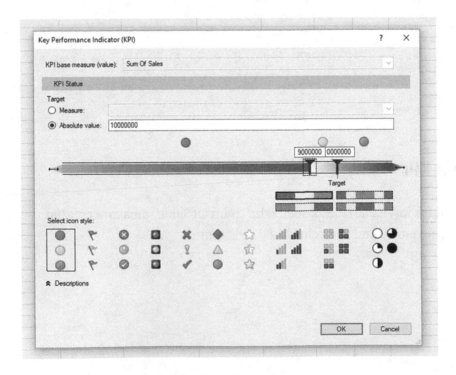

3. Once the KPI is done, click "OK" and then analyze the model in Excel again.

4. Drag the "Sum Of Sales" measure into the values box to display the total sales across all dimensions. Expand the "KPI's" node recursively until you locate "Values" (Sum Of Sales," "Goal," and "Status"). Drag each of those into the values box.

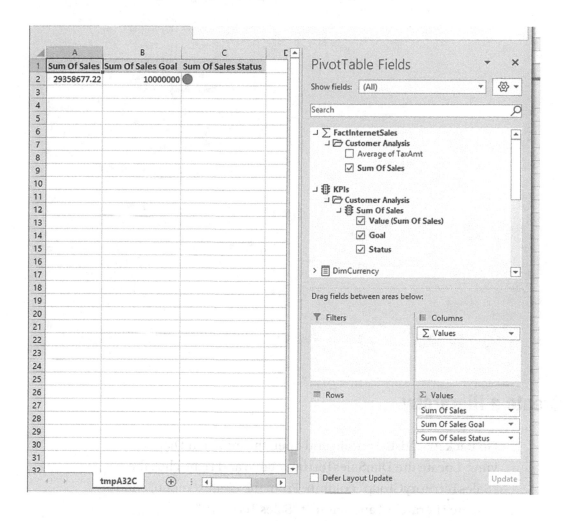

5. Now locate the "DimSalesTerritory" table and drag the "SalesTerritoryGroup" column into the Rows box. You should now see the KPI values split by Europe, North America, and Pacific.

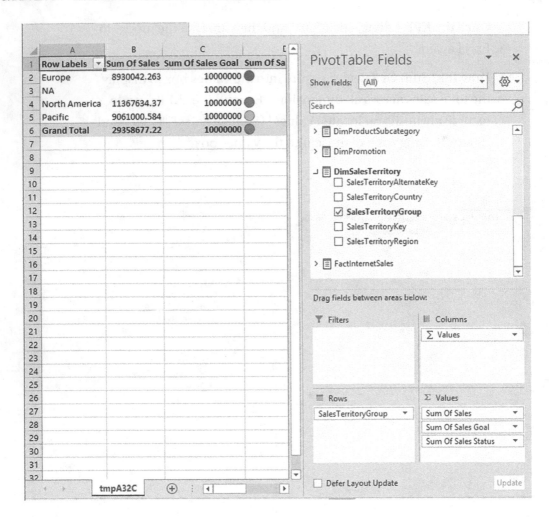

Create a Hierarchy

1. Go back into Visual Studio and open the model in Diagram view. Locate the DimSalesTerritory table and right-click the "SalesTerritoryGroup" column. From the context menu, choose "Create Hierarchy" and name it "Sales Territory."

2. Now drag the "SalesTerritoryCountry" and "SalesTerritoryRegion"
   columns onto the hierarchy parent (SalesTerritoryGroup). Once
   done, right-click each column and rename to match the following
   image.

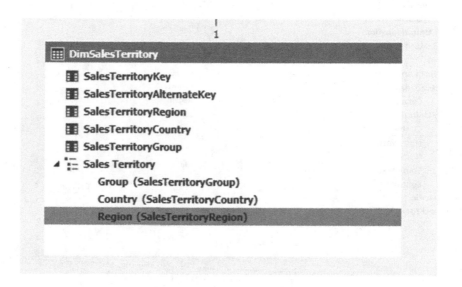

3. Save the model and analyze in Excel. Once Excel opens, expand
   the "DimSalesTerritory" table and note that all fields are now
   grouped under "More Fields." The hierarchy is also named and
   kept at top level.

4. Drag the "Sales Territory" hierarchy into the "Row" box. In the
   pivot table is each level of the hierarchy which can be expanded as
   required.

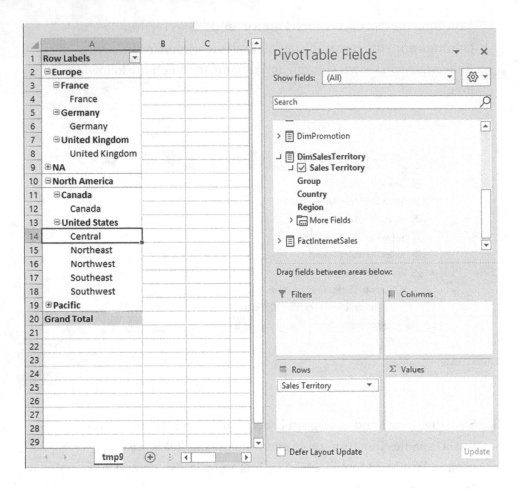

Create a Perspective

1. Go back into Visual Studio and open the model in Data view. Click the "Perspectives" button ▦ . Click "New Perspective" and give the perspective a name. Select a subset of tables, columns, and measures to add into the Perspective.

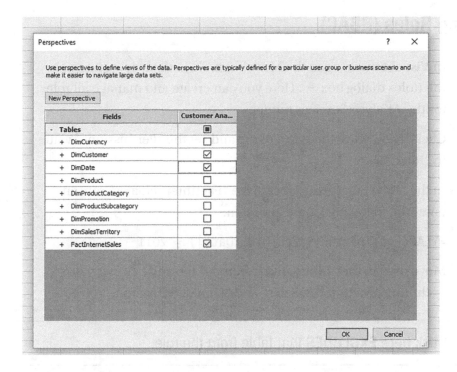

2. Click "OK" and analyze the model in Excel. When prompted,
    choose your new perspective from the drop-down menu.

3. Once Excel opens, you will see that the list of tables is now
    reduced to only those listed in the perspective.

Creating Roles (RBAC)

1. In Visual Studio, open the Model.bim file in data view and open the Roles dialog box  . Here you can create and manage all roles for the Analysis Services model.

2. Click "New." Give the role a name and set the "Permissions" value to "Read."

3. In the "Row Filters" box, locate the "FactInternetSales" row and enter the following DAX expression:

    ```
    =YEAR(FactInternetSales[OrderDate]) = 2011
    ```

4. Move over to the "Tables and Columns" tab and tick every box excluding "FactInternetSales" and "DimSalesTerritory."

Note   A tick here **EXCLUDES** that table from the role.

---

5. Test the role is working by analyzing the model in Excel and choosing the Role that you created (similar to how you would choose a perspective). The following image should be similar to what you can see:

Filtered to 2011 because of Row Filter

Reduced list of tables due to object limits

Complexity can be layered within numerous different roles for different levels of access

Deploy Analysis Services to Azure

1. Navigate back to the Azure portal and create an Azure Analysis
    Services instance. Supply a name, configure the Resource Group
    and Location, and choose "D1" for the Pricing tier. Ensure the
    Administrator is correct and leave the storage key expiration as
    "Never." Click "Create."

2. Once the resource is deployed, click "Go to resource" to validate
    the deployment completed successfully.

3. From the newly deployed AAS server, open the "Overview" tab
    and locate the "Server name" property. Copy it to the clipboard.

4. Go back into Visual Studio and open the "Solution Explorer" view.
    Right-click the tabular project and choose "Properties."

5. Set the "Server" to the one copied to your clipboard and ensure
    the "Database" name is correct/descriptive. Click "OK."

Note   You can rename the model here; otherwise it will be named "Model."

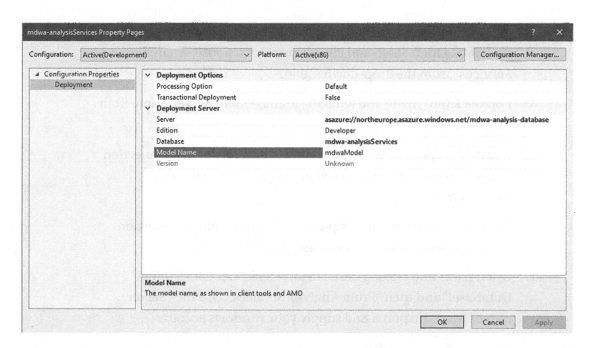

6. Right-click the tabular project again and choose "Deploy." This will prompt SSDT to build the project, and provided it builds successfully, deploy it to your Azure Analysis Services server.

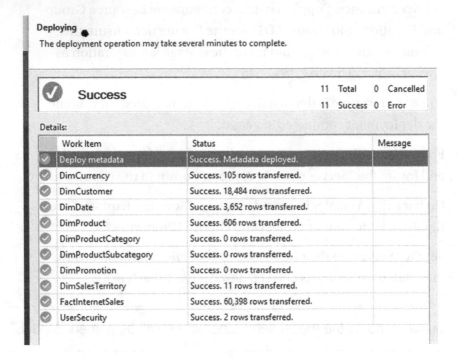

7. Validate that the model deployed successfully firstly by connecting via SSMS. Open SSMS and click "Connect." Choose "Analysis Services" from the drop-down menu.

8. Pop back into Azure and fetch the Management Server Name from the overview blade.

9. Use this property in the "Server name" property of the connection dialog and click "Connect." You may need to use MFA to connect here.

10. Once the connection is complete, review the tables, connections, and roles that can be managed using SSMS.

11. Open Excel and choose the Data tab. Click "Get data," "From Database," and then "From Analysis Services." Use the "Server name" from the portal and supply your windows account.

12. Once the connection is made, you will be offered to choose either the full model or a specific perspective. Choose the full model and click "Next."

13. You can change the connection name if you want to reuse. Once done, click "Finish" and "OK" on the subsequent dialog. You should then see a pivot table appear, exactly like the one seen using "Analyze in Excel."

14. Once finished with testing/development, be sure to pause the Analysis Services server to avoid any unwanted costs.

Processing an Azure Analysis Services Model

Once an Analysis Services model has been developed, it will contain not only data but also analysis objects such as calculations (or measures), calculated columns, and hierarchies. Obviously, the data contained in the model does not stand still and so these objects regularly need to be refreshed and recalculated to ensure they are accurate. Azure Analysis Services tabular models are easily refreshed using common protocols such as REST or PowerShell cmdlets.

A processing job can be carried out in a number of ways and at a variety of levels; the options are listed as follows:

1. **Process default**: This option at a model level processes any unprocessed tables and calculates all columns and hierarchies. At a partition or table level, the same steps are carried out but only for the objects in the partition or table.

2. **Process full**: This option will do a full process of all the objects in the model, partition, or table depending on the processing option, as well as calculating columns and hierarchies.

3. **Process data**: This option simply processes data into the model, partition, or table; however, it does not recalculate any columns or hierarchies.

4. **Process clear**: This final option clears data from a model, partition, or table.

In order to invoke any of these actions at any of the potential levels in an automated way that can be orchestrated along with the other ETL elements, a Data Factory pipeline can be deployed that uses Web Requests to interface with the Analysis Services server. The steps to build such a pipeline are described as follows.

The first job is to create a service principal that will be used to authenticate the process request:

1. Open Azure AD and locate the "App Registrations" blade. Click "New Registration" and supply a name, for example, "ASProcessor."

2. Open "API Permissions" and click "Add permission." Switch to the "APIs my organization uses" and type "Azure Analysis Services" in the search box. Click this API and click "Add permissions."

3. Open the "Certificates & Secrets" blade and create a new client secret with the name "Primary Key." Be sure to copy that secret into a text doc for later use.

4. Navigate back to the "Overview" tab and open "Endpoints." Locate the "OAuth 2.0 token endpoint (v1)" and copy it to a notepad.

With the service principal created, it now needs to be added to the server as an admin so that it is authenticated to perform the request:

1. Open SQL Server Management Services and connect to the Analysis Services instance.

2. Right-click the server node and choose "Properties" and then "Security." Click "Add" to reveal the security dialog box.

3. In the "Manual entry" box, type "app:" followed by the service principal client id and the tenant id joined by an "@" sign. An example is shown here:

```
app: <service principal client id>@<tenant id>
```

Now that the authentication is in order, the Data Factory pipeline can be built:

1. In ADF, create a new pipeline named "Process AS Database." Add two web activities to the pipeline and join them together with the "On Success" predicate.

2. On the first activity, set the URL to the endpoint copied earlier. Set the method to "POST" and add a content_type header of "application/x-www-form-urlencoded." Name the activity "Fetch Access Token."

3. In the body, add the following:

grant_type=client_credentials&client_id=*<your app id>*
&client_secret=*<your client secret>*&resource=https%3A%2F%
2Fnortheurope.asazure.windows.net

Note   The preceding code snippet works only for an Analysis Services instance in the North Europe region; you can change the region as required.

Be sure to replace the values with your new SPN details.

URL *   https://login.microsoftonline.com/6771b25a-

Method *   POST   ▼

Headers *   ＋ **New** | 🗑 Delete

              ☐ NAME   VALUE

                  Content-Type   application/x-www-form-urlencoded
                                        Add dynamic content [Alt+P]

Body   grant_type=client_credentials&client_id=12b74767-
                8d18-4ef3-bdae-
                26aad4601f68&client_secret=IDzs1IN%2B%40.GQ%3F
                EMwqPjucTQ3EwNHI51G&resource=https%3A%2F%2
                Fnortheurope.asazure.windows.net

4. On the second web activity, set the URL to

    `https://northeurope.asazure.windows.net/servers/<Your server name>/models/<Your model name (with spaces replaced with "%20")`

5. Create a `content-type` header with `"application/json"` as the value

6. Create an "Authorization" header and choose to "Add dynamic content…" for the value. In the dynamic content box, paste the following:

    `@concat('Bearer ', activity('Fetch Access Token').output.access_token)`

7. Set the body to the following:

    ```
    {
        "Type": "Full",
        "CommitMode": "default",
        "MaxParallelism": 10,
        "RetryCount": 2
    }
    ```

URL *   https://northeurope.asazure.windows.net/sen

Method *   POST ▾

Headers *   ＋ New | 🗑 Delete

	NAME	VALUE
	Content-Type	application/json
	Authorization	@concat('Bearer ', activity('Fetch Access Token').output.access_token)

Body
```
{
    "Type": "Full",
    "CommitMode": "default",
```

8. Now debug your pipeline to kick off the refresh operation.

9. Validate the debug run finishes and review the outputs of each activity.

10. To validate the refresh has completed, connect to your AAS database using SSMS and right-click the database node and choose "Refresh." Once the refresh is complete, choose "Properties" and note the date of the "Last Data Refresh" property – it should be today.

Azure Cosmos DB

The previous two examples explore analytical routes for data moving on from the data warehouse; however, a final route to explore is less about analytics and more about further integration. This example will dig into Azure Cosmos DB and look at how analytical data can be obtained from the warehouse and integrated into a website's back-end database. This integration can allow a degree of analytical intelligence to be exposed via the website without placing any unprecedented load on the data warehouse, as this is absorbed by Cosmos DB.

The Cosmos DB Architecture

Cosmos DB is a NOSQL (Not only SQL) database that provides the ability to store JSON documents in a globally distributed, highly resilient environment that offers unrivaled service level agreements and extremely low latency times, therefore making it an ideal platform for web development. Cosmos DB also boasts a multi-model capability, meaning it can be treated as a SQL-like document database, a table storage database, or a graph database built using Apache Gremlin. Figure 9-16 shows how a Cosmos DB account is structured to provide this multi-model capability by implementing the notion of a container that stores JSON *items* that can fulfil different purposes depending on the model type chosen. Figure 9-17 explains how each container is broken down into resource partitions based on contextual partition keys.

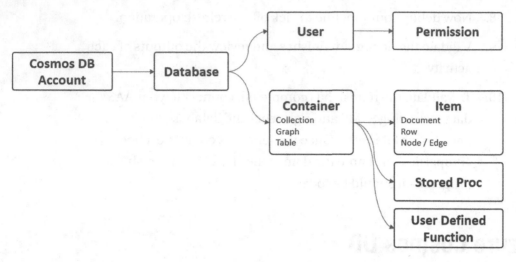

Figure 9-16. *A diagram explaining the layers of a Cosmos DB account*

Horizontal Partitioning

The data stored with a container is horizontally partitioned using a customer provided partition key and managed by resource partitions. As the container is scaled up by a user, the system internally manages resource partitions to deliver on the throughput required by the scale.

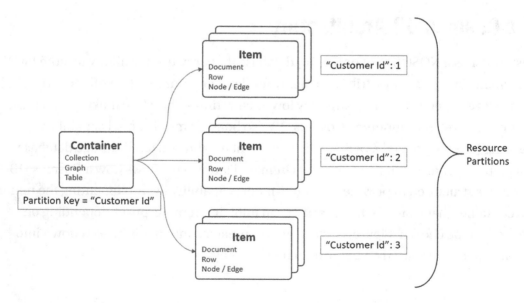

Figure 9-17. *A diagram showing how documents are organized into resource partitions based on a user specified partition key*

In addition to the horizontal partitioning explained previously, which always happens within a region, there is also the ability to replicate the data globally, into other Azure regions as specified through either the portal or an API request. This also enables multi-master capabilities whereby data can be written from multiple regions and read from all others within seconds. It is this global distribution of data that allows Cosmos DB to provide such low latency times to application users in any part of the world. Figure 9-18 shows how the preceding diagram is extended to partition globally.

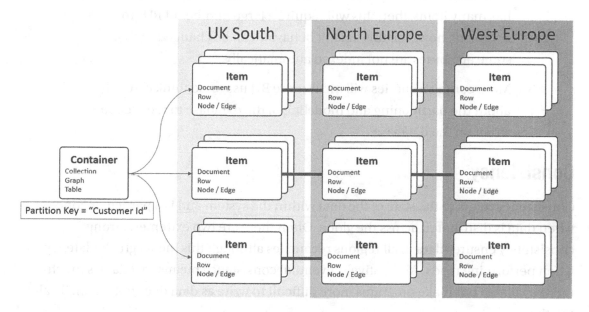

Figure 9-18. *This image shows how locally replicated resource partitions are further replicated globally, across Azure regions*

Resource Units

As with DTUs and cDWUs, Cosmos DB uses Resource Units (RUs) as the handy metric that abstracts the complexity of the internal IOPs, memory, and CPU consumption so that developers can manage a single slider instead of several. RUs can be provisioned at two levels, either the container or the database, and the same metric is used regardless of the container model type. The number of RUs provisioned to a container is often referred to as throughput, and the throughput is spread evenly across each physical partition of the container, assuming a good partition key is chosen and resource partition skew is low. Container level RU assignment is recommended when consistent throughput is required; otherwise database level RU assignment can be used and this spreads the throughput across each container, therefore not making the performance of each container consistent.

When thinking about Resource Units, there are some things to consider:

1. As documents in the database increase in size, the number of RUs required to read the document will increase as well. One RU is equivalent to reading 1Kb of data from the database.

2. As items are written, by default they are indexed. If a document has many items, then this will require a large number of RUs to complete; however, this default behavior can be changed so that some attributes are not indexed automatically.

3. More complex queries will incur more RU usage, so think carefully about the partitioning and modeling of the database to reduce the strain on the database.

Consistency

Consistency refers to the state of the data within the system and is a particular concern when data is distributed across the globe. Often there are two extremes. Strong consistency ensures data in all regions reconciles although this incurs greater latency when performing reads. Alternatively, eventual consistency means that data is much more available but make programs more difficult to write as data does not reconcile all the time.

Azure Cosmos DB offers more than two extremes and instead proffers a spectrum of consistency options, with several levels between strong and eventual consistency. The full spectrum of consistency options are listed as follows:

1. **Strong**: This level guarantees all reads from the database return the most recently committed version of a record. No uncommitted or partially written data will be returned to a client.

2. **Bounded staleness**: This level allows developers to create a boundary of either record versions (updates) or time. Global consistency is guaranteed outside of this boundary for all regions except where writes are accepted; in these cases, strong consistency guarantees are applied.

3. **Session**: Reads within a single client session have the ability to read your own writes; however, there is not a guarantee that the read is based on the latest record version. That said, the reads are supplied in order, meaning the data read is approaching consistency.

4. **Consistent prefix**: Reads that are made show some set of all the previous record versions with no gaps. This level guarantees that reads will not see out-of-order writes.

5. **Eventual**: There is no ordering guarantee for reads and so consistency is eventually achieved by the lack of incoming writes.

Now that Azure Cosmos DB is better understood, the steps here can be followed to copy some warehouse records into Cosmos DB so they could be presented to website users, regardless of their position on Earth.

Write Data to Azure Cosmos DB

1. To begin with, you will need to create an Azure Cosmos DB account using the Azure portal. You will simply need to provide a name, resource group, and a region. Once the account is created, you should open the "Data Explorer" blade and create a database and container.

   DATABASE CREATION IMAGE...

2. Navigate to Azure Data Factory and create a new linked service to connect to the Cosmos DB account.

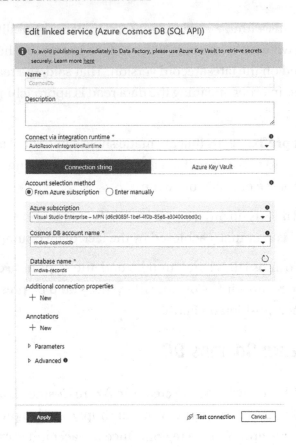

3. Create a new dataset that uses this linked service.

4. Now that you have the connection, a simple copy activity can be used to move the records from a SQL warehouse into the JSON-based Cosmos DB.

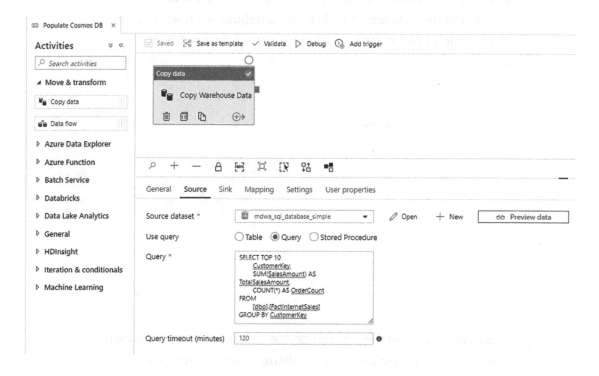

The following query is used here to create a sum of sales and count of orders record for each customer in the fact table.

```
SELECT TOP 10
    CustomerKey,
    SUM(SalesAmount) AS TotalSalesAmount,
    COUNT(*) AS OrderCount
FROM
    [dbo].[FactInternetSales]
GROUP BY CustomerKey
```

Set the sink option to be the newly created Cosmos DB dataset.

5. Debug the pipeline and validate it completes successfully. Once done, navigate back to Cosmos DB and refresh the list of items. You should now see ten records in the database, each with a sum of sales and order count attribute in a semi-structured JSON format.

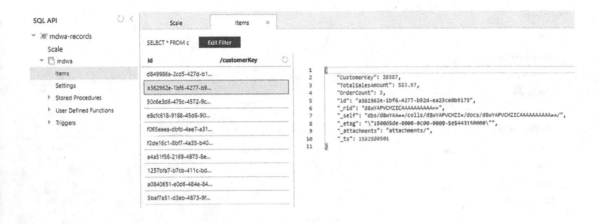

These records could then be integrated with a front-end website to provide analytical enrichment to existing customer records.

Index

A

Analytical objects creation
  calculated column, 249
  hierarchy creation, 256–258
  KPI button creation, 253–256
  measurement, 250–253
  perspectives, 258–259
  roles (RBAC), 260
Auditing process
  control database, 194
  copy activities, 196–197
  data volumes, 193–196
  operational process, 192
  processing times, 196–198
  requirements, 193
  storing high
    watermarks, 198–199
Azure Analysis Services (AAS)
  analytical objects (*see* Analytical object
    creation)
  calculating engine types, 241
  deployment, 261–263
  implementation, 240
  PaaS benefit, 241
  processing model (*see* Processing
    model)
  project link
    extensions menu, 247
    firewall rules, 248
    required details, 247

    search options, 245–246
    steps, 245
    tables list, 249
    workspace database, 246
  security model, 242–243
  semantic abstraction, 241
  standard tier, 241
  vertiPaq engine, 243–245
Azure Data Factory (ADF)
  alert messages
    action group creation, 206
    email, 208
    HTTP request option, 209
    JSON schema, 209–210
    logic app creation, 208
    mailing service, 210–211
    parameter value, 212
    web activities, 213–214
  alert rule creation
    configuration pane, 204–210
    metrics activities, 203–204
    new rule creation, 203
    notification, 206–207
  data integration, 45–46
Azure Data Lake Gen 1 (ADL Gen1), 136
Azure Data Lake Gen 2 (ADL Gen2)
  data lake technologies, 137
  directory resource, 146
  key principles, 146–147
  manage access dialog, 148

M. How, *The Modern Data Warehouse in Azure*, https://doi.org/10.1007/978-1-4842-5823-1

B

Batch ingestion tools
Azure synapse analytics, 111–116
CETAS statement, 116–117
data warehousing project, 108
ETL solution, 109–110
investigate issues, 110
risks/opportunities, 109
tools, 111
troubleshooting, 110
Blob storage/Azure storage, 136

C

Cleaning directory, 151
Azure Data Factory, 155
database, 152–154
data lake, 154–155
data storage, 139–140
Clean layer, 107
Column mapping pattern, *see* Dynamic
column mapping
Compute Data Warehouse Units
(cDWUs), 20
Cosmos DB architecture
layers, 267–268
horizontal partitioning
consistency options, 270–271
data explorer, 271–274
dataset creation, 272
linked service, 271
preceding diagram, 269
resource partitions, 268
resource units (RUs), 269–270
semi-structured JSON
format, 274
SQL warehouse data, 273

NOSQL (Not only SQL), 267
Create External Table As Select (CETAS)
statement, 116–117

D

Databricks job cluster, 56
Data contracts
definition, 164
design/integration considerations,
165–169
entity diagram, 164–165
integration, 170
scripting code generation, 220
SQL table implementation, 164
Data factory
dataset, 54–55, 72–74
debugging activities, 78
integration runtime, 49
invoke monitor script, 222–224
linked services, 47–49, 65–72
managed service identity (MSI), 62
monitoring portal, 78–79
parameters-driven (*see* Parameters-
driven pipelines)
pattern (*see* Pattern processing)
pipelines/activities, 55, 74–77
security, 62
self-hosted integration runtime, 50
solution structure, 63
SSIS integration runtime, 50–51
templates, 63
triggers, 52–53
V2 resource, 64
Data integration projects, 163
Data Lake
attributes, 143
benefits, 134

definition, 133

functional perspective, 135–137

enterprise implementation, 143–157

modern enterprise, 134–135

planning structure, 138–143

polyglot architectures, 157–161

research/experimentation

capabilities, 133

technologies, 134–137

WAREHOUSE directories, 142–143

Data Management Views (DMVs), 18

Data movement process

auditing process, 192–199

incorporating resilience, 199–216

logging, 181, 182

monitoring method, 216–218

Decoupled processing

cleaning process, 120

data warehouse scenario, 119

layers (loading data), 119–120

optional/mandatory files, 122

simplistic resolution process, 121

warehouse table, 121

Data streaming, see Stream ingestion

Data warehouse

cloud revolution, 1

database backups/lakes, 2

key tools, 4

modern data warehouse, 229

multi-region support, 3

naming convention, 7

on-premises tool, 1

resource group/tagging, 3–4

security standpoint, 4

terms/definition, 6–7

Deployment options (SQL database)

elastic pools, 39

features, 38

managed instance, 38–39

SQL DB/synapse analytics, 38

V-Core tiers, 39–40

Designing data contracts

consistency, 166

generation process, 166–169

modification, 170

storing, 169–170

validation, 168

Dictionary encoding, 244

Dynamic column mapping, 99–102

E, F, G

Error handling, 96

Event ingestion

Azure Synapse Analytics, 125

decoupled (see decoupled processing)

event-based ingestion, 118

event processing, 125–127

listening data, 123

risks/opportunities, 118

single file batches, 117

SQL database, 125

Extract, transform and load (ETL/ELT)

patterns

ADF V2, 46

anti-window, 110

ingestion mode, 105–106

mapping data flow process, 90

solution structure (ADF), 63

window, 109–110, 118

H

Hadoop distributed file system (HDFS), 48

HASH distribution, 15–17

HDInsight cluster, 56

Hyperscale databases
  accelerated disaster recovery, 37
  application intent parameter, 36
  architecture, 36–37
  cheap storage/flexible resources, 35
  features, 35

I, J, K

Ingestion modes
  approach, 132
  architecture, 108
  batch (*see* Batch ingestion tools)
  data streaming, 126–129
  event ingestion, 117–125
  lambda architecture approach,
      129–131
  layers, 105–108
Integration (data contract)
  code generation
    Azure SQL database, 178
    key parameters, 177
    ObtainEntityMetadata stored
      procedure, 177
    PowerShell script, 175
    process of, 175
    SQL database, 176
    templates, 178
  entity metadata, 174–175
  fetching metadata, 170
  harmonizing schema evolution,
      179–180
  JSON source code, 172
  orchestration metadata, 171–172
  requirements, 170
  utilizing orchestration
      metadata, 173–174

Integration engine
  activities, 55
    bucketed up, 56
    configuration properties, 57–58
    external compute, 56–57
    looping/conditional logic, 58–60
    output constraints, 61
    web activities, 60
  ADF, 45–46
  data factory (*see* Data factory)
Integration runtime (IR), 49
Internal activities, 57–58
Invocation methods, 85–86
Iteration/conditional activities, 58–60
Iterative parent-child pattern, 98–100

L

Lambda architecture approach
  blending streams/batches, 130
  cohesive/contextualized view, 129
  definition, 129
  serving layer, 130–131
Linear pattern, 96
Linked service connection
  access policies, 66–67
  author/monitor button, 67
  connection, 71
  data lake storage Gen2 option, 70
  key vault secret, 65, 71
  resource, 69
  security, 65
  UI/points, 68
Linked services, 47–49
Logging process
  aggregating data, 190–192
  alerting metadata, 183

definition, 182
events
    JSON data storage, 188
    approaches, 187
    parent-child processes, 185
    pipelines, 184
    platform track, 184
    processing hierarchy, 187
    structures, 185
    table code, 188
    table recreation, 185
    tabular data, 189
extended capabilities, 189
requirements, 182
storage, 182–183

M, N

Machine learning resource, 56
Managed service identity (MSI), 49, 62
Mapping data flows
    advantages, 87
    categories, 87
    data types, 94
    ETL steps, 90
    inputs/outputs, 88
    manipulation, 87–95
    mapping tab, 91–94
    pipeline, 89
    projection tab, 90–91
    row modification, 88
    schema modification, 88
    sink source, 92
    source options tab, 90
    transformation step, 93
    trim function, 93
Massively parallel processing (MPP), 6,
    11–12, 153

MERGE statement, 167
Metadata, *see* Integration (data contract)
Monitoring method, 216–218

O

Online analytical processing (OLAP)
    systems, 30
Online transactional processing (OLTP)
    systems, 30

P, Q

Parallel execution, 98
Parameters-driven pipelines
    configuration, 80
    control database, 84–85
    definition, 79
    invocation approach, 86–87
    lookup activities, 82–83
    mapping data flows, 87–95
    steps, 80–81
    stored procedure, 83
Parent-child pattern, 96–97
Parquet/Optimized Row Columnar
    (ORC), 54
Pattern processing
    boxed activities, 98
    column mapping, 99–102
    definition, 95
    iterative parent-child pattern, 98–100
    linear pattern, 96
    parent-child pattern, 96–97
    partitioning option, 103–105
Pipelines
    configuration, 76
    copy data activity, 75
    debugging activities, 78

Pipelines (*cont.*)
    ellipsis menu, 75
    input parameters, 79
    mapping data flows, 89–97
    monitoring portal, 78–79
    sink dataset, 77
    source dataset properties, 76
PolyBase technology
    components, 26
    credential creation, 26
    CTAS syntax, 28–29
    external data source, 26
    external table, 27
    file format, 27
    value/percentage, 28
Polyglot architectures
    characteristics, 157–160
    data cleaning/preparation, 160
    lake processing, 161
    SQL preference, 158
    Synapse Analytics/Azure Data Lake
        Gen 2, 159
Power BI (Microsoft Power BI)
    data visualization, 230
    key components, 230–231
    reports
        columns, measures/
            hierarchies, 235–236
        connect menu, 231–232
        data warehouse, 231
        navigation panel, 236–237
        output window, 237–238
        relationships, 234–235
        server information, 232–233
        splash screen, 231
        tables details, 233
    service process, 238–240
    working process, 230

PowerShell scripts, 219
Processing model
    authorization process, 266
    data factory pipeline, 264
    options, 263
    process request, 264
    service principal creation, 264
    SPN details, 265
    web activities, 266

R

Raw directory
    data lake implementation, 149
    data storage, 138–139
    file formats, 151
    key benefit, 149
    partitioning, 149–151
    sink dataset directory, 150
Raw layer, 106–107
Recovery point objective (RPO), 42
Recovery time objective (RTO), 42
Recurse data lake structures, 225–227
Replicated distribution, 18–19
Resilience
    alert data factory rules (*see* Azure Data
        Factory (ADF))
    data factory, 214–216
    defensive checks, 199
    troubleshooting (metadata), 200–202
Resource management
    classes, 20
    data factory pipeline, 23
    dynamic classes, 22
    pause/resume warehouse, 23–26
    service objective, 20
    static classes, 21
ROUND ROBIN distribution, 14–15
Run length encoding (RLE), 244

S

Scripting language
    code generation
        approach, 220
        data contracts, 220–221
        elements, 220
        ForEach loops, 222
        output folder, 222
        PowerShell code, 221
        tables/procs details, 221
    invoke/monitor, 222–224
    PowerShell, 219
    recurse structures, 225–227
Security configuration (Data Lake)
    ADL Gen2, 146–148
    default permissions, 145
    key information, 144
    parent folders, 145
    permission setup, 144
Self-Hosted Integration
        Runtime (SHIR), 50
Semantic layer, 241
Source controlled option (data factory), 63
SQL storage engine
    database (SQL DB)
        adaptive join, 34
        adaptive query processing, 33
        artificial intelligence, 32
        automatic tuning, 33
        batch mode memory grant
            feedback, 34
        benefits, 30
        cloud-based OLTP engine, 30
        concurrency, 20deployment
            options, 29, 38–40
        hyperscale, 35–37
        interleaved execution, 34
        trickle-fed data warehouses, 31

four Vs (volume, variety, value/
        velocity), 9
    synapse analytics (see Synapse
        analytics)
SSIS Integration Runtime (IR), 51
Static resource class, 21
Stored procedure, 56
Store linked services, 48
Stream ingestion
    benefit of, 126
    event-based/batch-based
        processing, 125
    implementation
        analytics jobs, 127
        Azure Event Hubs, 127–128
        blob storage, 128–129
        SQL database, 129
    risks/opportunities, 126–127
Symmetric multi-processing (SMP), 12
Synapse analytics
    batch ingestion
        CTAS pattern, 112–113
        DDL statement, 116
        external table, 112
        file structure, 115
        PolyBase engine, 111
        warehouse fact table, 113
    distributions
        columns, 17
        compute nodes, 13
        HASH distribution, 15–17
        MPP vs. SMP, 12
        REPLICATED distribution, 18–19
        right column, 18
        ROUND ROBIN approach, 14–15
        SMP single storage point, 12
        storage nodes, 13
    event ingestion, 125

Synapse analytics (*cont.*)
    PolyBase, 26–29
    resources (*see* Resource management)
    SQL database, 41–43
    workload management/importance,
        25–26

T, U

Transformed directory
    data storage, 141–142
    ELT approach, 156
    ingestion architecture, 107–108
    key points, 157
    warehouse, 155
Triggers, 52–53

V

Value encoding, 243
V-Core tiers, 39–40
VertiPaq engine, 243–245

W, X, Y, Z

Windows Azure Storage Blob (WASB), 136

Printed in the United States
By Bookmasters